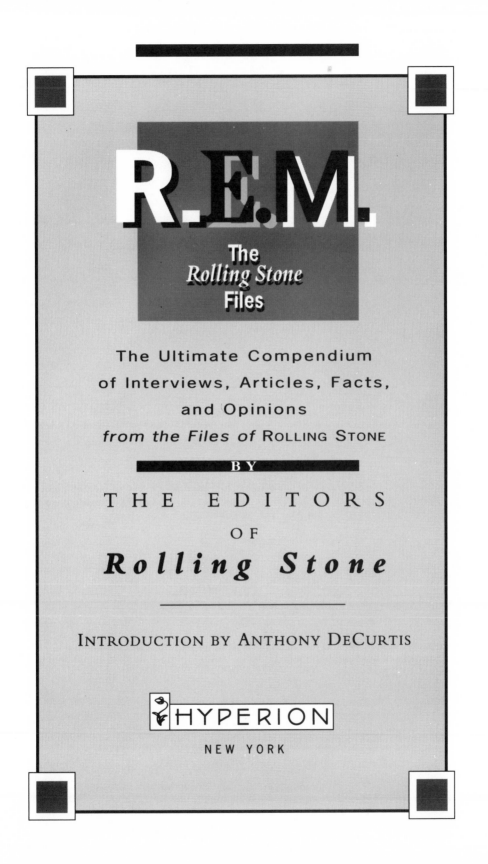

R.E.M.
The *Rolling Stone* Files

The Ultimate Compendium
of Interviews, Articles, Facts,
and Opinions
from the Files of ROLLING STONE

BY

THE EDITORS

OF

Rolling Stone

INTRODUCTION BY ANTHONY DeCURTIS

HYPERION

NEW YORK

Library of Congress Cataloging-in-Publication Data
R.E.M., the Rolling Stone files : the ultimate compendium of interviews, articles, facts, and opinions from the files of Rolling Stone / by the editors of Rolling Stone ; introduction by Anthony DeCurtis.
        p.   cm.
    Includes discography and videography.
    ISBN 0-7868-8054-6
    1. R.E.M. (Musical group)—Criticism and interpretation. 2. Rock music—United States—1981–1990—History and criticism. 3. Rock music—United States—1991–2000—History and criticism. I. Rolling Stone (New York, N.Y.)
ML421.R22R2 1995
782.42166′092′2—dc20
[B]   94-37354
                                                                                              CIP
                                                                                              MN

First Edition
10 9 8 7 6 5 4 3 2 1

DESIGN BY ROBERT BULL DESIGN

CONTENTS

FOREWORD

ROM CULT FOLLOWING to mass popularity. Wet-behind-the-ears small-town boys to jet-setting millionaires. Jangly guitar-pop to thrash-and-burn power chords. R.E.M.'s audience, personae and music have all transmogrified since those heady days of their early shows in tiny clubs across America. Barely two years old, R.E.M. was first profiled in ROLLING STONE back in October 1982 as a "New Face." At that point in time, the Athens, Georgia–based band, with one single and an EP to its credit, was quick to distinguish itself from its hometown's well-known groups, the B-52's and Pylon. Of course, fourteen years, eleven albums and four ROLLING STONE cover stories later, any comparison is ludicrous.

This volume chronicles the band's ascent as it was presented in the pages of ROLLING STONE, via news stories, Random Notes, record and concert reviews and, of course, in-depth interviews and profiles. We've also dug up two behind-the-scenes stories written in 1984 and 1985 by ROLLING STONE senior features editor Anthony DeCurtis, then a resident of Atlanta, Georgia, for ROLLING STONE's now-deceased sister publication, *Record*.

A number of people are responsible for *R.E.M.: The ROLLING STONE Files:* Anthony DeCurtis, Shawn Dahl, Greg Emmanuel, Jann S. Wenner, Kent Brownridge, John Lagana, Ben Hunter, Sidney Painter, Anthony Bozza and Carrie Smith. We salute you. Many thanks to the folks at Hyperion: Lauren Marino and Robert Miller, as well as our previous editor Mary Ann Naples. We also appreciate the help given by Sarah Lazin and Marianne Burke, Karen Moss and Carla Mercer at Warner Bros. and R.E.M.'s Jefferson Holt, Bertis Downs, Meredith Williams and Kevin O'Neil. In addition, we want to thank those hard-working Random Notes authors: Christopher Connelly, Merle Ginsberg, Mark Coleman, Sheila

Rogers, Chris Mundy and Jancee Dunn. And an extra heapin' helping of thanks to all those writers whose work appears here.

Most of all, our thanks to R.E.M. for keeping the faith—and creating a *Monster*.

HOLLY GEORGE-WARREN
Editor, Rolling Stone Press
September 1994

ANTHONY DeCURTIS

INTRODUCTION

IN THE LAST MAJOR interview he did before he died, Kurt Cobain told ROLLING STONE's David Fricke, "I know we're gonna put out one more record, at least, and I have a pretty good idea what it's going to sound like: pretty, ethereal, acoustic, like R.E.M.'s last album. If I could write just a couple of songs as good as what they've written . . . I don't know how that band does what they do. God, they're the greatest. They've dealt with their success like saints, and they keep delivering great music."

Nirvana, alas, would never make another album and, if they had, who knows if it would have sounded anything like R.E.M.'s *Automatic for the People*. But that's not what's important about Cobain's remark. However self-destructive he may have been, part of him wanted to find a way to survive—and that part of him was drawn to R.E.M. as a model of success with integrity. Over the course of a career that is now nearing the fifteen-year mark, R.E.M. have managed to pursue a highly personal, highly idiosyncratic artistic vision while simultaneously amassing an audience well into the millions. All the while, as Cobain noted, consistently "delivering great music."

R.E.M.'s beginnings were modest but extremely weird. I first saw the band in the spring of 1981 while working on a story about the then-burgeoning music scene in Athens, Georgia, R.E.M.'s hometown. The B-52's had burst out of Athens onto the national stage in 1979. Then, the following year, Pylon unleashed the jagged mentalist funk of their splendid first LP, *Gyrate*. At that point people began to wonder about the down-home surrealism that seemed to be taking shape in a sleepy Southern college town previously best known for its life-or-death devotion to the University of Georgia football team, those down and dirty Dawgs.

After moving to Atlanta in August of 1979, I began writing for ROLL-ING STONE in 1980. My first piece for the magazine was a live review of the B-52's in Atlanta; my second was a short profile of Pylon. The feature I was researching on the Athens scene—which, unfortunately, ended up never running—was supposed to be my first big story for ROLLING STONE and I was thrilled at that prospect.

I was also thrilled by the try-anything energy of Athens. The tedium of small-town Southern life and a university far too gripped by football fever to satisfy its most interesting students created a place in which, if you had any imagination at all, you had to create your own good times. The Athens crowd did that with impressive flair, and music became their primary outlet.

Students and the inevitable college-town hangers-on, many with affiliations of one sort or another with UGA's art department, formed bands that had infinitely less to do with technical expertise than with some bizarre brand of zany self-expression. The town's endless supply of huge, cheap ramshackle houses provided perfect settings for the crazed bohemian dance parties that further honed the Athens aesthetic. Groups like Pylon, Love Tractor, the Method Actors, Oh OK and the Side Effects all quickly cropped up as if by spontaneous generation. After rehearsing a few times and writing some songs, they began spinning around the Athens party circuit, often departing for club gigs in New York not long afterwards.

R.E.M.—a name the band used to insist meant nothing, but which stands for "rapid eye movement," the physical indicator of the deepest state of dreaming—formed in the self-consciously arty environment of Athens but also stood apart from it. One acknowledgment of that distance was the way other Athens bands invariably—and somewhat condescendingly—referred to R.E.M. as a "pop band." When I got to see R.E.M. perform for the first time at Tyrone's, the club that had virtually become the group's Athens headquarters, it was easy to see how they had earned that tag. While nearly all the other Athens bands mimicked the spindly guitar lines and herky-jerky rhythms of the B-52's and Pylon, R.E.M. had fashioned a more traditional sound that rested on Peter Buck's folk-rock, pick-strum guitar style, the passionately indecipherable slurring of Michael Stipe's vocals, Mike Mills's unusually melodic bass lines and Bill Berry's elemental, almost-steady drumming.

If you knew your rock history you could instantly identify R.E.M.'s musical sources, most prominently the Byrds and the Velvet Underground, but still the band sounded bracingly fresh. I remember the R.E.M. sets I saw over the following year or so as one long, unstopping song—ringing versions of "Radio Free Europe," "Sitting Still," "1,000,000," "Shaking Through," "Ages of You" and "Gardening at Night," one tune bleeding unidentifiably into the next. Stipe's choruses—often with Mills providing harmonies or background vocals—would rise out of the jangle and drone of Buck's guitar and inspire further frenzy in the dancing crowd. The audience would climb onstage with the band as the show would rock to a close, everyone smiling and drenched with sweat.

From the first, R.E.M. radiated optimism, and that was a rare, welcome virtue in the early Eighties. The campy, self-reflexive fun of the Athens scene could be delightful, but at times it also seemed to suggest that it was uncool to care about things. Why not just dance the mess around? More broadly, punk had run its self-destructive course, leaving its audience shell-shocked and groping for a new direction that neither America's arena bands nor England's synth-pop brigade could provide. And the social climate had grown ominous as well. The election of Ronald Reagan to the presidency in November of 1980 made the country seem a meaner, less forgiving place than anyone had yet imagined. Whatever vestiges of Sixties hopefulness had survived the Seventies were now stone cold dead.

None of these issues was addressed by either of the songs on R.E.M.'s extraordinary first single, "Radio Free Europe" b / w "Sitting Still," released in July of 1981 on the tiny, Georgia-based Hib-Tone label, but depressed spirits were lifted nonetheless. Everything "wrong" about the songs seemed right in some larger, more evocative, more significant sense. The absurdly muddy mix that caused Peter Buck to smash an early copy of the single in disgust was taken by listeners as a grassroots rebuke to the sterile studio wizardry that had dominated the music industry during the previous decade. In fact, Mitch Easter's Drive-In Studio, which he had built in his parents' garage in Winston-Salem, North Carolina, became a shrine of the independent recording scene largely because R.E.M. cut those tracks there.

And if Stipe's vocals were not only buried but entirely incomprehensible, who cared? It seemed as if he was ardently pursuing some truth that was deeper than mere sense, more emotional than literal, more sensual than verbal, more associative than specific, more evanescent than solid, fully as much yours as his. "Decide yourself," he called out from the throbbing murk of "Radio Free Europe," urging you to make the meaning of the song your own. The single's hints of desperation—part of the pleasure of life "on top of the big hill / Wasting time, sitting still" is being able to "get away from here / Get away from me"—only made its oblique messages of hope and forbearance seem earned. Even the photo on the back cover, in which none of the band members is looking at the camera, would prove hugely influential. For years it seemed as if the jacket of every independently released single referred to it.

One of those singles that shapes the way you hear all the music that comes after it, "Radio Free Europe" / "Sitting Still" established the R.E.M. cult. Critics raved; indeed, smart, literate and musically allusive, the band was the virtual definition of a critics' darling. Equally important, R.E.M. soon began the relentless touring that would not only build the group's base of evangelical fans—turning your friends on to R.E.M. became something of an Eighties rite of passage—but that would blaze a trail that other progressive underground bands could follow.

The single also won R.E.M. a worldwide deal with I.R.S. Records, a large, independent label based in Los Angeles. I.R.S., which had a distribution deal with A&M Records, did not pack the commercial clout of the major labels that were also interested in signing R.E.M., and certainly the band could have gotten a much larger advance from those majors. But I.R.S. agreed to allow R.E.M. virtually complete control over every aspect of their creative life, an issue about which the band was adamant. Then, as now, R.E.M. were extremely wary of any influence that did not originate with the band's four members, its manager Jefferson Holt or its attorney Bertis Downs (Holt and Downs are credited as members of R.E.M. on the band's albums). They would listen to suggestions from anyone—in fact, they often seemed open to just about anything—but they were almost obsessively determined never to *have* to do anything they felt uncomfortable doing.

This attitude resulted from a characteristic, if somewhat contradictory, combination of insecurity and confidence. R.E.M. simultaneously hated situations in which their naïveté and inexperience might be revealed *and* felt completely certain that, left to their own intelligence and instincts, they could figure out the best way for them to proceed under any circumstances. More important, if they were going to fail, they wanted it to be because of their own poor judgment, not someone else's. Joe Boyd, who produced *Fables of the Reconstruction,* described this strange blend of attitudes as "absence of doubt without arrogance."

"We get away with a lot of shit," Buck told David Fricke for a 1985 ROLLING STONE story. "But it's reasonable shit. It's not like we're asking for the brown M&M's to be taken out of the dish. We want the power of our lives in our own hands. We made a contract with the world that says: 'We're going to be the best band in the world; you're going to be proud of us. But we have to do it our own way.' "

That insistence on an internally defined sense of direction, even sense of mission, extends not only to the band's record company and fans, but to each of its individual members as well. All of the band's songs, for example, are credited to "Berry, Buck, Mills, Stipe," regardless of who the primary writers are. That arrangement ensures that songwriting royalties—a crucial source of income for bands—are split equally, preventing friction in the band over money.

"We have a real socialist democracy," Buck explained to Fricke in 1990. "We sit around tables and vote just about as much as we write songs. We vote on where we're going to play, where we're gonna make the record, who's gonna produce it. We each have equal say and input when we bring songs into the studio. Everything is a total compromise between the four of us.

"We have a rule of no," he continued. "If we can't make up our minds, then we don't do it. It has to be all four in one direction. If one person really thinks that something is wrong and is passionate about it, even if we think he is wrong, we agree with him."

Part of R.E.M.'s deal with I.R.S. was that the label, rather than insisting on an album immediately, would put out the five-song *Chronic Town* EP that the band had recorded at the Drive-In Studio with Mitch Easter in October of 1981 and January of 1982. Released in August 1982, *Chronic Town* only served to deepen R.E.M.'s already considerable mystique. Believers had their faith, which had for a year rested precariously on one single and whatever live shows they had managed to catch, soundly confirmed. Doubters who asserted that "Radio Free Europe" / "Sitting Still" was a lucky one-off had to admit that, at the very least, R.E.M. had managed to weave its spell one more time.

On *Chronic Town* the band yielded nothing to its critics—or to tiresome complaints that "You can't understand the words." Stipe's unwillingness to enunciate turned his voice into an instrument; his words and singing contained meaning only in the sense that a melody or the sound of a guitar contains meaning. Much as the band eventually grew tired of the metaphor, dreams do provide the best analogue for the emotional effect of R.E.M.'s early songs. In dreams the overall atmosphere colors every specific detail, and no detail is less significant than any other—a shirt is as important as the sky, a shape is as important as a word. To this day, I have no idea what "Wolves, Lower" or "Gardening at Night" is "about"; I only know how powerful the experience of entering those songs and traveling within them has been and continues to be.

After the release of *Chronic Town*, R.E.M. hit the road again, often with Peter Holsapple of the dB's in tow as an opening act and, occasionally, as second guitarist and singer. As always, anyone showing up at a gig hoping, on the basis of some of the writing about the band, to encounter a passel of sensitive poets got a rude, if altogether pleasant, awakening. Stipe, somewhat despite himself, had become an entirely riveting frontman, revealing enough in his shy smiles and skinny-hipped dancing to disarm, holding enough back to seduce you further. Meanwhile, Buck's arsenal of leaps and windmill moves left no doubt that this was a rock & roll band in the grand tradition.

All the mileage, literal and figurative, personal and geographic, that R.E.M. had traveled found full poetic expression on their first album, *Murmur,* recorded in January of 1983 at Reflection Sound Studio in Charlotte, North Carolina, with Mitch Easter and Don Dixon co-producing. Released the following April, *Murmur*—which included rerecorded versions of "Radio Free Europe" and "Sitting Still"—again found R.E.M. mining the folk-rock vein they had defined as their own.

As often happens, the band took its own increasing notoriety as a subject, however obliquely, on the album. It's hard not to hear Stipe's eager declaration that "The pilgrimage has gained momentum / Take your turn, take your fortune" as a kind of message of encouragement to himself and the other members of the band. Similarly, his simple assertion that "Not everyone can carry the weight of the world" can be read as a response to the growing numbers of people willing to read every manner of meaning into his songs.

Overall *Murmur* stirringly intermingled a heady sense of excitement with a vague but persistent air of apprehension. Writing in ROLLING STONE, Steve Pond described the album as "a restless, nervous record full of false starts and images of movement, pilgrimage, transit." That depiction so struck Michael Stipe as true that he's mentioned it any number of times since—often, incidentally, attributing it to me. (The truth, at last—and alas—comes out.) In ROLLING STONE's 1983 Critics Poll *Murmur* was voted Album of the Year—edging out Michael Jackson's *Thriller* and U2's *War*— and R.E.M. was named the year's Best New Artist.

Propelled by the rapturous response to *Murmur,* R.E.M. climbed back in their van and continued to tour. Stipe, the member of the band most averse to the rigors of the road, has described those days as "harrowing—but a blast."

"If there's an extension of *On the Road* and that whole Kerouacian— can I possibly use that term, Kero-*whack*-ian? If there's an extension of that, probably forming a rock band and touring clubs is the closest you could get," Stipe told me in an interview for a ROLLING STONE cover story in 1989. "Peter and I certainly had romantic ideas along those lines, and damned if we didn't do it."

Buck's reminiscences aren't quite so literary. "We really soon got the reputation of 'Well, they'll do anything,' " he said in the same story. "We were broke and we had to sell some fucking records, so 'Yeah, sure, we'll play the pizza parlor.' "

It's necessary to emphasize in this age of multiplatinum debut albums that *Murmur,* while a critical smash, was not remotely a commercial hit (though it did squeak into the Top Forty, a fact Buck noted with pleasure). At the time, it was all but unthinkable that a band like R.E.M. would get played on the radio—except on college stations, an "alternative" means of exposure that R.E.M. helped bring to maturity. The band's ultimate ambition was to be successful enough to be able to continue making records—in other words, not so unsuccessful that no record company would have them on their terms—and playing live.

It's a prosaic, but important, point that keeping costs low is one way of maintaining independence in the music business, and R.E.M. were masters at working economically. Because *Chronic Town* was essentially completed before R.E.M. even signed to I.R.S. and *Murmur* only cost around $25,000 to make, the label could hardly complain when they didn't sell millions of copies. It doesn't take much in the way of sales to earn back such a small advance, and staying in the black keeps the record company off your back. No executive can say to you, "Well, we gave you a million dollars to make your last record and it only sold fourteen copies. We'll give you another million to make your next one—now you owe us $2 million—and to recoup our investment we'd like you to fire your drummer, use an established producer and make an album we can get on the radio."

In addition to staving off corporate interference, making records cheaply gave R.E.M. every incentive to play live. Because they didn't get large advances, the band only made money when it toured and sold records, activities that go hand in hand. All those frequent visits to small towns, college towns and big cities really paid off in the long run. For the first few years of the band's life it seemed as if everyone who liked R.E.M. knew them personally, an emotional fact that filled their fans with fervor.

In December of 1983 and January of 1984 R.E.M. returned to Reflection Sound in Charlotte to record *Reckoning,* again with Mitch Easter and Don Dixon producing. As the album's title suggests, the band was quite conscious of having to live up to its critical reputation, but the mood at the sessions—confident, casual, incredibly good-humored—was exhilarating, even inspiring.

R.E.M. were recording *Reckoning* just as the age of the blockbuster album was taking hold. Michael Jackson's *Thriller* had dominated the charts throughout 1983 and Madonna, Prince and Bruce Springsteen were just about to assert their grip on the Top Ten. After that, any album that didn't achieve multiplatinum sales and spin off a series of big-selling singles would be considered a commercial failure.

R.E.M. represented an absolute contrast to that trend. At Reflection no one was thinking about hit singles, though you can be sure the band would have been delighted to have one. "We want to sell records that we *want* to make" is how Buck put it.

When I arrived at the studio to do a story for *Record* magazine in January, it seemed as if the kids had taken over the candy store. The band, Easter and Dixon had all grown their hair down to their shoulders, an unheard-of gesture at the time, very un-Eighties. Despite Easter's description of the album as "field recordings," the band felt free to put a plethora of bizarre effects on songs like "Camera" and "Time After Time (Annelise)."

Stipe would record his vocals in a secluded room off the main studio, sometimes while lying down, sometimes in the nude, to achieve the sense of overwhelming intimacy and vulnerability hinted at but ultimately denied by his lyrics. In short, there was an assumption of complete aesthetic and personal freedom, the ability of interesting, creative people to do whatever they wanted. As we drove to his motel after an ice storm late one night during those sessions, Buck told me he had earned a grand total of $8,000 the previous year; that didn't diminish a whit his conviction that "It's a *privilege* to do what we do." Those days of radiance were amazing to witness and share, easily one of the most powerful experiences of my professional life. Everything seemed possible.

While anything but a blockbuster, *Reckoning,* which was released in April of 1984, sold better than *Murmur.* The album also completed the first phase of R.E.M.'s recording career. Essentially, "Radio Free Europe" / "Sitting Still," *Chronic Town, Murmur* and *Reckoning* are all of a piece musically—impressionistic, mysterious folk-rock driven by Peter Buck's ringing guitar. After *Reckoning,* each R.E.M. album would represent a departure of one sort or another.

On *Reckoning,* also, Stipe continued his evasion and flirtation with literal meaning, a dynamic that, for all intents and purposes, has continued into the present. "To give away everything is never good, at any time," he told me for the *Record* story about the making of the album. "Even in a marriage or love affair, you never reveal everything to the other person in that love. There's always something you want to return to yourself. I think that's real important."

"Are you trying to second-guess me? / I am tired of second guessing / What will be your look this season? / Who will be your book this season? / Here we are," Stipe sings in "Second Guessing," asserting—or affecting—a ready openness. At the same time, amid the tangled emotions of "South Central Rain (I'm Sorry)," he reserves the right to keep his meanings, his "rivers of suggestion," open-ended: "The lines are down / The wise man built his words upon the rocks / But I don't have to follow suit."

If those shifting meanings lead to painful misunderstandings, "I'm sorry," the singer wails to a "girl without a dream," all apologies, but, finally, unwavering. To the degree, again, that R.E.M. records are "about" anything, *Reckoning* seems to be about missed connections and the pain—and anger, and regret—they cause. "She will return," the singer insists over Buck's strange, beautiful riff in "7 Chinese Brothers," that very insistence suggesting more hope than belief. For now, she is gone. The girl in "Pretty Persuasion" has clearly sent signals she has no intention of honoring, much to the singer's consternation. Gentleness, affection and fond remembrance are all in a "Letter Never Sent."

Underlying the individual situations those songs address is a tone of moral inquiry. Essentially, in its many interrogative moments, the album asks, What are the obligations of one human being to another? "If a friend took a fall / Are you obligated to follow?" Stipe wonders in "Time After Time (Annelise)," one of the two slow, spooky songs on *Reckoning* that I think of as "mystery ballads." In the other of those songs, "Camera," he asks, "When the party lows / If we fall by the side / Will you be remembered? / Will she be remembered?" Unknowable, even a bit frightening in real life, other people take on their full dimension only in one's imagination, the song suggests—where encountering them is emotionally safer, more controllable. Memory, then, becomes the consolation for loss—and the breeding ground for creation.

If on *Murmur* R.E.M.'s pilgrimage was excitedly gaining momentum, on *Reckoning* it has careened out of control. The apprehension underlying *Murmur*'s good spirits came further to the fore. *Reckoning* ends with the propulsive rocker "Little America," another of Stipe's oblique (and, in this case, anxiety-stricken) evocations of the road. The song concludes, "The biggest wagon is the empty wagon / Is the noisiest . . . Jefferson, I think we're lost," borrowing manager (and former van driver) Jefferson Holt's first name for its historical resonance. It's a stark vision of the band traveling down the road into the American night, directionless, its future unclear.

Making strict correlations between what's in a band's songs and what's happening in the lives of its members is always a dangerous business. Still, it does seem evident that R.E.M. went through something of an identity crisis by the time their next album, *Fables of the Reconstruction* (or, as the band coyly insisted, *Reconstruction of the Fables*) was released in June of 1985. While the band has never really had a great deal to say about it, it's widely assumed that R.E.M. nearly broke up during this period.

In many ways the band was experiencing the worst of both worlds at this time. *Fables* sold about 300,000 copies in its first three months of release—nothing by the platinum standard of the times but enough to take the underground sheen off the band. The ultra-hip backlash against the group first began to be articulated around this time. In tougher days R.E.M. took considerable satisfaction in the support of critics and like-minded fans; if everyone in R.E.M.'s audience felt a personal connection to the band, that feeling was mutual. "The idea that we were kind of successful meant that there were other people who felt like we did" is how Buck expressed it to David Fricke in 1990. To be denounced, however unjustifiably, as sell-outs then had to have been painful, even though the band would likely never admit it.

To make matters worse, despite that criticism, R.E.M. hardly had the option to be smug superstars, even if they had wanted it. Still chronicling his salary, Buck told David Fricke that he anticipated making $24,000 in 1985. R.E.M. were still working like dogs, touring at a merciless pace. The unevenness of their popularity became more glaring at this point, as well. In some cities they could fill 5000-seat theaters; in others they could barely fill clubs. In Europe, outside of England and France, they were still virtually unknown.

In planning for *Fables,* R.E.M. decided they had gone far enough with Mitch Easter and Don Dixon and chose to make the album with Joe Boyd, who had produced Fairport Convention and Richard Thompson, artists whose work the band much admired. It was a rather impetuous decision. "We met [Boyd] on Wednesday, and we decided on Thursday to fly to England and we left Friday," Buck recalled in an interview with me for *Record*.

Fascinating in its way, *Fables* is murky, dark, nearly impenetrable; it's probably R.E.M.'s most difficult record, reflecting the confusions within the band at that time. Bill Berry hates the album—"*Fables* sucked," he told Steve Pond bluntly for a ROLLING STONE cover story in 1987. R.E.M.'s ambivalence about their relative prominence at that point is nicely captured in a remark Boyd made to Pond for that same story: "When you mix a record, traditionally the singer wants his voice louder, and the guitar player says, 'Turn up the guitar,' and the bass player says, 'Can't you make the bass parts punchier?' With R.E.M., everyone wanted themselves turned down."

Speaking about *Fables* for my story in *Record,* Buck said, "There's more of a feeling of place on this record, a sense of home and a sense that we're not there." Indeed, recording in England, the band made their most Southern record—except it's the rural South of highly eccentric characters and folk artists like Howard Finster (who designed the cover of *Reckoning*), a land Buck described as "a strange, slow, surrealistic place."

In that same story, Stipe admitted that, in opposition to the free-floating associative writing on the earlier records, he had grown more interested in narrative for the songs on *Fables,* although, he added, "I hesitate to use that term because all along we've said that our songs are not stories—not a beginning and an end with a middle and some kind of crisis point that has to be resolved. Most of these, I would say, would be a slice somewhere out of the middle; there's not really a beginning or an end. If you had to call it a narrative, it's probably not a complete one.

"I found myself surrounded a whole lot when we were writing these songs by fables and nursery rhymes and *Uncle Remus* and old tales," he continued. "The idea of stories being passed down and becoming a tradition, and having those stories become as much a part of a way of living or a particular area that you live in as the religion or the trees or the weather, I like the connection between that and the South."

Stipe chopped his hair and dyed it blond during this period, an extreme departure from his previous hippie poet look. Musically, R.E.M. began to become interested in moving away from their signature sound on *Fables.* On "Feeling Gravitys Pull"—a telling title for a band that once seemed to feel it could float off to anywhere—the band used a string section for the first time. "Can't Get There From Here" experimented with funk rhythms and horns. That title, too, seemed suggestive of the band's sense of fatigue and aimlessness, a theme also picked up on "Driver 8": "And the train conductor says / Take a break, Driver 8 . . . We've been on this shift too long . . . We can reach our destination / But it's still a ways away."

On tour—needless to say, the band continued to work at a relentless pace—R.E.M. staged truly confounding shows that mirrored the turbid sound of *Fables*. The lighting, designed by Stipe, was dark to the point where it was often difficult to make out the band members amid the shifting shadows onstage. The singer's always complicated relationship to his emerging stardom had achieved such an extreme degree of ambivalence that it was really quite stunning.

Amid all this, Stipe also maintained the remarkably introspective quality of his writing. In particular, he continued his penetrating examination of the complex interplay between distance and desire, a dynamic that attains dramatic force on the ballad "Good Advices." While employing the rhetoric of homilies to craft a kind of Dadaistic folk poetry ("When you greet a stranger / Look at his shoes / Keep your memories in your shoes / Put your travel behind"), the song is an empathetic, though completely unsentimental, exploration of faith and faithlessness. "Familiar face, boring place / I'll forget your name," Stipe sings, telling the saga of everyband in anywhere-town on allnights (and recalling the lines about memory in "Camera," from *Reckoning*), "I'd like it here if I could leave / And see you from a long way away."

The character in the song is more capable of engaging his *feelings* about a person than the actual person—the farther away someone is, the easier it is to conjure a loving image. Distance breeds desire; nearness breeds detachment. The personal isolation that results from that emotional dilemma is difficult to bear, however, and the singer unleashes an indictment perhaps of himself, perhaps of a lover: "At the end of the day / When there are no friends / When there are no lovers / Who are you going to call for? / What do you have to change?" Through the years, Stipe has maintained a regard for his writing on *Fables,* and there is an intensity burning at the core of the album's dense musical layers.

R.E.M. switched producers again for their next album, *Lifes Rich Pageant,* returning to the U.S. to work with Don Gehman, who had established his reputation making records with John Cougar Mellencamp. In April of 1985 the band traveled to Belmont, Indiana, to record with Gehman at Belmont Mall, the studio Mellencamp had built in a small town not far from Bloomington, the site of Indiana University. R.E.M. found the setting congenial. Bloomington is "a lot like Athens," Mills said in ROLLING STONE's Random Notes. "There aren't many distractions."

Somewhat less congenial, apparently, was the band's relationship with Gehman. R.E.M. had always been extremely wary of big-name producers. Their one experience along those lines—a few tryout sessions in Boston with Stephen Hague (Human League) at the urging of I.R.S. before the band made *Murmur*—had been a disaster. Hague, as meticulous in the studio as the band was loose and untamed at the time, had R.E.M. do take after take of "Catapult" in a desperate (and futile) attempt to get them, particularly drummer Bill Berry, to play in time. The band was angry and frustrated—and, truth be told, intimidated. They went back to the label and insisted on working with Mitch Easter and Don Dixon. Easter described the band as "whipped dogs" when they showed up at the homier confines of the North Carolina studio. "I thought, 'If that's what it takes to make records, we'll just play live and not make records,' " Buck told me afterwards.

Relations with Gehman were by no means so negatively charged—the band still speaks of him with respect, and even appreciation for the way he was able to bring their sound a greater clarity and force. But this was still a situation in which R.E.M., essentially a band with an underground reputation, was working with a producer who, with John Mellencamp, had made some of the best-selling records of the Eighties. More seriously, Gehman—perhaps more accustomed to Mellencamp's unalloyed directness—seemed thrown by R.E.M.'s elliptical ways. If you ask Michael Stipe what a song is about, Gehman complained to *Musician,* he'll tell you it's about "hyperspace." For the band's part, Buck has described *Pageant* as R.E.M.'s "Bryan Adams" record.

While obviously not a marriage made in heaven, R.E.M.'s collaboration with Gehman produced *Lifes Rich Pageant,* which was released in July of 1986. It was a much harder rocking album than *Fables* and the band's first gold record. *Pageant*'s tougher sound suited its more public—by R.E.M.'s standard, anyway—themes. It's as if the band woke up from its own collective dream, looked around and discovered where the country was heading in the Age of Reagan. In one way or another, political consciousness would be an element of R.E.M.'s music from that point on.

"The insurgency began and you missed it," Stipe sings on the album's charging opening track, "Begin the Begin," in something of a generational call to arms. "I looked for it and I found it." *Pageant* also touches, however indirectly, on subjects like acid rain ("Fall on Me"), environmental pollution ("Cuyahoga") and American covert political actions in Central America ("The Flowers of Guatemala"). In a quieter way than Bruce Springsteen and U2, R.E.M. had joined the ranks of artists who were attempting to combat the cynicism and greed of the Eighties with an exhortation to idealism and social awareness.

R.E.M. followed up *Lifes Rich Pageant* with *Dead Letter Office,* which was released in April of 1987. A hodgepodge of previously recorded B sides, outtakes and other obscurities, the album spoke in particular to the collector's soul of Peter Buck. Buck, in fact, wrote the album's off-handedly charming liner notes, in which he pointed out that the compilation offered R.E.M. the opportunity to "clear the closet of failed experiments, badly written songs, drunken jokes, and occasionally, a worthwhile song that doesn't fit the feel of an album. This collection contains at least one song from each category. . . . Listening to this album should be like browsing through a junkshop." Filled with pleasures for R.E.M. devotees—"Ages of You" and covers of Pylon's "Crazy," the Velvet Underground's "There She Goes Again" and Aerosmith's "Toys in the Attic" are my personal choices—*Dead Letter Office* is most notable for including the only available CD version of *Chronic Town* in its entirety.

Document, R.E.M.'s next album, marks the first time they worked with Scott Litt, who has coproduced every one of their new studio albums since. (The band also began taking coproduction credits at this point.) Recorded in Nashville, mixed in Los Angeles and released in September of 1987, *Document* might be considered the first of R.E.M.'s "mature" albums in that it was clearly made by a band no longer interested in dodging or denying its prominence. Confident and poised even in its most casual moments, *Document* has all the earmarks of a major statement by a major band.

Aptly described by Stipe as "a brutal kind of song"—and comparable to another menacing love song, Sting's "Every Breath You Take"—"The One I Love" was also (gasp!) a Top Ten hit, the band's first. In perfect R.E.M. fashion, the song both exploited the conventions of pop love songs (singalong verses, catchy instrumental hooks) and subverted them. The classic request-night line, "This one goes out to the one I love," gets instantly undermined by a description of the lover as "a simple prop to occupy my time," complicating the song's point of view and the listener's relationship to the singer. Meanwhile, "Finest Worksong," "Welcome to the Occupation" and "Disturbance at the Heron House" extended the rhetoric of slanted social commentary Stipe developed on *Lifes Rich Pageant,* as did "Exhuming McCarthy" and "Its the End of the World as We Know It (and I Feel Fine)."

On those last two songs—and on R.E.M.'s uproarious cover of Wire's "Strange"—however, R.E.M. achieved something they hadn't really managed before: being funny without being silly. Those songs were savage indictments of Eighties greed and self-absorption—"You're sharpening stones and walking on coals / To improve your business acumen," Stipe wryly chided his listeners in "Exhuming McCarthy"—that were only more effective for their tart humor. On "Strange" Stipe even poked fun at his own ambiguous relationship to stardom in the lines, "Michael's nervous and the lights are bright / There's something going on that's not quite right." Largely on the strength of "The One I Love," *Document* became R.E.M.'s first platinum album and the occasion of the band's first appearance on the cover of ROLLING STONE, which declared them "America's Best Rock & Roll Band." Incredibly, all this acclaim had come to R.E.M. on their own terms. The band had truly become, in Buck's phrase, "the acceptable edge of the unacceptable stuff."

With the release of *Document,* which was R.E.M.'s fifth album, the band's contract with I.R.S. was completed. Relations between the band and the label were generally good, but if in 1982 people were impressed that R.E.M. had convinced a label as large as I.R.S. to consent to all its demands, by 1988 the insider consensus was that the band would be foolish not to sign with a record company with more thorough distribution and greater international muscle. Eventually the group decided to sign with Warner Bros. Reportedly the terms of the deal were five albums for $10 million (needless to say, Buck was no longer revealing his annual earnings to journalists). Warners was chosen because of its reputation as an artists' label—such eccentrics as Prince, Neil Young, Randy Newman, John Fogerty and Van Dyke Parks were on its roster at the time—and because its overseas distributor, CBS International, would help expand R.E.M.'s audience throughout the world.

Predictably, R.E.M. took some heat for signing with a huge multinational conglomerate. After speaking with a group of high school students, Bill Berry remarked that the kids seemed to "think of Warner Bros. as literally like a monster, just something that consumes and spits out. I think a lot of kids wonder how we fit." But Berry had no patience with the argument that R.E.M. had sold out. "My response is, like, Guns N' Roses," he told me for a ROLLING STONE cover story in 1989. "Great band, by the way. I love 'em. But it's like they've got this 'fuck you' 'rock & roll kid' attitude, and they sell seven million records. Their *first* record. And here we are . . . *Document* was our fifth full LP, it sells a million records, and 'R.E.M. has sold out.' But Guns N' Roses gets all these accolades. I don't know what we're supposed to do. I really don't."

Buck was equally impatient with the sell-out charge, though for more humorous reasons. "There are a lot of people who like bands when they're smaller—and *I'm* one of them," he said in the same story. "I really love the Replacements, but I don't go see them now. I saw them in front of twenty people fifty times, and the same with Hüsker Dü. The last time I went to see Hüsker Dü, I was, like, 800 people back and getting elbowed in the gut by a fat guy with a leather jacket. So whenever people say, 'You're just too big, I don't enjoy going to your shows,' I say, 'That's fine.' " I.R.S. retained control of the albums R.E.M. made while on the label and in October 1988 released the twelve-song *Eponymous,* the band's first—and, thus far, only—best-of collection.

On November 8, 1988, the day George Bush was elected to succeed Ronald Reagan as president of the United States, R.E.M. released *Green,* their first album for Warner Bros. The album's title suggested innocence, hope and environmental conviction—though R.E.M. were also certainly not above making a sly allusion to their newfound wealth. During the presidential campaign Stipe (who characterized the Eighties in ROLLING STONE as "the Reagan-Garfield era") had actively supported the Democratic Party candidate Michael Dukakis, placing ads in college newspapers in Georgia and California that read: STIPE SAYS / DON'T GET BUSHWHACKED / GET OUT AND VOTE / VOTE SMART / DUKAKIS. *Green* was intended, in part, to combat the apathy that might come in the wake of a Bush victory. "It was no coincidence that such a hopeful record was released on an election day whose outcome was a foregone conclusion," Michael Azerrad wrote, reviewing the album for ROLLING STONE. "Now is not the time for despair, R.E.M. seems to be saying, but for a redoubling of efforts."

Stipe confirmed Azerrad's view in the cover story I wrote for ROLLING STONE after the album's release. "I decided that this had to be a record that was incredibly uplifting," he said. "Not necessarily *happy,* but a record that was uplifting to offset the store-bought cynicism and easy condemnation of the world we're living in now." "Get Up" is an upbeat encouragement to keep the progressive faith, and the equally ebullient "Stand," the album's first single, became the band's second Top Ten hit. Meanwhile on *Green*'s propulsive opening track, the archly titled "Pop Song 89," Stipe seemed to be sending up his new persona as millionaire rock superstar (and his general air of befuddlement): "I think I can remember your name / Hello, I'm sorry, I lost myself / I think I thought you were someone else / Should we talk about the weather? / Should we talk about the government?"

Since *Lifes Rich Pageant,* R.E.M. had cut back considerably on their breakneck touring. But with a new album for a new record company—and the prospect of finally building a worldwide audience—the band (with

Peter Holsapple along on guitar and keyboards) took off on a monstrous international tour that ran through virtually all of 1989. The tour ended on November 13 with a benefit show at the Fox Theatre in Atlanta at which the band played all of *Murmur* and all of *Green* back to back—an acknowledgment of the degree to which they felt that *Green* had represented a new beginning. At that point, though, no one fully understood how emotionally draining that tour had been, particularly for Stipe, whose role as frontman gives him the biggest burden to carry. The band would not tour again until January of 1995.

Despite their exhaustion at the end of the *Green* tour, R.E.M. went back to work in January of 1990, beginning the sessions for what would become their best-selling album to date, *Out of Time*. The band altered its recording method at this point, working at a far more leisurely pace than it had in the past. The basic tracks for the album were done at Bearsville Studios in upstate New York over a seven-month period, with additional recording done at studios in Georgia, and the album was mixed at Prince's Paisley Park Studios in Minneapolis. As on *Document* and *Green,* Scott Litt coproduced with the band. With no tour in the offing, the band was free to work as casually as it cared to.

While R.E.M.'s sound had evolved considerably from the jangling folk-rock that had been the band's initial signature, *Out of Time,* which was released in March of 1991, represented an extreme departure. Rapper KRS-ONE did a turn on "Radio Song," the album's opening track, and Kate Pierson of the B-52's sang with Stipe on "Shiny Happy People," "Country Feedback" and "Me in Honey." String arrangements by Mark Bingham graced a number of songs on the album, and Peter Buck played mandolin on "Losing My Religion" and "Half a World Away." "Losing My Religion" and "Shiny Happy People," a song that Stipe rather appealingly insisted was not in the least ironic, were both Top Ten hits, and *Out of Time* was the first R.E.M. album to reach Number One on the *Billboard* charts.

Out of Time was a quieter album than either *Green* or *Document* had been, and that reflected where R.E.M. had arrived in their lives and career. "For me, age brings—if not wisdom—at least a little understanding," Buck told Jeff Giles for R.E.M.'s third ROLLING STONE cover story. "I like to play quiet songs, and I really didn't when I was twenty-one. I don't think I've ever, in the last five years, played the electric guitar for fun. . . . I usually play acoustic or mandolin. I really have no interest in going back to being a rock & roll band."

Their quieter sound also suited R.E.M.'s desire not to tour. "We're in our prime as far as writing songs goes," Bill Berry told Giles, "and that's what we feel like right now—we feel like a studio band." *Out of Time* also reflected changes that had taken place on the music scene at large. R.E.M. didn't identify with much that was going on in music at the time. "I think the days of rock & roll bands' being Number One on the charts are over," Buck said in the same story. And as for Guns N' Roses, the hot band of that moment, Buck had little patience for them: "They're a Benny Hill parody of what a rock & roll band should be." Accompanied by Peter Holsapple, R.E.M. did a handful of promotional acoustic shows in Europe and then performed sets for *MTV Unplugged* and American Public Radio's "Mountain Stage" in support of *Out of Time,* which went on to sell four million copies in the U.S.

With the band's identity shifting, it's tempting to read a collective spiritual confusion as one element of "Losing My Religion"—along, of course, with Stipe's ongoing cat-and-mouse game with self-exposure. "That's me in the corner / That's me in the spotlight / Losing my religion," the lyric runs. Having clearly invited such speculation, Stipe was characteristically exasperated when it was raised. "I wish I'd said, 'That's me in the kitchen' or 'That's me in the driveway,' " he told Jeff Giles.

On the strength of *Out of Time,* R.E.M. swept ROLLING STONE's 1992 Readers Poll, winning in the categories of Artist of the Year, Best Album, Best Single ("Losing My Religion"), Best Band, Best Male Singer (Stipe), Best Songwriter (Stipe, though in fact all of R.E.M.'s songs are credited to the entire band) and Best Video ("Losing My Religion"). The critics were barely less generous, honoring the band in the Best Album, Best Single, Best Band and Best Video categories.

R.E.M.'s fascination with acoustic music reached an apex on their next album, the remarkable *Automatic for the People,* which came out in October 1992. *Automatic* was done in much the same manner as *Out of Time,* with the band recording and mixing in a number of different studios and cities, including Bearsville, Miami, Athens, Atlanta, New Orleans and Seattle, over a long period of time. The album is filled with acoustic guitars, strings, cellos, violins, violas and an oboe, and it features only one guitar-driven song, the anti-Reagan / Bush screed "Ignoreland," that could be considered rock & roll as that term is typically understood.

Despite its flip title—as the album's credits indicate, "Automatic for the People is the motto and service mark of Weaver D's Delicious Fine Foods in Clarke County, Georgia"—*Automatic* is thoroughly haunted by intimations of mortality. "Drive," the album's brooding opening track, ironically evokes David Essex's "Rock On" to portray a youth culture perilously adrift in sensation-seeking and fabricated thrills. Nothing could possibly sound emptier, more devoid of meaning, than the "live fast, die young" ethic Stipe blankly intones in the song ("Hey, kids, rock & roll / Nobody tells you where to go, baby"). You can attempt to "rock around the clock," the song suggests, but the "tick, tock, tick, tock" Stipe repeats indicates that time will inevitably exact its toll.

Prematurely dead figures from popular culture, like Montgomery Clift ("Monty Got a Raw Deal") and Elvis Presley and Andy Kaufman ("Man on the Moon") wander through the album like lost souls. "Try Not to Breathe" and "Sweetness Follows" deal explicitly with death and mourning. And the album's last two songs—the ballads "Nightswimming" and "Find the River"—are so deeply suffused with longing and a wrenching nostalgia that it's difficult to ground their emotion in anything less elemental than a yearning for life itself.

If the musical performances on *Automatic,* including orchestral arrangements by former Led Zeppelin bassist John Paul Jones, are studies in intelligence and subtlety, Stipe completely outdoes himself as a lyricist. In his writing on this album he discovered a language that enabled him to be simpler and more direct than he had ever been before as well as more poetically resonant. His themes may be ambitious, but he handles them with a truly impressive grace. He also conveys, as he never had even attempted before, the strange sweetness of his sensibility, the part of him that once prompted Bill Berry to say, "Sometimes Michael says things, and the rest of us will be biting our tongues, trying not to laugh."

One of those instances occurs in "The Sidewinder Sleeps Tonight," a delightful children's verse catalogue of nonsense that runs, "Baby, instant soup doesn't really grab me / Today I need something more, some stuff sub-sub-sub-substantial / A can of beans or black-eyed peas / Some Nescafé and ice / A candy bar, a falling star or a reading from Dr. Seuss." (Stipe's laughter at the end of the verse resulted from Mike Mills's having repeatedly corrected his pronunciation of "Seuss" as "Zeus.") And "Man on the Moon," with its string of loopy, disconnected references to pop singers, board games, philosophers, comedians, the Bible, Cleopatra and sports could pass for a transcription of what passes through Stipe's brain in the course of a day. That in the midst of such a weighty album, Stipe was relaxed enough to be so playful—and, in a certain sense, so open—says a great deal about how much he'd grown as a songwriter, and as a person.

In the 1993 ROLLING STONE Critics Poll, *Automatic for the People* won in the Best Album category; R.E.M. won for Best Band; and Michael Stipe won for Best Singer. While not as hugely successful as *Out of Time, Automatic* sold more than two million copies in the U.S. And as with *Out of Time,* R.E.M. didn't tour to support *Automatic.* Astonishingly, after nearly a decade on the road the band enjoyed its two biggest selling albums while playing live with the greatest infrequency. It's virtually unheard of for multiplatinum bands—or bands at any level, really—to refuse to tour after they release albums. Along with the unique music R.E.M. were creating during this period, a highly individual brand of chamber pop, staying off the road demonstrated the degree to which R.E.M., however successful they had become, continued to play entirely by their own rules.

Not everyone viewed their decision so simply, however. When R.E.M. failed to tour for the second consecutive time, rumors of various kinds began to fly—the most serious and troubling being that Michael Stipe had AIDS or was HIV-positive. The rumors were further fueled by *Automatic*'s obsession with death; Stipe's refusal to grant interviews after the album came out; his activism in support of AIDS causes (and that he is, by his own description, of "questionable sexuality" and "queer-friendly"); and that, physically, his body had taken on the hard, angular, painfully thin quality of an Egon Schiele self-portrait.

I ran into Jefferson Holt one night in a bar in New York after *Automatic* had come out and asked him about the rumors. "Michael is healthy as a horse," he told me. That wasn't quite what I wanted to hear—you could be completely healthy and still be HIV-positive. I didn't want to press it, though. Sometime later I saw Peter Buck at a Lindsey Buckingham show at Town Hall in Manhattan, and we went out afterwards with some other friends. Someone brought the rumors up, and Buck strenuously denied them. That reassured me somewhat, but I also knew that Buck was loyal enough to Stipe to lie in his behalf if he thought Stipe would want him to. If Stipe wanted to keep the condition of his health to himself, Buck would absolutely respect that.

So when I went to Los Angeles in June of 1994 to do a ROLLING STONE cover story on R.E.M., I knew I would have to ask Stipe about his health. Before I had left for L.A., everyone who knew I was doing the story had asked me if I knew if Stipe was well or not. I felt the story couldn't be done without the issue being raised; if Stipe didn't want to discuss it, he could always refuse to.

Living in New York City and working in publishing and the arts, I've had far too many relatives, friends and acquaintances fall ill with AIDS. While it's never easy, I'd grown used to speaking with people about their HIV status. But only once or twice in my life had I ever had to ask directly if someone was HIV-positive—and the answer, thank heavens, was no. While we're hardly best friends, I'd known Stipe for twelve years, liked him a great deal and deeply admired him as an artist. Suppose his answer was yes? Were we then supposed to continue our chat about the band's new album and plans for the future?

Finally Michael and I were alone one night after midnight in the lounge at Ocean Way Studios where the band was working and I asked him. He seemed sympathetic to my asking and didn't hesitate to answer. "I don't know how smart it is to say this," he said, "but I purposely did not come forward and say, 'No, I am not HIV-positive,' because I thought that it might be good for a lot of people who did respect me or think highly of me to wonder about that and think about it, you know? And think, 'Wow, if it can affect somebody who I really look up to, maybe I should be a little bit more careful myself.' Now that might be *unbelievably* naive on my part.

"But getting back to the HIV thing: I'm not HIV-positive. I've been tested many times, for various reasons, whether insurance or personal. I guess I'm glad that people are concerned about my health. That makes me think that they might want me to stick around. I'm really, really okay." I was completely delighted at the news.

That good news aside, however, things were not going well at the *Monster* sessions that I attended. Because *Out of Time* and *Automatic for the People* were each recorded over relatively long periods and the band hadn't toured in years, Stipe, Buck, Mills and Berry had, in an odd way, become superstars without really having to be R.E.M. for any extended period. Having to work as a unit was not coming easily—quite uncharacteristically, they were peevish and tense. They were staying in different hotels and houses and seemed to be living very different lives, with each band member negotiating the demands of his own family, friends and personal life and the album getting done (or not) as those other commitments permitted.

Of course, by the time I arrived in Los Angeles the band had spent far more time on the album than they had anticipated. Deadlines had come and gone. R.E.M. had always been an extremely efficient outfit, but from the time they began working on *Monster* various pitfalls had arisen that prevented them from working as assiduously as they would have liked. As the band bounced from studios in Georgia, Miami, New Orleans and Los Angeles, Mike Mills had an appendectomy, Berry took ill with the flu for a week, Buck's girlfriend gave birth to twins and, most devastatingly, Kurt Cobain committed suicide.

The entire group, as well as producer Scott Litt (who had done some remixes on Nirvana's 1993 album, *In Utero*) had become friendly with Cobain and the other members of Nirvana. Stipe had even recently discussed doing an independent project with Cobain. So when Cobain died, R.E.M. were profoundly shaken and had a hard time going on with its work.

"Everything stopped—cold," Stipe said. "We all really loved and respected and admired him a great deal. But it was not an incredible shock, because I had been in contact with Kurt. We were speaking to each other daily, a couple of times a day, and when he disappeared, I knew it. We all knew it. For seven days, I guess, nobody knew where he was. I knew that a phone call was going to come and I was just hoping that it was going to be a good one. And it wasn't. So we were a little prepared. But it was bad. Really bad."

Crushing as that personal loss was and stressful as recording had been, none of those issues hurt the music at all. In fact, all the tensions fueled R.E.M.'s creativity. The songs on *Monster,* which was released in September of 1994, bear the mark of everything the band had been through. The album, unquestionably, is the edgiest music R.E.M. has ever made. Stipe seems to have taken all the speculation about his sexuality and turned it into a subject—the aspect of the album he terms "gender-fuck"—as well as into an exploration of the shifting nature of identity itself. Musically, the band—and, particularly, guitarist Peter Buck—is noisy and abrasive, a far cry from the delicacy of the songs on *Automatic for the People*. Clearly, R.E.M. felt far more comfortable being a rock & roll band in an environment shaped by Nirvana and Pearl Jam—bands who both cited R.E.M. as an inspiration—than one defined by Guns N' Roses.

R.E.M. also wanted to make a more upbeat album, since they planned to go back out on the road after *Monster*'s release, their first tour since 1989. A year of shows in Europe, Asia and North America would no doubt make R.E.M. one of the most popular bands on the planet—not that, needless to say, the entire group was relishing the prospect of touring again. "I'm dreading it," Stipe said bluntly, aware that his squeamishness, like his ambivalence about overt meanings in his lyrics and his role as the band's frontman, had taken on an almost comic character over the years.

With the release of *Monster,* R.E.M.'s time had come. They would dominate the musical scene in ways they never could have while not touring in support of their most popular albums. It is a dramatic moment for them. They had always joked about breaking up on New Year's Eve of the year 2000, and they'd backed off that joke as the date loomed nearer. While never stepping back from mass success, R.E.M. had never pursued it with the singlemindedness of the other artists—U2, Bruce Springsteen, Prince—to whom it has come at one time or another. It will be intriguing to see if their peculiar, finely balanced chemistry weathers that experience.

No one has a crystal ball, but this much is certain: After fourteen years of creating challenging, adventurous music—music "by genuine people trying to *say* something," as Billy Bragg described it—R.E.M. deserve what has come to them. And, as artists and as people, they deserve to survive it in splendid form.

ANDREW SLATER

R.E.M.: NOT JUST ANOTHER ATHENS, GEORGIA, BAND

"**W**E'RE NOT A PARTY band from Athens, we don't play New Wave music, and musically, we don't have shit to do with the B-52's or any other band from this town. We just happen to live here." So says Michael Stipe, the twenty-two-year-old singer of R.E.M., a beguiling pop quartet from Athens, Georgia. And if his admonitions seem a bit emphatic, it's just because he's tired of reading otherwise.

Ever since the group's 1981 single, "Radio Free Europe," catapulted R.E.M. to national prominence (the 45 turned up on several ten-best lists in the *Village Voice*'s critics' poll and led to a worldwide record deal with I.R.S.), Stipe has been up to his adenoids in reviews that throw R.E.M. into a food processor with other notables from the Athens cabal.

"It's ridiculous," he moans. "You'd think anyone with an ear for music, anyone who was really listening, would be able to distinguish between R.E.M. and the B-52's, or R.E.M. and Pylon." Perhaps *Chronic Town,* a new five-song EP on I.R.S., will help discourage that kind of pigeonholing. Such songs as "Carnival of Sorts (Box Cars)," "Stumble" and "Wolves, Lower" recall some of the best elements of mid-Sixties hard pop. There are vague traces of the Velvet Underground, the Who, the Monkees, the Byrds and a host of others. Through it all, Michael Stipe's foggy, nasal baritone and neo-Beat poetry foster R.E.M.'s dreamy, elusive sound.

"Basically, we're just four pretty vague people," says Peter Buck, R.E.M.'s twenty-five-year-old guitarist. "We're definitely not writing in one specific tradition, and I can't think of any one group or attitude that we subscribe to. Rather than join a particular club, we'd like to be free to join them all."

The band formed in March 1980, when Stipe and Buck met bassist Mike Mills and drummer Bill Berry, who were both twenty-one, at an Athens party. The quartet lived in an abandoned church before going public, taking its name from "rapid eye movement," a term for the stage of sleep most associated with dreaming.

Though R.E.M. has garnered plaudits for its limited work on vinyl, the group is most compelling onstage. Buck's leaping, pick-strum guitar style leads the propulsive rhythm section in an urgent call to the dance floor, while Stipe whirls, watusis and croons with teasing teen appeal. R.E.M. has turned down several tour offers (the B-52's, the Clash), and when I.R.S. recently talked of sending the band out on the Go-Go's Vacation tour, the group expressed its disinterest.

"There's no reason to play in front of 5000 or 10,000 people who want to hear 'Rock Lobster' or 'Our Lips Are Sealed,' " explains Buck. "Besides, I don't think we're ready to play big halls. Right now, we're more concerned with writing songs and becoming the best live band we can."

"Well," adds Stipe, "that and clearing up our complexions."

STEVE POND

MURMUR ALBUM REVIEW

★ ★ ★ ★

R.E.M. 'S *CHRONIC TOWN* EP was one of last year's more invigorating, tuneful surprises: a record from an Athens, Georgia, band that cared not a whit for the fashionable quirks of that town's dance-rock outfits like the B-52's or Pylon. R.E.M. fashioned its own smart, propulsive sound out of bright pop melodies, a murky, neopsychedelic atmosphere and a host of late-Sixties pop-rock touches. The execution wasn't always up to the ideas—instrumentally, the band was still stumbling at times—but *Chronic Town* served notice that R.E.M. was an outfit to watch. *Murmur* is the record on which they trade that potential for results: an intelligent, enigmatic, deeply involving album, it reveals a depth and cohesiveness to R.E.M. that the EP could only suggest.

Murmur is a darker record than *Chronic Town,* but this band's darkness is shot through with flashes of bright light. Vocalist Michael Stipe's nasal snarl, Mike Mills's rumbling bass and Bill Berry's often sharp, slashing drums cast a cloudy, postpunk aura that is lightened by Peter Buck's folk-flavored guitar playing. Many of the songs have vague, ominous settings, a trait that's becoming an R.E.M. trademark. But not only is there a sense of detachment on the record—these guys, as one song title says, "Talk about the Passion" more often than they experience it—but the tunes relentlessly resist easy scanning. There's no lyric sheet, Stipe slurs his lines, and they even pick a typeface that's hard to read. But beyond that elusiveness is a restless, nervous record full of false starts and images of movement, pilgrimage, transit.

In the end, though, what they're saying is less fascinating than how they say it, and *Murmur*'s indelible appeal results from its less elusive charms: the alternately anthemic and elegiac choruses of such stubbornly rousing tunes as "Laughing" and "Sitting Still"; instrumental touches as apt as the stately, elegant piano in the ballad "Perfect Circle" and the shimmering folkish guitar in "Shaking Through"; above all, an original sound placed in the service of songs that matter. R.E.M. is clearly *the* important Athens band.

PARKE PUTERBAUGH

R.E.M.'S SOUTHERN ROCK REVIVAL

"**W**E WANTED TO MAKE a noncool, nontrendy record, and we particularly didn't want to go to Los Angeles or New York or London," says Peter Buck, the lanky, outspoken guitarist for R.E.M. "We really wanted to do it in the South with people who were fresh at making rock & roll records."

So *Murmur,* R.E.M.'s first full-length album, was recorded in Charlotte, North Carolina, at a small studio whose chief customer is the Praise the Lord Club. The LP is as original a piece of music as has been heard in 1983: its twelve tunes embody all the best virtues of classic pop—concise, artful arrangements, subtle hooks and a perfectly modulated small-combo sound—while incorporating a good measure of between-the-lines eccentricity, particularly in Michael Stipe's words and singing.

R.E.M.—a name taken from the state of deep dreaming known as "rapid eye movement"—instantly achieved favored status among critics with their 1981 debut single, "Radio Free Europe," and last year's *Chronic Town* EP. And the band is attracting a growing legion of fans—but on their own terms, since they reject many of the standard pathways to pop success. They've declined offers to tour with such big-time acts as the Clash, the Go-Go's, U2 and the B-52's, for example. "Opening for other bands is just the rankest sort of masochism," Buck says, scowling. And they passed over name producers to work with a relatively unknown North Carolinian named Mitch Easter.

Easter, who runs a recording studio out of his home in Winston-Salem, North Carolina, came to the attention of R.E.M. through a mutual friend, Peter Holsapple of the dB's. "There was something about them that I immediately liked," says Easter. "They have this kind of old-fashioned thing about them that made me feel real good—like the way four guys get together and decide to form a group."

At the heart of the R.E.M. aesthetic is that rapport. Though Buck stands out as the most garrulous of the bunch and Stipe is the most introverted, they share a kind of bemused casualness about the world that reflects their upbringing in the Deep South and their coming of age in Athens,

Georgia, where they were students at the University of Georgia, a party school of great renown. "At Georgia, all you wanna do is avoid having a job for four years, so you drink and raise hell," Buck explains. "I didn't study, I didn't even go to classes. I was . . . lazy."

Nongraduates all, the four members of R.E.M.—Buck, Stipe, bassist Mike Mills and drummer Bill Berry—met one another in the extracurricular melting pot of Athens night life. Berry and Mills, both twenty-three (as is Stipe), were childhood friends who'd come to Athens from their hometown of Macon. Buck—at twenty-six, the eldest band member—hailed from Atlanta, and Stipe was an army brat who'd grown up in Texas and Georgia. The latter two were living in an abandoned church outside of Athens, and Berry moved in after getting thrown out of school.

"It was a real zoo," Buck remembers. "We lived with some girl who dealt drugs—all of these sickos coming over at four in the morning with *the urge.*"

"One of the guys who lived there before us was named Purple Hayes," says Stipe, chuckling. "That church has been through generations of real bad hippies."

The main part of the church made a good rehearsal hall for a rock band, though, and R.E.M. could stay up all night cutting their craft on such venerable standards as "Gloria" without having to worry about the neighbors. "We played on the altar," says bassist Mills, "since it made a kind of natural stage."

When the rectory got claustrophobic, there was always the good life in downtown Athens. After the bars closed, the owners would sometimes move their big speakers into the windows, and the main drag would suddenly become a drunken block party. So, life was cool, rent was cheap, school made no demands on them, and gradually, they began to work up a repertoire of original songs that had little to do with the arty-party dance-band sound of fellow Athens musicians like Pylon, the B-52's and the Method Actors.

In fact, getting a handle on R.E.M.'s music is not all that easy, though some have tried. "We're not much of a drinking band, and we're certainly not a drug band," says Buck.

Does neopsychedelia apply to the band's music?

"Nope."

What about the claim that they seem detached?

"That's weird," Buck says with a perplexed look. "I would say quite the opposite; I would say we're really passionate."

"Maybe the ideas are a little detached," offers Stipe. "There's what Peter always calls the nonlinear sense, which is a good way of saying it."

Stipe's lyrics do aim at impressionism rather than straightforward narrative, sending out images drawn from mythology, literature and even Biblical parables in a free-associative way. And the music, though instantly familiar, is difficult to pin down. Not that R.E.M. are trying to be tight-lipped or vague about it.

"If we steal a whole lot from any one type of music, it's country," says Stipe.

"It's true," says Buck. "I know I put country licks all the way through what we do."

"On the vocals, too," Stipe continues, "I go for what I call the acid *e* sound, which is that nasal thing where you take the sound of *e* and make it as terrible as you possibly can. Tammy Wynette and Patsy Cline knew a whole lot about it."

All of this might come as a surprise to the new-music types who have picked up on *Chronic Town* and *Murmur,* which, to the unaided ear, seem to sound more like Dire Straits in the Twilight Zone than Chet Atkins or Patsy Cline. But a certain amount of mystery and subterfuge is basic to the concept of R.E.M., and they aim to fuse words and music into a total experience that defies any single, literal interpretation. "It's all part of the philosophy of the band," Buck says. "We never wanted to spell things out. If you want that, go and listen to the Clash. They're a newspaper; we're not."

R.E.M. like to spend a lot of time touring, and though they still make their homes in Athens, they rarely get back anymore. Playing live, they maintain, is their bread and butter, and they prefer to hit clubs and small towns, where people can get up close to them. "Our idea," says Buck, "has always been that we could walk into any bar in America and play, and if you didn't enjoy the band, it wouldn't be because you were too far away to see or hear us."

In the high-finance world of rock, the members of R.E.M. are on welfare wages, relatively speaking, allowing themselves each a $350-a-month salary and a modest per diem for food. But, Buck notes proudly, he'll have money in the bank when he gets back to Athens this summer. "None of us has expensive habits like cars, drugs, big houses," he says. "We don't even have our eyes set on the top of the charts, really. We just want to make records and play."

All modesty aside, things are looking good for *Murmur.* Buck notes happily that I.R.S., the band's label, is putting a lot of money into marketing the record, and the fact that *Murmur* was a recent Pick of the Week in Bill Hard's *FMQB Album Report* certainly won't hurt its chances with radio. Yet even though all the signs herald some sort of imminent arrival for R.E.M., Buck waves it off, laughingly looking down the road at life after rock & roll. "I think if this fails," he says, deadpan, "I'm going to start raising sea monkeys for a living."

1983 MUSIC AWARDS

CRITICS PICKS

BAND OF THE YEAR
U2
Police
R.E.M.
X
Five tied for fifth place

BEST NEW ARTIST
R.E.M.
Culture Club
Big Country
Nine tied for fourth place

ALBUM OF THE YEAR
Murmur, by R.E.M.
Thriller, by Michael Jackson
Synchronicity, by the Police
War, by U2
More Fun in the New World,
   by X

ARTIST PICKS
BONO (U2)
"Waterfront," by Simple
   Minds

"December," by the
   Waterboys
"Under My Skin," by the The
Proof through the Night, by
   T-Bone Burnett
"The Stand," by the Alarm
Murmur, by R.E.M.
Benefactor, by Romeo Void
Summit, by In Tua Nua
"Don't Turn Around," by Big
   Self
"The Lights Go Out," by Blue
   in Heaven

■ **RANDOM NOTES** "ZEVON BOUNCES BACK" (April 12, 1984)

"I'M IN THE PROCESS of cheering myself up and saving the world—in that order," declares **Warren Zevon,** the dry-witted singer / songwriter who's bouncing back from a yearlong labelless hiatus with the aid of **R.E.M.** The one-time **Jackson Browne** protégé, who now makes his home in Philadelphia, is shopping around a series of demos that he recorded with the Athens, Georgia, band. He says the tracks represent a distinct change in direction: "The excitement of playing Jackson Browne acoustic for 50,000 angry punks had started to wear thin. These songs are a little less pious than the last few."

CHRISTOPHER CONNELLY

RECKONING ALBUM REVIEW

★ ★ ★ ★

Brooding emotion and inventive playing highlight R.E.M.'s latest

MURKY YET EMOTIONALLY WINNING, brainy but boyishly enthusiastic, R.E.M.'s debut album, *Murmur,* burst onto the pop scene last year with minimal fanfare. Though some critics lumped the Athens, Georgia, quartet with the big-guitar bunch (the Alarm, Big Country), R.E.M.'s approach was more delicate and pastoral, a curious fusion of vocalist Michael Stipe's bookish, still-wet-behind-the-ears pretension and guitarist Peter Buck's cheerful folky energy. The tunes aside, there was something positively seditious in a song like "Laughing," where an engagingly bright acoustic guitar arpeggio accompanied a lyric like "Laocoon . . . martyred, misconstrued." Stipe's words may largely have been indecipherable, but *Murmur* was consistently intriguing. In short, the best LP of 1983.

On *Reckoning,* R.E.M. has opted for a more direct approach. The overall sound is crisper, the lyrics far more comprehensible. And while the album may not mark any major strides forward for the band, R.E.M.'s considerable strengths—Buck's ceaselessly inventive strumming, Mike Mills's exceptional bass playing and Stipe's evocatively gloomy baritone—remain unchanged.

If *Murmur* showed Buck to be a master of wide-eyed reverie, *Reckoning* finds him exploring a variety of guitar styles and moods, from furious upstrumming to wistful finger-picking. "Letter Never Sent" displays Buck at his sunniest, whirling off twelve-string licks with hoedown fervor, from a lock-step part in the verse that recalls early Talking Heads, to a cascading, Byrds-like riff in the chorus. Mills proves to be an infectious keyboard player; his echoey chords slide easily underneath Stipe's cry of "sorry" on the album's single, "So. Central Rain." And on "7 Chinese Brothers," Buck combines curt, distorted background chords, warm chordal plucking and high-string riffs with Mills's icy piano notes. Within their drone, Stipe sketches, in a mournful hum, the fairy-tale story of a boy who swallowed the ocean. Yet, for all that aural activity, the song flows with elegiac grace.

Stipe, whose voice is usually mixed way back, comes up front for "Camera," an enigmatic account of failed love that's enhanced by an eerie single-string solo from Buck. While less powerful than *Murmur*'s "Perfect Circle," this ballad demonstrates a surprising degree of emotional depth in Stipe's singing. On "(Don't Go Back to) Rockville," a more traditionally structured country rocker, Stipe stretches himself even further, singing in an exaggerated, down-home twang.

There's an off-the-cuff feel to much of *Reckoning*—even some of the band's jams and coproducer Mitch Easter's exhortations are preserved on side two. Unfortunately, improvisational songwriting has its pitfalls. The group, for example, could benefit from a tougher drum sound. Bill Berry shows a deft touch on the cymbals in the peppy "Harborcoat," but the martial beats of "Time after Time (Annelise)" are about as threatening as the Grenadian army. Stipe's amelodic singing also poses problems at times. While the band tends to use his voice as an instrument, his vocalizing in such songs as "Second Guessing" and "Little America" seems out of place, unsatisfying.

As a lyricist, Stipe has developed considerably over the past year. In "So. Central Rain," he notes, intriguingly, that "rivers of suggestion are driving me away." Yet he still waxes pedestrian on occasion, as in "Pretty Persuasion," which finds him griping, "Goddamn your confusion." His erratic meanderings may give the band some hip cachet, but they are an impediment that will prevent R.E.M. from transcending cult status. With skill and daring like theirs, the tiniest commercial concessions—some accessible lyrics from Stipe and a major-league drum sound—could win this band a massive audience.

Even without those changes, however, R.E.M.'s music is able to involve the listener on both an emotional and intellectual level. Not many records can do that from start to finish. "Jefferson, I think we're lost," cries Stipe at *Reckoning*'s end, but I doubt it. These guys seem to know exactly where they're going, and following them should be fun.

ANTHONY DeCURTIS

AN OPEN PARTY
R.E.M.'s Hip American Dream

A SUBDUED SUNBELT SPRAWLTOWN and would-be convention center paradise, Charlotte, North Carolina, has striven for years to
broker good manners and mild winters into boomtimes. But attracting out-of-state business, even from nearby Athens, Georgia, can trig-
ger unpredicted results.

It's hard to imagine, for example, what the local Chamber of Com-
merce would make of the wild scene unfolding here at Reflection Sound
Studios, where R.E.M. has camped in bohemian splendor to record *Reckoning,* the followup LP to their 1983 poll-conquering debut, *Murmur.*

At this precise moment the four lads are swept up in a rush of lunatic
activity to produce what guitarist Peter Buck calls "spectral, ghostly
sounds" for "Camera," a foreboding ballad that graces *Reckoning*'s second
side. Incited to gleeful mayhem by producers Mitch Easter and Don Dixon,
singer Michael Stipe seizes a T-shirt from manager Jefferson Holt's valise,
records the sound of himself ripping it to shreds and then wanders through
the studio endlessly mouthing two muted harmonica chords; guitarist Buck
alternately shakes bells and noodles psychedelic guitar riffs for backwards
recording; drummer Bill Berry raises a piercing, feedback-like howl by
whipping his finger around the rim of a drinking glass; and bassist Mike
Mills hammers at the vibes.

An earlier session featured Easter prone on the studio floor clanging a
metal pipe against a steel chair leg to get atmospheric percussion for "Time
After Time (Annelise)," *Reckoning*'s other mood piece. With his partner
down for the count, Dixon intoned big-time professional advice from the
control room. "It still doesn't have quite the 'ping' the other one had," he
muses. "Try to get more pitch." Stipe, as usual, has been recording his
vocals in a secluded room off the main studio, often while lying down. "He
likes the sound he gets that way," Buck explains.

But, lest you and the good folks at the Chamber think it's all fun and
no hump at Reflection, let auteur producer Mitch Easter disclose how his

R.E.M. buddies cramp his distinctive and much celebrated style. "I can always think of a million little noises to put on songs, and that's what most people want—but these guys don't want it," Easter sighs about his spartan work on the album he refers to exclusively as *Led Zeppelin II.* "These are like field recordings compared to most pop records."

Indeed, despite the occasional chaos and outburst of zany effects, the key word around Reflection these days is "stripped down." "We came in trying to do something different from *Murmur,* which sounded very textured and layered, filled with musical colors, concerned with tone," states Buck. "As far as arrangements and what instruments we play on it, this record is much more direct. And, really, that directness has something to do with the fact that we've matured. We don't want to be a band whose music is all right there on the surface, but we're not trying to make this a closed party."

To the degree that R.E.M. ever was a "closed party," vocalist Michael Stipe was the man checking psychic credentials at the door. "Michael is curious," is how drummer Berry understates it. "Everybody tries to figure him out."

In his singing, his lyrics and his life, Stipe continually vacillates between warmth and distance, freedom and commitment, trust and wariness, revelation and concealment. He writes by an ever-shifting set of private "rules" (for a time he wouldn't allow himself to write a lyric with "I" or "you" in it—too personal) and dresses in comically elaborate layers of clothes onstage to "protect" himself. He is also extremely suspicious of any potential influence originating outside R.E.M.'s tight circle of associates.

Characteristically, Stipe is attracted in principle to *Reckoning*'s "directness"—"If I ever see the word 'indecipherable' again I might vomit"—but he's convinced that even directness is an ambiguous virtue. "To give away everything is never good, at any time," he insists as we sit in an empty, half-lit studio. "Even in a marriage or love affair, you never reveal everything to the other person in that love. There's always something you return to yourself. I think that's real important."

An essentially introverted person who aspires to being an "open, friendly guy," Stipe will go to absurd lengths to protect anyone who approaches him from feeling discomfort. This trait, combined with a repertoire of lyrics so open-ended as to permit the most wildly subjective interpretations, makes for some bizarre happenings. Stipe relates how a theology student trailed him for hours around a Connecticut club to explain how he "knew" that the "two-headed calf" in "Pilgrimage" was the singer's conscious symbolic description of two parts of the student's room and two aspects of his life.

And as Jason and the Scorchers were tearing apart the 688 Club recently, some Atlanta politicos accosted Stipe, demanding a little on-the-spot *explication de texte.* "They were nice and sincere," Stipe recalls, "but they were convinced—and they just had to hear it from my mouth—that 'Shaking Through' was about fear of nuclear holocaust. They had the words figured out—it was really great. I said, 'Yeah, sure, it is,' but I couldn't come right out and say, 'Yes, that is what I wrote it about,' because that's *not* what I wrote it about. They wanted so bad for me to say that, and they thought I was kidding them. But I wasn't. All this was going on with incredibly loud music blaring and people milling all around us. And at the end of the day, it's still a pop song!"

While Stipe's voice and vision are the main ingredients that lift R.E.M. into the highest rank of American bands, the twenty-four-year-old singer was never the likeliest candidate for the glamorous grind of rock frontman. An art student, aspiring painter and prototypical denizen of the Athens fringe, Stipe met Buck when the guitarist worked behind the counter of a local record store. By all accounts Stipe was the sort of customer who selected albums based on how weird the cover looked. His knowledge of the rock & roll canon has, shall we say, some significant gaps.

As a St. Louis high-schooler, things pretty much kicked in for Stipe with Patti Smith and Television, who are still the primary influences on his writing. An earnest, lively and good-hearted participant in discussions about pre-wave sounds, he routinely sends jaws crashing to the floor with questions like "Was Donovan in the Turtles?" Stipe's lately developed a taste for country music (particularly female vocalists like Patsy Cline), an interest most likely derived from the stark contrast that music's complete emotional guilelessness presents to his own much more guarded sensibility.

P ETER BUCK, THE KEITH Richards of the post-punk scene, is another story. In Mike Mills's words, "Peter has rock & roll in his soul. He adds fire and enthusiasm." R.E.M. is the first band the twenty-seven-year-old Buck ever belonged to, and their success has transformed his life into a dream he never would have dared imagine. His energy and unremitting optimism are the glue that makes R.E.M. stick.

An irrepressible stage-hound, rock archivist and no stranger to the sunrise, Buck will strap on a guitar at a moment's notice to do sessions (most notably with Warren Zevon) or to jam with local or visiting bands. And he is the instigator behind such classic R.E.M. episodes as opening for the Cramps at New York's Peppermint Lounge under the alias "It Crawled From the South" and doing a Southern metal cover set.

With Stipe and Buck as complementary point men and Mills and Berry holding down the rhythm section, R.E.M. comprises a classic rock configuration. Mills and Berry, now both twenty-five, have played together since their high school days in Macon; their experience, intelligence and versatility would enable them to hammer the bottom under many different types of bands. Without Stipe as a counter-balance, however, Buck's encyclopedic knowledge of rock history would inhibit him, making it impossible for him to believe he was doing anything that added value to the tradition he reveres so totally. For his part, without Buck's tough rock instincts, Stipe's arty aspiration would probably consign him to the terminal fringe. As it is, Buck's sense of the past and Stipe's freedom from it simultaneously enhance and temper each other, and Berry and Mills can swing either way with grace. This tension and balance forge R.E.M.'s heat.

But tension, heat and the Chamber boys aside, this band does like its fun. In fact, days here at Reflection resemble nothing so much as an ongoing episode of *The Monkees,* a group that not incidentally numbers Buck and Easter among its most fervent adherents.

A stealthy glance over the shoulders of Easter and Dixon intently conferring at the mixing board reveals that they have turned the track identification chart into a cartoon strip. The fan mail pours in and, whoa, does it run the gamut. A Florida woman sends Stipe a copy of *Finnegans Wake* and compares his lyrics to Joyce, while a North Carolina kid writes to apologize for Charlotte's dullness and invites the band to dine with him and his parents, after which formality perhaps they could repair to his room to check out his videocassette of *The Kids Are Alright*.

Berry and Mills are locked in a momentous duel-of-the-titans pool tournament, and the indefatigable Buck holds forth to whoever drifts by about what he's been reading (Thomas Pynchon's *V.* and the story of *The Andy Griffith Show*), watching (teen movies) and listening to (Richard Thompson and hardcore). Berry and Buck sport new-grown beards, and the entire combo has hair so long that—forget about similarities in sound— they now actually *look* like the Byrds.

A S FOR THE NEW record, the title *Reckoning* is both a pun on R.E.M.'s southern roots and an expression of the group's sense that, after *Murmur*'s virtually unanimous acclaim, this is a disc about which important judgments will be made. But Buck ardently believes that if R.E.M. is to last, quality and the band's own creative desires must override concern about sales.

"There are things we could do that would make it a lot easier for us to sell records and get on Top Forty radio," Buck argues, "but that wouldn't be what we want to do. We want to sell records that we *want* to make. And, hopefully, they will sell. If they don't sell now, maybe they'll sell in five years. You know, Talking Heads finally had a hit album, and they didn't do anything other than make records they wanted to make. I think it ultimately pays off to do what your heart says to do and not worry about the commercial thing."

As with *Murmur* and the *Chronic Town* EP, all the tunes on *Reckoning* are group compositions. According to Berry, R.E.M.'s songwriting habits have changed little since their earliest days. Stipe's lyrics—much clearer on *Reckoning* than they've ever been before—undergo a process of "emotional editing" which involves the rest of the band either identifying parts they don't like or suggesting alternatives. "We don't clarify things," Buck explains. "When we first started, Michael and I used to say how much we hated most rock & roll lyrics. We had this idea that what we'd do is take clichés, sayings, lines from old blues songs, phrases you hear all the time, and skew them and twist them and meld them together so that you'd be getting these things that have always been evocative, but that were skewed just enough to throw you off and make you think in a different way. It seemed like a really pretentious thing to do, but that concept does work its way in."

Lyrics that ring true emotionally and yet leave broad room for interpretation in part explain R.E.M.'s profound impact on their audience. Stipe himself finds the meaning of his lyrics shifting in unforeseen ways as time passes, and he often alters lyrics in performance to test the types of meanings the songs will bear. Similarly, when listeners interpret a song, they actively complete a process he intentionally set in motion when he wrote it.

"One of the things Peter always says about videos is that he hates them because they're so passive," Stipe states, referring to Buck's denunciation of "image fascism." "It's all handed to you—you just sit and watch them," the singer continues. "I think a lot of music is that way too. The idea is there and it's very clear-cut; you don't have to think about it at all. If you had to think about it some or come up with your own idea of it, the song might have more personal meaning for you."

This emphasis on "personal meaning" in R.E.M.'s music inspires their fans to action, whether that action is lyric interpretation; opening a record store and naming it Murmur, as some guys in Orlando, Florida, have; starting a rock magazine because you're tired of "wasting time, sitting still" as some Chicagoans did; or forming a band and calling it "7,000 Gifts," from a line in "Seven Chinese Brothers" on *Reckoning*.

These personal responses derive from the message R.E.M. embodies that, in a time when cagey career moves and bald-faced hankering for mass success dominate the scene, when rock has been reduced, in Buck's words, to "a shallow series of gestures and conventions," you can still do things your way and make it. In the course of earning a deserved reputation for independence and outspokenness, R.E.M. has repeatedly blown off the "opportunity" to open arena dates for big-name acts (outside of a few shows with the Police last summer), opting instead to tour clubs and small halls, building their own intensely devoted audience as they go.

They are also committed to the local scene in Georgia and the Southeast in ways that count. Mitch Easter, a North Carolina native, has produced all their records (with help on the albums from another Carolinian, Don Dixon), and his trio, Let's Active, got the opening dates on R.E.M.'s national tour last year; Atlantan Howard Libov, who directed the "Spin Your Partner" video for the Athens-based Love Tractor, got the nod to do the "S. Central Rain (I'm Sorry)" video from *Reckoning;* and *Reckoning*'s cover was designed by the Reverend Howard Finster, an extraordinarily eccentric religious visionary and Georgia folk artist.

But R.E.M.'s deep grounding in a specific local scene has not made them hick snobs, but ardent supporters of local scenes everywhere. "I guarantee that I have more records from 1983 in my collection than any other year," Buck says. "I mostly buy independent records by American bands, and there's a lot of good ones. All over the country we go, and every town has at least one really top-notch group. Maybe they're too uncompromising or maybe they're all not pretty boys, or maybe they're just weird. From Los Angeles that has a million good bands now—Dream Syndicate, Rain Parade, Black Flag, Channel 3, Minutemen—to the Replacements and Hüsker Dü from Minneapolis, Charlie Burton and the Cut-outs from Nebraska, Charlie Pickett and the Eggs from Ft. Lauderdale, Jason and the Scorchers from Nashville. Good bands all over America doing exciting things, and no one really hears them. Hopefully things will pick up."

BACK AT REFLECTION, AFTER a week of fifteen-hour days doing final mixes, it's Friday night and party time. An ice-storm has slammed the lid on whatever Charlotte's night life normally consists of, so the combo and friends are relaxing and throwing back the brew in the studio itself. Jefferson Holt, R.E.M.'s manager, motors in from Athens, bringing word that an Atlanta high school has invited the band to discuss their profession on "Career Day."

Buck, a frustrated teacher who accepted an offer earlier in the day to address an English class at Emory University, leaps at the news. "We've gotta do it!" he exclaims, grinning maniacally. "I'll tell 'em, 'Look, there's no such thing in the real world as algebra, so don't worry about it!' "

Everyone laughs, but Bill Berry grows serious for a moment: "I'd like to do it. I want to tell them about how hard we really have to work and how we don't really make any money. They should know that it's not like what they read about."

"Aw, c'mon Bill," Buck counters with a speed and gentleness almost saintly in a man whose annual income has yet to crack five figures. "We live like *rich* people. We get to travel all over, and our meals and hotel bills are paid for. We sleep late and get to be creative and do what we want. It's a *privilege* to do what we do."

Two hard-working energetic musicians, one naive avant-gardist and one young man gripped by the vision of rock & roll promise, all striving to make music that is both popular and deserving of its popularity. If that's not the rapid eye movement of some hip American dream, who cares to think about what we'll have to wake up to?

■ **RANDOM NOTES** "NOTABLE NEWS" (February 14, 1985)
R.E.M. is writing songs and will go back to the studio in March to record its third album, for summer release.

■ **RANDOM NOTES** "NOTABLE NEWS" (June 6, 1985)
Why did **R.E.M.** call its new LP *Fables of the Reconstruction?* **Michael Stipe**'s answer: "It reminds me of two oranges being stuck together with a nail."

PARKE PUTERBAUGH

FABLES OF THE RECONSTRUCTION ALBUM REVIEW

R.E.M. turns to fable

O NE TIME, JACK KEROUAC asked William Burroughs to read and react to something he'd written. Burroughs did so, and said he liked what he read. But that wasn't enough for Kerouac, who pressed: What do you *specifically* like about it? Burroughs replied that he didn't know what he liked about it, specifically. He just liked it, that's all.

Fables of the Reconstruction, the fourth record by R.E.M., invites similarly non-specific praise. One absorbs the sound of these songs, one by one, mood by mood, without being greatly concerned with precisely what they might be about. Too much close scrutiny—trying to comprehend singer Michael Stipe's often hazy diction and imposing an interpretive framework upon the few lyrics that can be sussed out—is a self-defeating and frustrating exercise, as a day's worth of listen-guess-replay-guess-again made clear to me. Better to just accept Stipe's dusky voice as an extraordinarily evocative instrument, perhaps the lead instrument in this band, since there are no soloists per se.

Though attempts at analysis will probably be futile, some stray fragment of a lyric—"It's a Man Ray kind of sky" or "When you greet a stranger / Look at her hands"—might set off all sorts of intellectual resonances. Because R.E.M. suggests instead of spells out, leaving you to guess at what tantalizing secrets they're keeping, they have amassed a substantial following among the kind of discriminating fans who spurn contemporary-hit radio and Music Television.

Their latest record finds R.E.M. taking a few giant steps away from the format of the previous three, which were all cut in North Carolina with producers Mitch Easter and Don Dixon. *Fables of the Reconstruction* was made in England with Joe Boyd, the producer and creative midwife of some

Note: ROLLING STONE eliminated its star rating system for record reviews from April 25, 1985 to January 28, 1988.

of the most stirring British folk records of the past few decades, by artists like Fairport Convention, Nick Drake and Richard and Linda Thompson. R.E.M.'s liaison with Boyd makes perfect sense. Rural England and the rural South—the band members are all Georgians—share a deep tradition of myth and mystery that's nurtured in the bond between man and land.

R.E.M. draws upon the more haunting aspects of the South for inspiration and subject matter. Though they never deal with history head-on, the title of their album betrays an interest in history or, more exactly, the effect of a historical event in shaping the peculiar culture of their region. *Fables* is not a concept album, but there is a contextual frame here—more so than on R.E.M.'s other records. Perhaps making this album in another country gave them the distance to see their own more clearly.

Besides being a kind of cultural overview, *Fables of the Reconstruction* unfolds as a series of observations sequenced to suggest a dialogue between extremes: tension and languor, momentum and inertia, the natural and the surreal, accessibility and impenetrability. The band—Stipe, guitarist Peter Buck, bassist Mike Mills and drummer Bill Berry—establishes mood and texture without resorting to needless studio histrionics. Joe Boyd's genius is that his influence is almost undetectable; *Fables* is as devoid of the fifth-member diversions of a producer as R.E.M.'s previous records.

They do, however, toss in the occasional stylistic curve ball or quirky embellishment to flesh out the details of a song. "Can't Get There from Here" finds the band augmented by a horn section, though the way it's used seems to mock the idea of the big-band flourish of old soul records. A banjo enters toward the end of "Wendell Gee," plucking its doleful way around Stipe's surreal, lachrymose fable about some back-country oddball. A cello's murky drone seems to drag down and halt time in the unnerving, dirgelike "Feeling Gravitys Pull." At one point in "Driver 8," a faint harmonica conjures echoes of that folk-music staple, the train song, but the landscape passing by the locomotive's windows seems bleak and decaying.

Mostly though, *Fables* is unretouched R.E.M. in all their rough-cut glory, swinging from contemplative, Byrds-like balladry ("Green Grow the Rushes," "Good Advices") to careening, maniacally driven numbers like "Auctioneer (Another Engine)," which is dense with the mad torque of guitars and drums and Stipe's clenched, tense vocal. It appears to be about the strange motivations and betrayals that underlie a relationship as it comes undone, but who knows?

The guitars on "Maps and Legends" reverberate in the somber and grandscale mode of the Waterboys and Richard Thompson. Here and elsewhere, Buck's arpeggiated licks circle Maypole-style around the rhythm section's tight foundation until the subject, or object, seems entirely wrapped. This inventiveness makes the R.E.M. of *Fables of the Reconstruction* sound surer than they did on *Reckoning,* closer to the insular mood weaving of *Murmur.*

"Can't Get There from Here" is perhaps the boldest, most full-blooded song this band has recorded. With its scratch-funk guitar, bobbing bass line, spare yet potent drumming and Stipe's enthralling vocal, it deserves to become a hit. It also sets a tone of dislocation that pervades the entire record. Backup voices sing, "I've been there, I know the way," as Stipe growls contrarily, "Can't get there from here." The question is not only "How do we get there?" but "Where are we going?" *Fables of the Reconstruction* is an odyssey in search of a final destination.

And so it asks more questions than it answers. Listening to *Fables of the Reconstruction* is like waking up in a menacing yet wonderful world underneath the one we're familiar with. R.E.M. undermines our certitude in reality and deposits us in a new place, filled with both serenity and doubt, where we're forced to think for ourselves.

ANTHONY DeCURTIS

THE PRICE OF VICTORY
Confident but confused, R.E.M.
comes all the way home

STRIKING HIS CHARACTERISTIC foot-twitching posture of agitated patience, R.E.M. guitarist Peter Buck takes his place in line at an Athens, Georgia, utility office. Amid the townies and comforting environmental grays of the waiting area, the lanky Buck sports a tails-flying red and black striped shirt, a black vest and black skin-tight jeans. It's early afternoon, half the work of this sun-scorched Southern town's already done, but Buck, who'd been up till six doing interviews, watching *Dawn of the Dead* and reading Elmore Leonard, beams the engaging optimism of the just-risen.

An eon later the guitarist exchanges pleasantries with the ancient Southern matron behind the counter, who completes his forms with the exaggerated care and neatness of someone taking an exam in penmanship. Then the question comes: "May ah have the name and add-dress of yore landlor'?" Self-consciousness mingles with pride as Buck replies, "Um, there is no landlord . . . I *bought* the house." Yes, folks, Peter Buck—club-crawler, voice of renegade American rock, guitar hero of the underground—is now also a home-owner. Has R.E.M. arrived?

Sorta. With two LPs that sell consistently—both *Murmur* and *Reckoning* have cracked 300,000 and are still moving—and an EP *(Chronic Town)* that's by no means dead, R.E.M. has seen the last of the grinding, open-ended, van-propelled tours to everywhere that built their fanatical following and blazed an alternative trail for young combos with the urge to play and something to say. The band's progression has been so steadily gradual since the 1981 independent release of the now collectible "Radio Free Europe" / "Sitting Still" single that championing R.E.M. is almost reflexive, even though the uninitiated has for some time been a diminishing crew. But the success of devotees' ardent efforts to realize their cause and put the band over may ironically be the very factor that ends R.E.M.'s honeymoon with fans and critics alike. Even given the modest level of success the group now enjoys—don't forget, in this multi-platinum age, R.E.M. has yet to score its first *gold* record—strange things sometimes happen when cults become crowds, clubs concert halls and underdogs victors. The band that once could do no wrong can suddenly be seen as doing nothing right. Unrealistic, highly personal standards are set, and if they're not met (can they ever be met?): the backlash. I ask again, Has R.E.M. arrived?

Bassist Mike Mills and drummer Bill Berry consider what's changed for the band over the years as they throw back brew and munch on fruit and cheese on the R.E.M. tour bus. "A lot of people bitched because we charged $15 for a New Year's Eve show," Mills recalls, with a laughing seriousness, "with three bands and a whole lot of fun stuff, balloons and big lights that said 1985 and stuff . . ."

"To get it all together we had to rent the Atlanta Civic Center for two nights," adds Berry. "I figured out what we got for that, R.E.M. got *one dollar* of that fifteen."

Mills pitches in again: "And then there were people bitching, 'Oh, man, four years ago you coulda seen them for $2 at Tyrone's.' Well, *goddamn,* don't you get a *raise* when you work somewhere for five years? When you graduate from school, you're gonna go out and expect a raise when you've been somewhere for two years—don't bitch when we get one!"

Unless a single breaks out and carries the band to a truly mass audience, *Fables of the Reconstruction* will not be the LP that brings R.E.M. another big raise and broadens their following much beyond its current size. The faithful will willingly grant the album the time it takes for its virtues to unfold, but *Fables,* which lacks *Murmur*'s instant, disarming uplift and *Reckoning*'s lyrical expansiveness, is too dense and foreboding to welcome new listeners very easily. Buck acknowledges that certain aspects of *Fables* might not only throw newcomers to the band, but might upset widely held preconceptions among long-standing supporters about what an R.E.M. record should be like. "Listening to the record in retrospect," he allows, "it seems that something like, oh, 'Can't Get There From Here,' the first song, or 'Gravitys Pull' are pretty much stylistically unlike anything else we've ever done. It's not that shocking as far as what happens in rock & roll, but there's a horn section on one track and a really strange string section on another. There's a little bit of a soul feeling on 'Can't Get There From Here.' I think we just had a lot of divergent ideas about what we wanted to do with the album when it was being written, and we decided to encompass them all instead of one or two."

One way *Fables* diverges from its predecessors is that R.E.M. didn't use long-time pals Mitch Easter and Don Dixon for production. Instead the band journeyed to England to work at Livingston Studios with Joe Boyd, who's produced Fairport Convention and Richard Thompson. "Both Mitch Easter [who fronts the North Carolina combo, Let's Active] and Don Dixon were busy doing their own creative stuff," Buck explains, "and we all felt that it would be good to have a change, because they didn't want to get associated with us permanently any more than we wanted to be associated with them permanently . . . We had a list of producers who were interested in us, and Joe Boyd was one of them. We do things by intuition; we didn't think whether he had a track record or whatever—I liked his records, I liked him. We just decided on the spur of the moment, 'Okay, let's do it with him. Let's fly to England tomorrow and do the record.' It was that simple. We met him on Wednesday, and we decided on Thursday to fly to England and we left Friday."

Literally winging it to work with Boyd—"We didn't really want a producer who would give us the 'Steve Lillywhite sound' or the AOR sound," Buck insists—R.E.M. countered speculation that in their third LP outing they'd consciously shoot for a disc that, without compromising their characteristic style, would make them more radio-friendly. As it turns out, the swinging "Can't Get There From Here" and urgent "Driver 8" both are potentially stronger singles than anything R.E.M.'s previously come up with. But if you've been listening to the super-smooth high ends and bam-boom bottoms of radio hits these days, it won't take you more than a few seconds to realize that the straightforward, unspectacular Joe Boyd ain't Phil Collins. And that's just fine with Buck.

"There's a style of production that's predominant on AOR radio," the guitarist states. "It's mostly digital, real slick-sounding things, real high-tech drums, real crisp and real sterile, and our records don't sound like that. I don't like digital recording, I think it's completely dead sounding. Well, no, it's *live,* but it's lively just like an electric mannequin is lively. I think the human ear is designed to hear—at least we were brought up to hear—distortion in things. This natural built-in distortion from the word go has always been in electronic instruments and in electronic reproduction. And without it—which is what digital does, it cuts down the distortion in the transfer from the tape to, um, the *other* tape or whatever, I don't know, screw it, it's all technical stuff—but it takes away this distortion that people our age are used to hearing. All the rock & roll records I had when I was a kid have this built-in distortion, every record ever made did until five or six years ago.

"I've kind of come to terms with the fact that we're never going to be a singles band," he continues. "We might make good singles, but they're parts of albums. When you hear 'So. Central Rain,' it's a good song but it *really* makes sense in the context of the album. Out of that context, although it's a good song, it doesn't make as much sense as something like that Def Leppard song, 'Foolin'.' Now *that* makes sense on any radio station, any time you hear it, on video, TV *and* in the context of the album. Our stuff, you almost have to understand it before you hear it in between Joan Jett and Foreigner.

"I listen to the radio the way most people listen to it, for a snappy chorus or whatever. Again, that Def Leppard song, 'Foolin',' I don't know any of the words except 'Fuh-fuh-fuh-foolin',' you know? But that's the *hook,* it's so overpowering with the guitars and all that it carries you in. And our stuff just doesn't have that. The hooks are more subtle and emotional and colored than something that hits with a sledge-hammer. Another hook that's real heavy is 'We Got the Beat,' you know (sings) 'Hey, hey, hey,' where the girls sing that? You hear that and your head snaps around, it's in your head for the rest of the week. I don't think our stuff is really like that. I mean, it might be in your head, but it's the kind of thing where you go, 'What *was* that I heard?' "

SPINNING OFF IMPROVISED BIRD calls and leafing through art books, singer Michael Stipe stretches out on the lawn outside Waveform Media Rehearsal Studios in Atlanta, where R.E.M. is gearing up for a string of pre-album release college dates. An album called *Fables of the Reconstruction* and song titles like "The Auctioneer," "Wendell Gee," "Driver 8" and "Old Man Kinsey" led to speculation about thematic threads running through the new LP. "We suddenly had all these songs that were somewhat narrative," Stipe states. "Although I hesitate to use that term because all along we've said that our songs are not stories—not a beginning and an end with a middle and some kind of crisis point that has to be resolved. Most of these, I would say, would be a slice somewhere out of the middle; there's not really a beginning or an end. If you had to call it a narrative, it's probably not a complete one. That is real new for me, though, and it's real new for us. I found myself surrounded a whole lot when we were writing these songs by fables and nursery rhymes and *Uncle Remus* and old tales. The idea of stories being passed down and becoming a tradition, and having those stories become as much a part of a way of living or a particular area that you live in as the religion or the trees or the weather, I like the connection between that and the South."

And the South is undeniably a brooding, haunting presence on *Fables*—"There's more of a feeling of place on this record," says Buck, "a sense of home and a sense that we're not there"—but it's not the stereotypical South that governs the imagination of people who've never lived there. "I know we have a definite feeling of being Southern," Buck asserts. "I don't know if it shows up in the music much, but then again I don't know how it wouldn't. I read this article about the Del Fuegos—I really like them. It was this guy in the *Village Voice,* and he goes, Oh, you know, the Del Fuegos, they've got the soul of a real Southern band, unlike R.E.M., who could be from Chicago. And the reason he said that is because the Del Fuegos sing about getting their paycheck, driving around in their car and getting drunk. And I thought, well, gosh, *right,* that's all Southerners do. Being from the South is not Dukes of Hazzard country. Being from the South encompasses a lot of things that are slower and more reflective, that's the way I think of the South. I don't think of it as some redneck heaven. It's more of a strange, slow, surrealistic place, and that comes through in a lot of our records."

Like, for example, in the moody night-train tune, "Driver 8," where, in one of the album's recurrent blurrings of distance and desire, Stipe nervously assures that, "We can reach our destination, but it's still a ways away." "In 'Driver 8' there is this real kind of searching," the singer states. "It's not like an ignorant searching, people kind of know what they're looking for. But it's something that's almost unobtainable, it's almost an idea, it's almost this fantasy or this dream, and you're fooling yourself into believing that it is obtainable, when in fact it really isn't. Or, if it was at one time, it's gone away farther than that."

THE PERIOD OF RECONSTRUCTION after the Civil War was a time of agonizing dislocation in the South. The stir of promise only salted the sting of loss. Withdrawal overcame whatever urge for reconciliation existed in the region, and the South's eerie separateness was birthed as surely in defeat as it would have been in victory. Now from their four-year pilgrimage through "Little America" and the big world beyond, R.E.M. has returned to this real and mythical home for a time of recollection and soul searching as unsettlingly ambivalent as the tales they uncover on their new LP.

Speaking of *Reconstruction,* Berry states that "The first thing I thought of was literally the definition of the word, and that was what we did when we went in to write the songs and do the record. We pretty much just stripped down and started over, because we did write all those songs at one time." However, R.E.M.'s reconstruction, rebuilding and psychic retreat come as the price of victory, not defeat. After years of being the coming thing, their preeminence on the contemporary music scene is now virtually unquestioned. Their take-it-to-the-people, tour-till-you-drop approach to the independent music market is now an established path of progress for young bands. Almost all the kindred bands they've battled for have been signed to major labels. Their example has taught that it's at least possible to make it by doing nothing but what you want. Their outspoken demands in *Record* and elsewhere for a fair hearing for American bands has contributed in part to the surge in popularity American music is now enjoying worldwide. They helped create and shape the very American underground they're in the process of rising above.

So has R.E.M. arrived? Listen to "Driver 8" and the other songs on *Fables,* like the clashing background vocals on the opening track that argue "I've been there, I know the way" against Stipe's insistence that "You can't get there from here." Or Stipe's yearning claim in "Good Advices" that "Home is a long way away . . . I'd like it here if I could leave and see you from a long way away." "You learn a lot as you go along, but then you also learn there are a lot of things you just don't know," reflects Berry. "I'll tell you, one thing I think we've come around to is that our intuition is usually right." He illustrates his point with an anecdote from four years ago. "You know, Miles Copeland came into our hotel room at the Iroquois and said we didn't have the image," Berry says. "We should be going on all these monstrous tours opening for people all over the world. We should do this, we should do that, we should have a big-name producer, we should make high-tech videos. And we've proven pretty much that we were right in the past, and now we're confident in our assertions. But we're still confused."

Confident and confused, a triumphant R.E.M. has arrived back home, arrived in the ambiguous country to which their good efforts have led.

DAVID FRICKE

R.E.M.'S SOUTHERN-FRIED ART
The Thinking Fan's Rock Band
Just Wants You to Dance

F OR ABOUT TWENTY MINUTES in Ottawa last August, the four members of R.E.M. thought they were the most boring rock & roll band on the planet. Marching soberly into their first number, the harsh, funereal "Feeling Gravitys Pull," at a local club called Barrymore's, they trudged through half a dozen songs like studio zombies, hitting every note and plucking every string with numbing accuracy. Their performance was tight, absolutely correct—and utterly lifeless. The sellout crowd greeted them like conquering heroes, the hip generals of America's New Music revolt. But R.E.M. knew this was third-rate entertainment, rock by numbers, and they hated themselves for it.

So they hit the covers with a vengeance, starting with clumsy stomps through Brownsville Station's "Smokin' in the Boys' Room" and Lynyrd Skynyrd's "Sweet Home Alabama." Singer Michael Stipe recited the Sex Pistols' "God Save the Queen" and blew half the lyrics to "Secret Agent Man." Guitarist Peter Buck challenged a heckler who yelled "Fuck you" during their a cappella reading of "Moon River" to come backstage after the show, presumably for a good beating. By the end of the set, songs by Marc Bolan, Jonathan Richman and the Monkees had been fried beyond recognition, in spite of Bill Berry's yeoman drumming, and Buck had ripped most of Stipe's clothing to shreds. *This* is how R.E.M. is changing the face of American rock & roll?

"The most crippling thing for a band like us," bassist Mike Mills explains over a few Buds about two weeks later in a Washington, D.C. hotel room, "would be to feel that we have to do a really professional set. Once we decide that because people paid money that we have to give them the most perfect set we can, we're finished."

He recalls a similar free-for-all in Buffalo a couple of years ago. "We did maybe five of our own songs and the rest was all covers. A couple of guys came up after the show and wanted their money back because we didn't play enough R.E.M. songs. We told them they were completely missing the point. We were playing rock & roll, and we gave everything we had for it."

R.E.M. is now well paid for its sacrifice. Four years ago, they would return home to Athens, Georgia, from a six-week cross-country tour of slummy beer joints and creepy New Wave discos—sleeping five to a hotel room (including Jefferson Holt, their manager), doing up to five hundred miles a day in a green Dodge van—and split forty-five dollars in profit between them. This year, the band's third album, *Fables of the Reconstruction,* zipped straight into *Billboard*'s Top Thirty, selling over 300,000 copies in only three months, while on tour R.E.M. is selling out the likes of Radio City Music Hall. Buck, whose previous job experience includes washing dishes and cleaning toilets, expects to make at least $24,000 this year, not including future *Fables* songwriting royalties.

That is humble money compared to the megawealth of Prince and Bruce Springsteen, but R.E.M.'s real achievements transcend record-company arithmetic. In 1980 and 1981, when many top New Wave acts mostly toured major cities, R.E.M. whipped through such forgotten markets as Greensboro, North Carolina, and Louisville, Kentucky, establishing a vital link between small, active but heretofore isolated New Music scenes. Later on, they showed good taste in opening acts, booking fellow rebels the Replacements, Hüsker Dü and Jason and the Scorchers, providing national exposure that in some cases led to major-label deals.

More important, R.E.M.'s success has proven to America's postpunk generation the power of underground virtues in the overground world. *Fables* producer Joe Boyd describes the group's attitude as an "absence of doubt without arrogance." Hardly standard-issue rock & roll bullies, R.E.M. instead practices a kind of homespun sorcery, with Michael Stipe's onomatopoeic bleating and the pretzel twists of such haunting folk-pop carols as "So. Central Rain" on last year's *Reckoning* and "Driver 8," a panoramic train song, on *Fables.* Then they package the music in playful abstract videos and cryptic cover art, like the spooky kudzu still life on 1983's *Murmur.* Onstage they conduct their hoodlum punk business— Stipe's mutant frugging, Buck's frantic scissors kicks—in near darkness, the dusky lighting (designed by Stipe) creating the illusion of Who-like shadow puppets.

In short, by most record-company standards, R.E.M. gets away with murder. When they selected Boyd, the American-born godfather of British folk-rock (the producer of Richard Thompson and Fairport Convention), to produce *Fables,* I.R.S. Records, the band's label, raised a few commercial objections. R.E.M. flew to London to record with Boyd anyway, under the flimsy pretext of cutting some demos.

"R.E.M. has a very firm vision of what they want to do and how they want to do it," says Jay Boberg, president of I.R.S., sighing, "If their album covers are not good marketing tools, hey, too bad for us. They're not willing to compromise that." Their only notable concession to I.R.S. was a series of seven stadium dates opening for the Police in 1983. Buck claims that if the tour had gone on even a week longer, the band would have broken up just to get out of it.

"We get away with a lot of shit," grins Buck, 28, who's obviously hit the bottom of his road laundry in his grimy Iron Maiden sweatshirt. A Day-Glo-orange toy monkey dangles from his belt loop. "But it's reasonable shit. It's not like we're asking for the brown M&M's to be taken out of the dish. We want the power of our lives in our own hands. We made a contract with the world that says, 'We're going to be the best band in the world; you're going to be proud of us. But we have to do it our way.' "

Formed in Athens in April 1980, the embryonic R.E.M. was an unlikely alliance. Easygoing Bill Berry (a native of Hibbing, Minnesota, Bob Dylan's hometown) and chipper, bookish-looking Mike Mills had already played together in sock-hop bands in nearby Macon. Buck, who worked at a used-record store, was a motormouth from Atlanta, well versed in rock culture but "a little too cynical for his own good," according to Berry. The youngest of the four, Stipe was also the strangest. "Michael said he liked my eyebrows," Berry says, chuckling. "He claims to this day that's the reason he wanted us to get together."

Happy in the lazy groove of student life at the University of Georgia, R.E.M. lived only from weekend to weekend, playing student parties where they drew both punky hipsters and woolly frat animals. They released an indie single, "Radio Free Europe" / "Sitting Still," essentially to help get club gigs. To their utter amazement, it topped many critics' best-of lists for 1981. At the time, says Berry, 27, R.E.M. was basically "three chords and a six-pack of beer."

Even three chords is stretching it: self-taught guitarist Buck says that the first ten songs R.E.M. ever wrote all started with an A chord. "It was the only chord I really liked."

As singer and lyricist, Michael Stipe, 25, took the band on its first turns into deep left field. A well-traveled army brat born in Decatur, Georgia, he studied painting and photography at U. of G., developing a special taste for surrealism and medieval manuscript illumination. His songwriting soon mirrored those interests. On pivotal early originals, like "Gardening at Night" and "Carnival of Sorts (Boxcars)," both included on the 1982 EP *Chronic Town,* Stipe combined vivid imagery with pithy telegraphic phrasing, sacrificing grammar for impact. "He leaves out essential parts of speech," Berry warns. "People try to guess the next word before he says it. Then when it's not there, they completely lose it." "He can see the way things fall apart," adds Mills, 26, "rather than the way things fall together."

"A lot of my critics say the words are complete chaos," admits Stipe. With his severely cut hair, now dyed golden blond, and hushed, almost religious demeanor, he suggests nothing so much as a Hasidic surfer. "In some cases, they really are. But more likely than not, they are extremely linear." Indeed, many of the songs on *Fables* are narrative, pastoral travelogues rooted in a wistful, almost nineteenth-century yearning for decency and honesty. Yet Stipe finds that even sincere fans mistake his probing eccentricity for mere weirdness. Among the gifts he's received on tour recently are a ball-peen hammer, bouquets of human hair ("I don't even want the hair of people that I know") and a turtle.

"But let people think what they want to," Stipe shrugs. "That's probably entertaining to them, considering me some kind of weird jigsaw puzzle where they can't quite find out where the missing pieces are." It's just too bad, he adds, that "a lot of people don't see the humor in what we do."

Until recently, R.E.M. road life was one laugh after another. On their first tour above the Mason-Dixon line, the band got as far north as Princeton University, where they played a dance. "The theme for this party," Buck remembers, "was 'Lust in Space.' There were these Princeton guys, the young hearts and minds of America, walking around with big aluminum-foil penises." The band, of course, went "totally insane. We were leaping into the audience and attacking people. We got five encores, and people were throwing their metal dildos on stage."

Bill Berry's favorite story is about the night the band pulled into a Howard Johnson's during an all-night haul to Ohio. Berry, who was at the wheel, claims they drove sixty miles before they realized they'd left their manager back in the HoJo men's room. It was another forty before they could turn around on the turnpike. "I figured we eventually drove an extra two hundred miles to go back for him.

"Compared to what used to be a really ripe situation for weird things to happen, this is kind of predictable." Berry gestures, a little sadly, around the band's roomy tour bus (the sign on front says, NOBODY YOU KNOW). "The funny little things don't happen anymore."

They are content with their modest prosperity. Buck recently bought a house; otherwise, his chief indulgences are records and beer. Mills and Berry both own hot new wheels, a turquoise '66 Thunderbird and a lavender '60 Ford Galaxie, respectively. Stipe buys art, and he recently purchased two mud paintings by Juanita Rogers. Otherwise, he says, "I have a bicycle to get around, and in the winter my mom lets me borrow her car."

But R.E.M.'s growing popularity has brought with it responsibility for a movement they inspired—the current American guitar-based rediscovery of Sixties song values and Seventies punk spirit—but never asked to lead. New groups are already copying the jump-and-jangle of R.E.M.'s sound without understanding the message of their conviction. Upstate New York band 10,000 Maniacs, close friends of R.E.M., told Buck that of the local bands opening for them on a recent East Coast swing, half did "Radio Free Europe."

Those bands would do better to heed these words from Mike Mills: "We do it because around the corner is another thrill. Not another thousand bucks."

FRED SCHRUERS

YEAR-END REVIEW OF
FABLES OF THE RECONSTRUCTION

O R *RECONSTRUCTION OF THE FABLES,* right? Did you know that all the lyrics, with Michael Stipe's footnotes, are available for the price of a stamped, self-addressed envelope sent to—just kidding. Where would the fun be in that? It's a lot harder to hide meaning than to spoon it out, though there's a trace of the sophomoric in either approach. R.E.M. is often more about textures than anything else, and the refrain to the Byrds-like "Driver 8"—"And the train conductor says / 'Take a break, Driver 8' "—is just a foothold in the very pleasurable climb to some kind of sunny meadow where we'll bask in the mumble, lisp and twang of the next song. When Peter Buck throws a train-whistle guitar run into the headlong "Auctioneer (Another Engine)," that provides the listener as much of an emotional clue as Stipe's burring voice—which is somewhere midway between a horn and a stringed instrument. Producer Joe Boyd, a veteran of the British folk scene, has not altered the band's sound in any major way, and what we have here is simply a fourth well-made R.E.M. riddle to get nervously lost in the ozone with.

1985 MUSIC AWARDS

MICHAEL STIPE'S FAVORITE RECORDINGS OF 1985

Cabin Flounder, Fetchin Bones, DB

Project Mersh, Minutemen, SST

The Wishing Chair, 10,000 Maniacs, Elektra

Telephone Free Landslide Victory, Camper Van Beethoven, Independent Project

Rain Dogs, Tom Waits, Island

Mister Heartbreak, Laurie Anderson, Warner Bros.

Flip Your Wig, Hüsker Dü, SST

Fegmanial!, Robyn Hitchcock, Slash

Tragic Figures, Savage Republic, Independent Project

Squalls, Squalls, Mbrella

■ **RANDOM NOTES** NOTABLE NEWS (June 5, 1986)

John Cougar Mellencamp producer Don Gehman will produce X's next record after he wraps up work on the fourth R.E.M. album.

■ **RANDOM NOTES** SMALL-TOWN BOYS (July 17, 1986)

Early this summer, R.E.M. finished up its fourth album, *Lifes Rich Pageant,* which the band recorded in John Cougar Mellencamp's studio in Bloomington, Indiana, with producer Don Gehman. Bassist Mike Mills describes the result as "more accessible—the strongest, best album we've done. Bloomington was a lot like Athens. There aren't many distractions." But the band members weren't hermits. "We went out to bars and saw bands. The big thing there is cover bands." Mills has his own cover band, called the Corn Cobwebs, and he, R.E.M. guitarist Peter Buck (who may play on Robbie Robertson's LP) and drummer Bill Berry are in the Hindu Love Gods, along with Warren Zevon and singer Bryan Cook. R.E.M. vocalist Michael Stipe will probably tour briefly with the Golden Palominos, and he'll also produce a New York band called Hugo Largo.

ANTHONY DeCURTIS

LIFES RICH PAGEANT ALBUM REVIEW
R.E.M. Goes Public

OR R.E.M., THE UNDERGROUND ends here. *Lifes Rich Pageant,* the band's fourth LP, comes on with such full-throttle force that it's impossible to imagine AOR radio—if not Top Forty stations—failing to bring this group a broader audience. Moreover, *Lifes Rich Pageant,* as its partially ironic title suggests, is the most outward-looking record R.E.M. has made, a worthy companion to R.E.M.'s bracing live shows and its earned status as a do-it-yourself and do-it-your-way model for young American bands.

Thematically, *Lifes Rich Pageant* carries on the legacy of songs like the probing on-the-road rock-out "Little America" and the dark Southern folk artistry of last year's *Fables of the Reconstruction.* Suffused with a love of nature and a desire for mankind's survival, the LP paints a swirling, impressionistic portrait of a country at the moral crossroads, at once imperiled by its own self-destructive impulses and poised for a hopeful new beginning.

"Let's put our heads together, and start a new country up," lead singer Michael Stipe suggests in the environmentalist anthem "Cuyahoga," and that invitation to action stands at the heart of *Lifes Rich Pageant.* "Silence means security silence means approval," Stipe declares over the churning Yardbirds Orientalism of Peter Buck's guitars in "Begin the Begin," the LP's powerhouse opening cut and a searing indictment of apathy. Stipe's insistence that we "begin again" sets the stage for the equally torrid rocker "These Days." Its chorus defines a statement of generational purpose: "We are young despite the years / We are concern / We are hope despite the times." Still another guitar raveup, "Hyena," makes nuclear posturing its target: "The only thing to fear is fearlessness / The bigger the weapon, the greater the fear."

Of course, despite the social vision that unifies the LP, anyone who comes to *Lifes Rich Pageant* expecting "Eve of Destruction" directness will be sorely disappointed. *Lifes Rich Pageant* may be more manifestly focused than R.E.M. has been in the past, but Stipe continues his seductive dance of veiled meanings in both his vocals and lyrics. "Cuyahoga," for example, derives its emotive effect as much from Stipe's sensuous love of singing that beautiful Indian word as from the song's concern over the poisoning of the Ohio river—separating the tune's "message" from the timbre of Stipe's resonant, raspy baritone is pointless. And the Velvet Underground-like "The Flowers of Guatemala," with its incantatory choruses and poetic cadences, illustrates that his powers of personal observation are undiminished by the album's public concerns.

Ever since the compelling obliqueness of "Radio Free Europe" first brought the band to national attention in 1981, R.E.M.'s impact has always depended much more on sound than sense. Buck's ringing guitars, the inspirational reach of Stipe's singing, Mike Mills's musical bass parts, Bill Berry's subtle, steady drums, the uplifting choruses that sweep the vocal harmonies into a rush of feeling—these all communicate "meaning" in an R.E.M. song, rendering the much-belabored "obscurity" of Stipe's lyrics irrelevant.

On *Lifes Rich Pageant,* producer Don Gehman has done an outstanding job of hardening R.E.M.'s sonic jolt. Without sacrificing the band's lushness and texture, Gehman has crafted a sound that subordinates musical details and coloring to the main instrumental thrust of each song. The distractions that occasionally crept into Mitch Easter and Don Dixon's productions (the two LPs *Murmur* and *Reckoning* and the EP *Chronic Town,* which Easter produced solo), not to mention the ominous murkiness of Joe Boyd's work on *Fables,* are dispelled on this album. The most basic conventions of rock recording—clear, crisp, loud drums, for example—which R.E.M. had almost perversely avoided before (largely at Stipe's insistence), are observed. As a result, *Lifes Rich Pageant* has a contemporary feel, even as it sidesteps obvious modern electronics and indulges in such oldfangled touches as pianos, banjos, accordions and pump organs.

In its least successful tactic, R.E.M. attempts to leaven the seriousness of *Lifes Rich Pageant*—and counteract a widespread perception of the band as a bunch of precious psychedelic mystics—with humor. The album's (intentionally misspelled) title is taken from a remark by the Peter Sellers character Inspector Clouseau, to the effect that even the most absurd setbacks are part of "life's rich pageant"—a sentiment that became something like the band's motto. The album has a "dinner" and a "supper" side, and each side wraps with songs that are, if not throwaways, at best flip sides to singles.

The dinner-side closer is "Underneath the Bunker," a bit of spaghetti-western nonsense; it's merely a curiosity and of interest only to buffs. More winning is "Superman," which ends the supper side. An irresistibly cheesy psychedelic grunge rocker (originally recorded during the head-music hey-day of the late Sixties by the Clique), "Superman" gets an energetic treat-ment, with Mike Mills turning in a superb debut as lead vocalist.

But signing off both sides of an LP as rousing and raucous as *Lifes Rich Pageant* with self-consciously hip jokes is an unfortunate waste—an appar-ent effort to cling to insider status when every other aspect of the album is a lesson in how to assume the responsibilities of mass popularity without smoothing the subterranean edge. Two more top-flight R.E.M. songs might have made *Lifes Rich Pageant* a masterpiece—ranking with *Remain in Light* and *Born in the U.S.A.* as seminal American records of the Eighties. As it is, it's a brilliant and groundbreaking, if modestly flawed, effort by an immensely valuable band whose most profound work is still to come.

■ **RANDOM NOTES** R.E.M.'S PAGEANT PIT STOP (November 6, 1986)

The stage setup on R.E.M.'s current tour resembles an old-fashioned theater, with lights coming through black-curtained windows on both sides. The back wall is a screen on which occasional images are flashed—video outtakes and slides by **Michael Stipe.** Besides playing its familiar hits, R.E.M. is doing covers of **Iggy Pop** ("Funtime") and **Wire,** along with some originals so new they don't even have names yet. Bespectacled bassist **Mike Mills** says that overnight bus rides don't allow the band members as much musical extracurricular activity as they'd like, but so far R.E.M. has met up with Cajun legend **Clifton Chenier** in Houston and jammed with members of North Carolina's **Fetchin' Bones** and a horn section called the **Soul Capitalists** in a Memphis dive. "What kind of songs did we play?" Mills says. "Easy ones, real easy ones—like 'Rock & Roll,' by **Led Zeppelin.**" That seems appropriate, somehow.

STEVE POND

R.E.M.'S PREDICTABLE PAGEANT

I N SOME CIRCLES, R.E.M.'S new album has been hailed as a breakthrough on which a new producer has given the band's music the rock & roll kick it's been missing. In other circles, *Lifes Rich Pageant* has been dismissed as R.E.M.'s most blatant attempt yet to pass off vague feelings and sentimental yearnings as coherent songwriting. But onstage none of that means much, because the band's *Lifes Rich Pageant* tour is pretty much business as usual for the four Georgians who've become the archetype for regional American rock in the Eighties.

In other words, the guys who made jangling guitars and inspirational longing *de rigueur* on college radio still deliver lots of that in concert, with enough punch and verve to show why they've had such an impact. Many of the best parts of their L.A. show were those that were the most propulsive and sometimes the most daring: they flattened and roughed up the melodies of "Radio Free Europe," "Auctioneer" and "1,000,000," counting on their head of steam to put the songs across.

But the single most memorable moment of the concert had to do with melody, not momentum. In the evening's one indisputable standout, R.E.M. encored with an understated version of the cautionary "Fall on Me," its current single and one of the loveliest and most lyrically substantial tunes that the band's ever recorded.

Aside from that, though, R.E.M. didn't show the reverent crowd much that it hadn't already demonstrated at plenty of previous shows. In fact, despite the highlights, the set had an unsettling air of stagnation about it, as if the band had trotted out this kind of thing too many times before. R.E.M. is far too young a band to have turned a live show into this kind of comfortable ritual—and while "Sitting Still," from 1981, may have been a welcome song choice, there's a little too much irony in that title these days.

The boys in the band did try to throw a few curves: they did a Floyd Cramer cover; singer Michael Stipe added a few Patti Smith lines to one song; they used an uncharacteristically elaborate stage set (colored lights came at the band through what looked like big church windows and characteristically moody and hard-to-see films were projected on the back wall); and they made some onstage comments that were even more explicit than the relatively topical lyrics on the new album. "I pledge allegiance to no flag," said singer Michael Stipe at one point. "I pledge allegiance to the ground I stand on." For at least one night, though, he fell short of giving listeners any new reasons to pledge allegiance to his band.

YEAR-END REVIEW OF
LIFES RICH PAGEANT

WITH ALBUM NUMBER FOUR, R.E.M. made the quantum leap from underground sensation to mainstream sock-it-to-'em. Don Gehman's aggressively straightforward production gave the band's basic guitar-combo sound a forceful jolt, closer to the spirit and power of its celebratory live shows than any previous R.E.M. record. But the lustrous tone of *Lifes Rich Pageant* also had a lot to do with the group's top-drawer originals—the locomotive roll of "Begin the Begin" and "Hyena," the quiet radiance of "Cuyahoga," the velvet caress of the near hit "Fall on Me." Packaged with typical R.E.M. whimsy, this was without question one of the best made-in-the-U.S.A. albums of '86. The only thing missing was the apostrophe.

1986 MUSIC AWARDS

PETER BUCK'S FAVORITE RECORDINGS OF 1986

Element of Light, Robyn Hitchcock and the Egyptians, Relativity

Evol, Sonic Youth, SST

All-Night Lotus Party, Volcano Suns, Homestead

Daring Adventures, Richard Thompson, Polydor

Trudge, Savage Republic, Play It Again Sam

A Date with Elvis, the Cramps, Big Beat

Candy Apple Grey, Hüsker Dü, Warner Bros.

Out My Way, Meat Puppets, SST

Kicking Against the Pricks, Nick Cave, Homestead

Scarred but Smarter, Drivin' and Cryin', 688

JIMMY GUTERMAN

DEAD LETTER OFFICE ALBUM REVIEW

NEITHER THE NEW R.E.M. album nor the stopgap product that bands often spit out between real records, *Dead Letter Office* is what its title suggests, a clearinghouse for outtakes, cover versions and B sides of singles. If the fans don't like it, the next R.E.M. album will be out in September and this one will quickly fade. (CD purchasers get a bonus: the disc version of *Dead Letter Office* includes all of the songs from the band's 1982 EP *Chronic Town,* which was previously unavailable on CD.)

Dead Letter Office sets its sights far lower than any of the band's previous four LPs, but the first R.E.M. record wholly without pretension is something of an event. The self-deprecating, generous inner-sleeve notes, written by guitarist Peter Buck, prevent any stuffiness. For example, on his band's deconstruction of Roger Miller's fabled "King of the Road," Buck muses that Miller "should be able to sue for what we did to this song."

Dead Letter Office is R.E.M.'s loosest record. Singer Michael Stipe is as open as the best of *Lifes Rich Pageant* suggested he always could be, and on "Burning Hell" and "Ages of You," Buck's guitar work is his least studied and most unrestrained. Reverential covers of songs by the Velvet Underground, Aerosmith and Pylon nudge against the steady instrumental "White Tornado" and the wacky "Walters Theme," helping to define the sources of this wide-ranging band. *Dead Letter Office* isn't meant to be anything special. That's why it is.

ANTHONY DeCURTIS

IN BRIEF

R.E.M.'S NEW LP, RECORDED in Nashville with producer **Scott Litt**, is finished and set for an early-September release. Titled *Document,* the record includes "Exhuming McCarthy" (the title referring to the late **Senator Joseph McCarthy**), "The One I Love" and "Finest Worksong." Despite earlier reports, **Peter Buck, Mike Mills** and **Bill Berry** will not be touring with **Warren Zevon** this summer, but R.E.M. will tour after *Document* is released. Until then, fans can read *Pete Buck,* the tabloid-size pen-and-ink comic-book fantasy devoted to the R.E.M. guitar hero.

THE TOP 100: THE BEST ALBUMS OF THE LAST 20 YEARS
MURMUR

To celebrate ROLLING STONE's twentieth anniversary, the magazine's editors chose the 100 greatest albums of the past two decades. R.E.M.'s first LP made the cut.

#58 *Murmur*

Moody and stylish, retro feeling but forward looking, R.E.M.'s first full-length album announced the arrival of America's first major band of the 1980s.

The band, which hails from Athens, Georgia, made its debut with the 1982 EP *Chronic Town*. The song titles were arch—"Wolves, Lower" and "Carnival of Sorts"—but the music brimmed with weird noises and murky but catchy riffs.

Then I.R.S. sent the band into a Boston studio to make its first album with producer Stephen Hague, who had worked with the Human League. Hague set a rigid beat with a click track, tried to add synthesizers and had the band play "Catapult" forty-eight times. Terrified, R.E.M. fled back to the South and to *Chronic Town* producer Mitch Easter.

"We wanted to make a ghostly, floating, from-nowhere album," says guitarist Peter Buck. "I don't know why we felt confident enough to make such a weird record. Because live, we were still a rock & roll band, concentrating on vocals, falling down, whatever. But it was time to come up with something a bit more diverse, evocative."

"They were concerned about keeping themselves intact," says Easter. "R.E.M. wasn't the type of band that brought in someone else's record and said, 'Can you get us a mix this hot?' There wasn't a lot of concern with radio play. Bands from the South tend not to be tuned in to showbiz."

With Easter and Don Dixon at the helm in a studio where Tammy Bakker had recorded, R.E.M. laid down "Pilgrimage" as a test, and it worked brilliantly. Lead singer Michael Stipe recalls layering "thousands of vocals on it, to make it sound like a Gregorian chant. They're still there, way buried. We put everything in the world on that record, way buried."

Intriguing stray sounds permeate the texture of *Murmur* (so named because "it's one of the seven easiest words to say in the English language," says Stipe). On "We Walk" the booming noise is the electronically altered sound of drummer Bill Berry playing pool in a room underneath the vocal booth, and the opening futuristic rumbling of "Radio Free Europe" is the studio's inherent background hum, amplified and keyed into Mike Mills's bass. "Perfect Circle" is enhanced by a backward guitar part and the same thing played on two different pianos, one fancy, the other an untuned tack.

Out of the wondrous shimmer arise Stipe's echoey, highly impressionistic vocals. "A lot of reviews said his voice is buried in the mix," says Easter, "but it just comes out of his mouth like that. He didn't want to be one of those bombastic-lead-singer types."

"We knew we were onto something," says Buck. "I like some of our albums better, but it's the one that has the most weird soul to it."

Recorded at Reflection, Charlotte, North Carolina, January 1983. RELEASED: September 1983 PRODUCERS AND ENGINEERS: *Mitch Easter and Don Dixon.* HIGHEST CHART POSITION: *Number Thirty-six.* TOTAL U.S. SALES TO DATE: *375,000.*

■ **RANDOM NOTES** NOTABLE NEWS (September 10, 1987)

R.E.M. manager **Jefferson Holt** has started a new record label, called Sosumi Records. Sosumi will release its first LP, *Rebel Shoes,* by the **Squalls**, from Athens, Georgia, in mid-September: a single by the **Vibrating Egg** will follow in November.

■ **RANDOM NOTES** JUST RELEASED: *DOCUMENT* September 24, 1987

Document. *R.E.M. I.R.S.* Peter Buck recently described R.E.M.'s last album of new material, the surprisingly straightforward *Lifes Rich Pageant,* as the group's "Bryan Adams" record. *Document* is a looser, more typically idiosyncratic effort from Athens' finest. "Exhuming McCarthy" is an inspired piece of politically astute garage rock. "The One I Love" (the first single from the album) is the band's "Every Breath You Take," an extremely pretty but menacing love song that could be the band's first hit. Other high points are "Welcome to the Occupation" and the wonderfully titled "Its the End of the World As We Know It (and I Feel Fine)."

DAVID FRICKE

DOCUMENT ALBUM REVIEW

R.E.M.'s Valuable *Document*

I**T IS NO ACCIDENT** that R.E.M.'s finest album to date opens with the anthemic reveille "Finest Worksong," a muscular funky–metal wake–up call that is an unmistakable declaration of intent. "The time to rise / Has been engaged," bleats singer Michael Stipe over the industrial scrape of Peter Buck's guitar and the martial locomotion of bassist Mike Mills and drummer Bill Berry. "We're better / Best to rearrange." *Document,* the fifth in a series of singular state-of-our-union addresses by America's most successful fringe band, positively ripples with the confidence, courage and good, swift kick of a rock & roll band at the top of its form.

For R.E.M.'s latest step forward is actually the result of a key step backward. Stipe and company are hardly strangers to change. Without exception, their records combine a spirit of willful perversity with a healthy restlessness and a steadfast refusal to acknowledge either commercial or critical expectations. But in the beginning—before the enigmatic electric folk of *Murmur,* the exploratory smorgasbord of *Fables of the Reconstruction* and the consummate outlaw pop of *Lifes Rich Pageant*—there was the Beat, and R.E.M. knew how to use it. It was the band's incomparable stage rage, Buck's Who-like slice-and-dice guitar, Stipe's steely vibrato and Mills and Berry's rhythmic tug that wowed Deep South barflies and East Coast in crowds in the early days.

Document captures those thrills and chills in tight, vivid focus. Coproduced by the band and engineer Scott Litt with a striking technical clarity and a diligent respect for bar-band basics, it is the closest to the band's live sound that R.E.M. has come on record since its '82 EP *Chronic Town* and its 1981 indie single debut, "Radio Free Europe." Despite a few splashes of extra texture (the occasional faint keyboard, Steve Berlin's loco-Trane sax in "Fireplace"), the band assumes a tough instrumental stance, a reduction of possibilities into a spiked-fist thrust that in fact heightens the strange compound of telegraphic imagery and haunting vulnerability in Stipe's lyric transmissions. Indeed, his vocals, which are up front in the mix, are as crisp and distinct as they've ever been, full of emotional portent and physical insistence.

In "The One I Love," a straightforward expression of regret ("This one goes out to the one I left behind") becomes a cry of guilt and pain; Stipe wails, "Fire!" with 3-D torment as Buck's storm-cloud guitars open up with bassy thunder and stabs of lightning twang. "Fireplace" is more abstract in tone; for lyrics, Stipe used extracts from a speech by Mother Ann Lee, the leader of the American Shaker sect in the eighteenth century. But it too crackles with uncommon tension, the product of a fractured waltz rhythm, a weird circular chord structure and the clarion Stipe-Lee call to celebrate life amid hellish chaos—"Crazy crazy world / Crazy crazy times / Hang up your chairs / To better sweep / Clear the floor to dance / Shake the rug into the fireplace."

It is a theme that pervades and animates *Document*. "Disturbance at the Heron House," an otherwise sunny folk-pop number, has bitter lyrics that describe liberty gone amuck, free expression co-opted by the mob that shouts the loudest ("the followers of chaos / Out of control"). Two songs later, in the jangly, churning "It's the End of the World As We Know It (and I Feel Fine)," a joyous hymn to self-assertion and self-preservation, Stipe turns all of that rhetoric into a brilliant Gatling-gun litany of cheap clichés and TV newspeak, delivered in a frenzied Dylanesque monotone. It is his own "Subterranean Homesick Blues." It is also probably the only rock song ever written that mentions Leonard Bernstein, Leonid Brezhnev, Lenny Bruce and the late rock critic Lester Bangs all in the same line.

Document has its more placid, though no less disquieting, moments. "Welcome to the Occupation" is a blistering indictment of U.S. interference in Central America. In the eerie "King of Birds," Stipe's subtle debunking of his own mystique ("I am the king of all I see / My kingdom for a voice") is aptly framed by bittersweet sleigh bells and a John Fahey-like raga guitar. But where previous records by R.E.M. have essentially been selective refractions of the band's whole, concentrating on a particular spirit or mood, *Document* balls them all up into a clenched-fist manifesto of rebel bravado. Even the album's lone cover, "Strange," by the English postpunk band Wire, is worked into the script; the original's robot stomp is pumped up into an AC / DC-does-"Sister Ray" boogie as Stipe dryly intones, "There's something strange going on tonight . . . something going down that wasn't here before."

Those words date back to 1977, long before the members of R.E.M. played their first note together. But they suit the album perfectly. A vibrant summary of past tangents and current strengths, *Document* is the sound of R.E.M. on the move, the roar of a band that prides itself on the measure of achievement and the element of surprise. The end of rock & roll as R.E.M. knows it is a long way off.

STEVE POND

R.E.M. IN THE REAL WORLD
Rock's Most Influential College Band Graduates

I T'S A WARM, CLEAR fall afternoon in New York City; R.E.M.'s guitarist, Peter Buck, is shopping in midtown Manhattan, trying to answer the young clerk who rings up his Jim Carroll and John Waters paperbacks and keeps asking, "Are you from Boston? Do you know any musicians in Boston?" Unfailingly polite, Buck hems and haws, says that he knows a few Boston musicians and adds that he is himself a musician. But while he might well clear things up by telling her that he's in R.E.M., Buck steadfastly refuses to do so. Of course, if the clerk glanced at the floor, she'd see a stack of local music magazines with Buck and his R.E.M. colleagues—Michael Stipe, Bill Berry and Mike Mills—on the cover.

"I will never tell anyone I'm in this band," says an uncomfortable Buck afterward. "That's not why I got into this. If people ask me, 'Do I know you?' I say, 'Maybe.' I try not to be an asshole about it, but I certainly don't want to be one of those people who goes, 'Yeah, you might have seen my face on the cover of the *Dickville Daily Ball,* one of the new music papers around today. . . .' I mean, who *cares?*"

Then he walks a couple of blocks toward Central Park and is soon recognized by two young ladies riding in a horse-drawn cab along the perimeter of the park. "Peter! Peter!" they yell across several lanes of New York City traffic, and Peter Buck grins. "Yeah," he says, "this is a pretty good job I've got."

And how does he see that job? "We're the acceptable edge," he says, shrugging, "of the unacceptable stuff."

A ND THAT, IN A NUTSHELL, is R.E.M., circa 1987: more popular than ever before, enjoying the spoils of success, having fun in territory that's new, yet not completely comfortable with the trappings of fame. It wouldn't do for the members of this one-time cult band to embrace mass acceptance too readily, but on the other hand their underground status has all but disappeared—so it would hardly make sense for them to turn their backs on the mainstream.

Besides, it's been a good week. The night before, R.E.M. played the second of two sold-out shows at Radio City Music Hall. Moments before walking onstage, the band had learned that its new album, *Document,* was in the Top Twenty and the single "The One I Love" had jumped thirteen places to Number Thirty. Since 1982 each new R.E.M. record has outsold its predecessor, but this was an unexpected leap—an album nearing the platinum level and a bona fide hit single for a band whose singles *never* do well. And as he strolled through New York City, Buck was carrying one of the rewards of success: that afternoon he'd plunked down about $500 for an oddly shaped Italian mandolin-cum-lyre ("a mandolin with preten-sions," he says) that he'd liked because of its shape and figured he'd learn to play sooner or later.

Once upon a time it seemed that R.E.M. was the ultimate college band. R.E.M. was formed on a college campus, the University of Georgia in Athens, and its early support came from college radio. Its dense, sometimes obscure, folkish pop-rock songs, with enigmatic lyrics by the group's singer and resident eccentric, Michael Stipe, were perfect fodder for late-night dorm discussions. And its guitar-driven sound, take-it-to-the-clubs ap-proach to touring and low-key image helped shatter the prevailing Anglo-philia of the early 1980s and influenced regional bands in college towns across the United States.

But now, R.E.M. has finally and fully graduated. The band is out of the underground and into the real world, if you can call rock stardom a real world. And to an observer watching Peter Buck buy a new instrument or get recognized on the street, it's hard not to think of the chorus of R.E.M.'s next single. "It's the end of the world as we know it," sings Michael Stipe, and then he tosses out the punch line: "And I feel fine."

"**I** WILL NEVER, EVER, ever, ever play another general-admission show, ever. *Ever.* And I will never, ever, *ever* play a place that's bigger than the place we played tonight, ever." A pause. "Did I put enough *evers* in there?" It's one day later, and Peter Buck isn't feeling so fine. R.E.M. has just played to 12,000 fans in Williamsburg, Virginia, the only general-admission show of their 1987 tour—and while nobody was hurt, the crush down front was serious, and the band was upset.

Not that most people could tell. For about ninety-five minutes, the swarthy, genial drummer, Bill Berry, sat in back in an undershirt and white shorts, pounding with real authority; Mike Mills, whose clean-cut Poindex-terish looks contrast with the shaggier, grungier look of the rest of the band, played melodic bass lines and sang backup; Peter Buck stood on the side of the stage, cutting a Keith Richards-esque figure with his black jeans and vest, his white shirt and his low-slung guitar; and in the center Michael Stipe staggered about the stage spasmodically, peeling off layer after layer of coats, jackets and T-shirts and charismatically howling out his mostly dark, sardonic lyrics and introducing songs with deadpan, disjointed comments. It wasn't a great R.E.M. show by any means, but it was tough and force-ful—and its problems weren't apparent until the final encore, "The One I Love," when Buck, nailed twice by wet sweat socks thrown from the audience, threw down his guitar and stormed offstage.

After the show, Buck grabs a six-pack from the tour bus and heads toward his room. Like the other members of the band, he isn't sure that when it comes to venues, bigger is better. He for one isn't interested in having R.E.M. become an arena band. "People have been trying to con-vince me for a long time that we could play bigger places and enjoy it," says the lanky, fidgety, garrulous Buck. "And tonight proved, if nothing else, that there's no fucking way I can. If we ever did a stadium tour, I would imagine it would be about the last thing we'd ever do together."

Some longtime fans have already accused R.E.M. of selling out, of courting mainstream success. The band doesn't agree. "If you look at the album charts, the only thing up there on the charts that's weirder than we are is Prince," says Buck. "I mean, this record seems to me to be pretty uncommercial."

But one of the songs from that uncommercial record put R.E.M. over the top, hitting the upper reaches of the singles charts when no previous single—from "Radio Free Europe" to "So. Central Rain" to "Can't Get There from Here" to "Fall on Me"—had even made the Top Seventy-five. And typically enough for this band, "The One I Love" succeeded at least partly because a lot of the audience doesn't know what it's about. Listeners hear the opening lines—"This one goes out to the one I love / This one goes out to the one I left behind"—and miss it when what begins as a rueful love song turns hard: "A simple prop to occupy my time" and, in the last verse, "Another prop has occupied my time."

"It's a brutal kind of song, and I don't know if a lot of people pick up on that," says Michael Stipe. "But I've always left myself pretty open to interpretation. It's probably better that they just think it's a love song at this point." A shrug. "I don't know. That song just came up from somewhere, and I recognized it as being real violent and awful. But it wasn't directed at any one person. I would never, *ever* write a song like that. Even if there was one person in the world thinking, 'This song is about me,' I could never sing it or put it out."

Now, though, R.E.M. has got to figure out what kind of follow-up record to make, what kind of tour to do, what size halls to play, what kind of lyrics to write. "There's a little bit more weight on my shoulders as far as what I say," says Stipe, who long ago won a reputation for singing his lyrics in an often indecipherable mumble. "One lives in a world where things are not what they seem, and I see no reason not to reflect that," says Buck.

Stipe says that his new visibility means he ought to write clearer lyrics. "I guess I've figured out that I can't just blabber anything I want to anymore, which I've done before, though not a great deal. On some of the earlier songs, whatever I happened to be singing, we recorded it. Some had very distinct ideas: '9-9' has a very distinct idea, but, you know, it was purposely recorded so you could never be able to decipher any of the words except the very last phrase, which was 'conversation fear,' which is what the song was about."

Certainly it's easier to listen to the last two records and hear Stipe's personal distaste for much of modern living, or to hear the concerns of a band some of whose members belong to Greenpeace and quietly donate to selected causes. And while *Document* is a quirky, thorny record, there's enough clarity on it to help put R.E.M. in unaccustomed company.

"We're Top Twenty now, which is *unbelievable,*" says Stipe. "I can't believe that we're up there with Springsteen or whatever. It doesn't really mean that much, but it does to the industry, and I guess to kids that read.

"And my mom got kinda weepy," he says, grinning, then stops himself. "No, she didn't. But *she* couldn't believe it, either."

IT STARTED WITH A MACON, Georgia, high-school band that by all rights should never have existed. Bill Berry played drums, Mike Mills played bass, and the combination was unlikely—because Mills and Berry openly and unequivocally hated each other's guts.

At the time, Berry was a budding hoodlum who'd just moved to Macon from the Midwest (he was born in Bob Dylan's home town of Hibbing, Minnesota); Mills was a Georgia native and a self-described "goody-goody." "I hated him from the first time I saw him," Berry says with a laugh, " 'cause he had that same kind of nerd appeal that he has now, and I was just starting to experiment with drugs and stuff. He was everything

I despised: great student, got along with teachers, didn't smoke cigarettes or smoke pot. . . ."

But an unknowing mutual friend invited Berry to sit in with a band that included Mills. Berry wanted to storm out but couldn't because his drums were too heavy for effective storming; instead, he decided to endure Mills, and before long the two were best friends. Together, they moved to Athens to attend the university, where Berry wanted to study law and become a music-industry lawyer and manager. They'd all but given up music by then—but heartened by the first wave of Seventies punk bands, they took instruments with them to Athens.

Before long they met Peter Buck and another Georgia student, Michael Stipe, who had met each other in the record store Buck managed. Both had spent their childhoods traveling extensively; army brat Stipe, the youngest R.E.M. member (now twenty-seven), developed a keen interest in painting, photography and medieval manuscripts, while Buck, the oldest at thirty, grew up spending all his free money on records (the Velvet Underground, the Move, the Raspberries, the Kinks) and books (Jack Kerouac, Thomas Wolfe).

"My parents were pleased that I was well read," Buck says. "But the fact that I was well read and also listened to Iggy and the Stooges was kinda . . . well, they ended up being supportive. Much later."

Athens was full of new rock & roll bands, from the B-52's to Pylon to the Method Actors. R.E.M. wasn't looking to be the next big thing; the four formed a band to have fun and play a few frat parties. They also moved in together, taking up residence in an abandoned church that, says Buck, "has been romanticized beyond belief. It was just a rotten, dumpy little shit hole where college kids, only college kids, could be convinced to live."

Their early shows were mostly covers: "Needles and Pins," "God Save the Queen," "Secret Agent Man," "California Sun." "We just tended to play everything loud and fast," says Mills. They made $343 at one of their first shows; Berry still remembers standing under the stage counting the money, which seemed like a fortune.

They began writing their own songs: "Gardening at Night" came very quickly, and "Radio Free Europe" followed shortly thereafter. And when they did their first out-of-town show in North Carolina, part-time booker Jefferson Holt was impressed. "They'll hate me for this," he says, "but to me the first time I saw them was like what I would have imagined of seeing the Who when they first started. They blitzkrieged through some incredibly pop covers, then they had some of their own songs that were real pop but also some stuff that wasn't pop."

Jefferson Holt soon became their manager. Another friend from Athens, a young lawyer named Bertis Downs IV, helped them handle the legal side of things: he persuaded them to incorporate, even though their only asset was a $1250 van, to form their own publishing company and to trademark the band's name—a precaution Downs says he took because two other R.E.M.'s, one REM and one Rapid Eye Movement had already come and gone. (Downs is still the band's lawyer.)

It wasn't long before gigs got in the way of classes, and Berry was asked to leave the university; the rest of the band decided to drop out, made an independent single ("Radio Free Europe" / "Sitting Still"), toured incessantly and began to pick up college airplay, critical raves and major-label interest. "The thing is," says Holt, laughing, "the great reviews and the Top Ten lists didn't change the fact that we were in a '75 Dodge Tradesman lugging all our gear ourselves and still showing up and playing to eight or nine people."

I.R.S. signed the band and agreed to release the already-recorded EP *Chronic Town,* provided the band re-record "Radio Free Europe" and "Sitting Still" for their first full-fledged album. *Chronic Town* got some attention; the album, *Murmur,* was an instant college radio and underground rock classic.

Reckoning, in 1984, was more of the same—and suddenly it seemed as if the regional American rock scene was full of jangling, guitar-based bands that sounded like R.E.M. and toured like R.E.M. "I think maybe what we did," says Mills, "was give people a touchstone. As an alternative to the synthesizer-dominated electronic music that was being made, we were the most visible sign that something else was going on. It doesn't mean that we were the best, and we certainly weren't the first. But perhaps we were the most accessible and the most visible."

Visible and accessible and influential as they were, the members of the band went through one of their periodic dark spells when they went to London to record their third album, 1985's *Fables of the Reconstruction.* "A lot of things were catching up to us," says Mills. "We didn't realize we were going to be asked to do certain commercial kinds of things, and we thought, 'Is this what we really want to do?' It was, maybe, a crisis period, just an overall feeling of unease."

"Fables sucked," says Berry bluntly—though others in the band are somewhat happier with the moody, atmospheric record.

"It wasn't the best time in my life, either," says *Fables* producer Joe Boyd, who adds that despite R.E.M.'s inner turmoil at the time, "they seemed to get along better than most groups I've worked with." He also found mixing the record to be a singular experience. "When you mix a record, traditionally the singer wants his voice louder, and the guitar player says, 'Turn up the guitar,' and the bass player says, 'Can't you make the bass parts punchier?' With R.E.M., everyone wanted themselves turned down."

But the next time around, the band turned it up: *Lifes Rich Pageant* was clearly designed as a hard-edged response to *Fables*. By then, though, another complaint sometimes crept into R.E.M.'s once unanimously positive reviews: the idea that the band mapped out their musical territory on the early albums and wasn't changing it or challenging its audience.

"We're not so versatile that there's not going to be something in common in all our records," says Berry. "I think we've developed a little more now, to where we can get away with doing a 'King of Birds' on a record, and break it up a little bit. But that's still not going to stop 'Heron House' from sounding a little bit like 'Gardening at Night' slowed down. We try to diversify as much as possible, but a lot of our stuff does tend to sound the same. That's one of our weak points, I'll admit it."

And their strong points?

"I think we've kept our integrity intact pretty much," Berry says. "I'm not doing anything today that I'll be ashamed of in ten years. And we've all aged pretty well. I think we all weigh the same as we did. And we get along, which is pretty rare. I'm not saying we haven't had our flare-ups, but I've had more fights with my wife in the last two years than I have with any of these guys in the last seven years." He shrugs. "Amazingly, our chemistry hasn't broken down yet."

"**H**I, MY NAME IS MICHELLE, and I'll be your waitress today." Michael Stipe looks up at the perky Ramada Inn waitress standing above him and grins shyly. "I'm Michael, and I'll be your . . ." His soft, deep voice trails off. "Um . . . your customer, I guess."

Stipe, certainly, is R.E.M.'s resident oddball, a shambling, simultaneously intense and spacey conversationalist who's apt to interrupt the talk by pulling a couple of pressed leaves out of his pocket or by pointing at an interviewer's hand and saying, "You've got hair on the side of your hand, too." Some of the behavior is clearly due to what Peter Buck calls Stipe's "very weird sense of humor, which is actually two senses of humor. One is very Laurel and Hardy—we can watch *Animal House,* and he'll laugh at the stuff where I'll think, 'He can't *possibly* like that.' And then there's the other part of him, where I can barely tell that he's saying something funny, and people around him can't tell at all.''

Some of the eccentricities may be inherited: Stipe says his father has been hoarding bottles in his basement for years. "Now he's decided to build this extension onto my parents' house, made out of bottles," says Stipe. "And he's a math wizard. He and I had this discussion about Vietnam, and he went on for two and a half hours explaining a lot of his ideas about it, and about the draft, and about America and American foreign policy, and somehow it wound up working into rock & roll and how I fit into it."

During the discussion Stipe's father covered a sheet of paper with words and mathematical equations. The result, Stipe says, looked like it belonged in the Swiss museum that collects outsiders' art—the work of mental patients, convicts and others on the fringes of society. "It's really beautiful," says Stipe affectionately.

And some of the eccentricities seem to be the purposeful designs of a shy person who wants to keep the world at arm's length. "Michael is normal as hell, and as different as anybody you'd want to meet," says Jefferson Holt, who lived with Stipe briefly. "It's an act of will by which he creates his life and the space in which he lives."

But if Stipe is the band's shyest, most private member, he's also the one most often besieged by R.E.M. fanatics. "I think a lot of people get presumptuous, think they're soul mates, think Michael is speaking directly to them," says Mike Mills. "I mean, that's the point of some of his lyrics: to get to someone's insides. But that doesn't mean he wants them to come over to his house, you know?"

When the subject is broached, Stipe grows visibly uncomfortable. "Athens is full of people looking for R.E.M.," he says, shaking his head. "Not all the time, but . . ." He trails off. "I don't really want to talk about that because I'm still a little bitter about it."

Still, Stipe says he's learning out how to deal with the attention. "Not to be Cartesian," he says, "but, you know, I feel fairly well protected now from people coming up to me and wanting a piece of me. I'm able to dole out what I want, you know. Whereas before I was a lot more accessible for people to reach in and pull out vital organs."

So Stipe stays in more protected situations: a large, muscular personal aide stands beside him at backstage gatherings, and he rides from show to show in his own bus (accompanied, on the first leg of the tour, by 10,000 Maniacs singer Natalie Merchant, whom he joined onstage every night during the Maniacs' opening set), separate from the rest of the band. The separate buses, says the band, weren't planned—but Stipe, who eats health foods and can't stand to be anywhere where the windows won't open, couldn't tolerate the sealed windows in the band bus.

"I used to really hate touring," says Stipe. "But it's gotten easier for me. It's not that I've relaxed more, it's just that the rest of the world has relaxed a little bit, so it's easier for me to walk the streets and stuff. To find food and find water. And find windows that open occasionally."

But the separate buses also reinforce Stipe's separation from the rest of the band, a separation that already existed to some degree. "There is a difference, and it's always been there," says Bill Berry. "There's no doubt that he's an eccentric individual, that that's the way it should be. He is who he is, and R.E.M. is who they are because of who's in it."

Stipe concedes that there are differences between himself and the musicians in the band: for one thing, he prepares for a show by getting quiet and withdrawn, which means the hyperactive Buck has standing orders to stay away for a couple of hours before each concert. Still, Stipe says, "we share so much more in common than most people would ever give us credit for. We're very much a group."

Stipe glances across the room, then shakes his head. "I'm watching TV in a mirror," he says. "I just realized that. I've been focusing in on this thing, and it's a television set in a mirror." He grimaces. "Nothing really upsets me more, on a really regular basis, than television. And the whole culture that's built up around it is horrifying. The fact that I can sit here and talk to you, and there's a TV in the corner, and I'm attracted to it . . . The best comparison I can make is moths to a light."

Television culture provided part of the inspiration for "It's the End of the World As We Know It (and I Feel Fine)," a song, Stipe says, about "bombastic, vomiting sensory overload." But the first line of that song deals with another calamity—"That's great, it starts with an earthquake"—and when he finds out the reporter's from Los Angeles, Stipe's thoughts turn to the recent 6.1 tremor that he's been mentioning when introducing "End of the World."

"Wow, were you there when the earthquake and everything happened?"

Yep.

"Are you gonna move?"

Nope.

"A lot of my friends from the West Coast called me immediately, because they wanted to know when the next one was coming. I usually get headaches when an earthquake happens—when Mexico City went down, I was on my back for three days, really bad. But last week was the first time since I became aware of it that there's been an earthquake anywhere in the continent and I didn't know about it ahead of time."

He rambles on about earthquakes for a while, mentions the *Superman* movie in which Lex Luthor buys up soon-to-be beach-front property in Nevada, then admits that even if California were to fall into the ocean—*if* it does, he's not saying that it definitely will—the rest of the country would be in big trouble, too.

"My parents' farm is right on a fault line, in Georgia," Stipe says absently. "But it's not like the San Andreas."

He looks up and laughs and does his best to change the topic, albeit in his own disjointed fashion.

"Anyway, earthquake talk," he says with a shrug. "It's the end of the world."

With that, Michael Stipe raises his coffee cup. "Cheers."

"WE'VE ALREADY AGREED THAT we will not make Michael go to the West Coast in 1988," says Jefferson Holt, chuckling, as he sits backstage in Fairfax, Virginia, the Washington, D.C., suburb where the band is playing a welcome reserved-seating show. But then, calming Stipe's earthquake phobia isn't going to mean R.E.M. will cancel any shows or reroute any tours next year—because for now the band plans to follow up its biggest success to date with a year, in Bill Berry's words, "to clean out the closet and rearrange the shoes.

"We've been locked in this thing for the last six years," he adds. "We go in the studio, put out a record, tour, rehearse. It's getting to be a really predictable thing. And I'm not saying it's stifling us, but this record bought us the opportunity to take a year off." He laughs. "We were gonna do it anyway, so thank God the record's doing what it is."

After the tour, Berry plans to go fishing, play some golf, spend time on his boat, do some reading and simply hang out in Athens with his wife of a year and a half, Mari. Mills will likely hit the golf course himself, perhaps join a softball or basketball league and definitely spend some time working in his yard. Buck will go back to the big new house he recently bought, which is cluttered with the flotsam and jetsam of the road; he'll probably work with a few new bands or with friends like Fleshtones guitarist Keith Streng. Stipe—who's directed some of the band's videos in the past—has some video projects in the works. Once in a while, Mills and Berry will get together in the Corncob Webs, their Sixties-cover band. Many nights the whole band will wind up together, in one of Athens's three clubs. And next fall they'll go into the studio to make their sixth album, one they hope will be weird rather than commercial.

R.E.M. is also at another crossroads: with *Document,* the band's deal with I.R.S. Records has expired. Plenty of other labels have already expressed interest in signing away I.R.S.'s biggest band. "We may or may not sign with I.R.S.," says Berry. "That's undetermined."

The band's long-term plans are nebulous: the only constant is that they all assume that one day they'll stop working together. It's not that the band seems to be in the midst of any major personality conflicts—by all accounts they get on better now than they ever have—but that they simply don't plan on doing this indefinitely.

Stipe says he's not sure he'll even be in the music business in another decade; if he is, he says, he can see himself being like Tom Waits, with an offbeat, theatrical ensemble. Berry says he simply hopes that until record making gets to be tiring—which he assumes will happen long after they've stopped touring—they'll still work together in some form, even if not as R.E.M. But before they drift apart, Peter Buck has a goal.

"I think it's within us to make one of those Top Twenty all-time rock & roll great records," he says. "We haven't done that yet, and I don't know how you pull that out of you. Sometime, somewhere, the inspiration hits. And you hope it hits when you're awake and you have a guitar in your hands.

"All I want to do," he adds, "is make great records, and be a great band, and play great live. But I'm not sure that I want to keep going the way that we're going. I have no doubts that we *can* do it; it's just I don't know if I *want* to do it. For me, personally, I'd rather turn out a record that's really brilliant and then try to find some other way to present ourselves onstage, something that short-circuits the rock & roll rah-rah thing.

"I don't know how to do that, but I think there's some way to do this at an interesting level. Who knows? Maybe it means putting out a record that's really great and doesn't sell at all. That would be really cool."

In the meantime, R.E.M. has a hit album, a hit single, a new, bigger audience and a tour that'll run until the end of November. And when they take the stage in Fairfax, they've found exactly the right way to respond to their new situation, at least for a night: the show is a rock-hard, well-paced, furious blast of intelligent and provocative rock & roll. For more than two hours, Stipe reels around the stage, and his band mates play with surprising fury; with the repertoire drawn mostly from the last two albums, you can hear the hardening of this band's sound and clearly catch the vehemence and humor in Stipe's assaults on an environment he finds nearly unlivable.

For the encores, they pull out all the stops: first, there's a three-song set of covers, from Lou Gramm's "Midnight Blue" (the crowd laughs uneasily, then responds to the anthemic chords, while Stipe strikes exaggerated arena-rock poses and the rest of the band plays hard on a song they really do like) to Television's "See No Evil." They do the hit, with a gorgeous, hushed introduction; they do *Chronic Town*'s "Wolves, Lower" after Stipe says, "Moving way back to the Pleistocene era . . ." And at the end, Stipe and Buck stand side by side at center stage for an exquisite slow version of "So. Central Rain," which ends with Stipe tossing in a few revealing lines from Peter Gabriel's "Red Rain": "I come to you, defenses down, with the trust of a child."

THREE HOURS, A FEW six-packs and a couple of bottles of champagne later, the members of R.E.M. straggle into the lobby of their hotel. It's 2:30 in the morning, and the only other guests in the lobby are a group of Continental Airlines pilots and stewardesses, who pile into one elevator and then yell out, "Don't any of you want to ride with us?"

With that, Michael Stipe—his flyaway hair tied back in a ponytail and tucked under a beret, his tattered clothes more disheveled than usual and his eyes still caked with heavy black eye makeup—strolls into the elevator. As the doors start to close, his voice can just be heard: "So, are you all with an airline?"

And when the other members of the band take another elevator to their floor, Stipe is waiting on the landing, a huge grin on his face. "They asked if I was in a band," he says enthusiastically, "and when I said I was in R.E.M., they got all excited and said, 'Is the whole band staying in *this* hotel?' "

In the hotel hallway the guy who's supposed to be R.E.M.'s shyest member breaks up laughing, and exclaims, "It was *great!*" And suddenly it looks as if this arty college band might have the temperament for the real world after all.

DAVID FRICKE

YEAR-END REVIEW OF
DEAD LETTER OFFICE AND *DOCUMENT*

R.E.M. CRACKED IT. IT took five albums to do it, but the fringe-rock band consistently voted most likely to succeed by critics since its '81 indie debut finally stormed the Top Ten. *Document* succeeded where equally worthy R.E.M. albums—*Murmur* and *Lifes Rich Pageant*—had failed because it captured with exhilarating crispness the bar-band dynamics fueling even the most eccentric beat expeditions. The poignant immediacy of "The One I Love," R.E.M.'s first bona fide hit single, didn't hurt, either.

Dead Letter Office, released early in the year, was a rather less serious enterprise, a Whitman's Sampler of discarded outtakes and weird B sides. In his liner notes, guitarist Peter Buck wrote, "Listening to this album should be like browsing through a junkshop." But the haunting Velvet Underground covers and, on "Voice of Harold," Michael Stipe's beguiling delivery of some obscure gospel-album liner notes over the backing track to "Seven Chinese Brothers" proved that one band's excess baggage is another fan's treasure.

1987 MUSIC AWARDS

READERS PICKS

ARTIST OF THE YEAR
U2
R.E.M.
Madonna
Bruce Springsteen
Bon Jovi

BEST SINGLE
"With or Without You," U2
"Where the Streets Have No
 Name," U2
"I Still Haven't Found What
 I'm Looking For," U2
"The One I Love," R.E.M.
"Here I Go Again,"
 Whitesnake
"Brilliant Disguise," Bruce
 Springsteen
"Touch of Grey," the
 Grateful Dead

"Alone," Heart
"I Want Your Sex," George
 Michael
"Learning to Fly," Pink Floyd

BEST VIDEO
"Where the Streets Have No
 Name," U2
"With or Without You," U2
"Learning to Fly," Pink Floyd
"The One I Love," R.E.M.
"Touch of Grey," the
 Grateful Dead

BEST ALBUM
The Joshua Tree, U2
Document, R.E.M.
Tunnel of Love, Bruce
 Springsteen
A Momentary Lapse of
 Reason, Pink Floyd

Whitesnake, Whitesnake
Hysteria, Def Leppard
Sign o' the Times, Prince
Tango in the Night,
 Fleetwood Mac
. . . Nothing Like the Sun,
 Sting
Bad Animals, Heart

BEST BAND
U2
R.E.M.
Fleetwood Mac
Whitesnake
The Grateful Dead

BEST GUITARIST
The Edge
Eddie Van Halen
Eric Clapton
Peter Buck (R.E.M.)
Prince

■ MUSIC IN BRIEF (March 24, 1988)

R.E.M.'s contract with I.R.S. Records is up, and the band is talking to a number of labels—Island and Virgin among them—besides I.R.S. The band is said to be seeking an advance of more than $2 million. For now, the group has recruited Los Lobos sax man Steve Berlin and the Uptown Horns for a reworked version of "Finest Worksong," which will be released as a single on March 21st. I.R.S. will also release a dance mix of the track. The flip side of both releases will be a live medley of "So. Central Rain" and "Time After Time," from the band's *Reckoning* album, and "Red Rain," by Peter Gabriel. . . .

■ MUSIC IN BRIEF (April 7, 1988)

Word is that R.E.M. has narrowed its list of prospective record companies to four: Warner Bros., Columbia, Arista and its original label, I.R.S.

■ MUSIC IN BRIEF (May 19, 1988)

After six years with I.R.S. Records, R.E.M. has signed a multimillion-dollar, medium-term deal with Warner Bros. I.R.S. will retain control of R.E.M.'s current catalog, which includes the band's first six albums and the *Chronic Town* EP. A compilation drawn from those records may be released before the end of the year. R.E.M. will record its first album for Warners this summer at Ardent Studios, in Memphis, and Bearsville Studios, near Woodstock, New York, with Scott Litt producing.

■ MUSIC IN BRIEF (June 2, 1988)

R.E.M.—whose five-record deal with Warner Bros. is said to be worth $10 million—won't be going into the studio until this summer, but Peter Buck has had no trouble keeping busy. He and Grant Hart, formerly of Hüsker Dü, produced Run Westy Run's album *Hardly, Not Even,* which was recently released by SST. Buck also produced *The Wilderness,* a new album by Charlie Pickett, due out on Safety Net in June; Buck plays on two of the album's tracks. The guitarist is also assembling a compilation of tracks from the Seventies by the pioneering Atlanta band the Fans.

JEFFREY RESSNER

R.E.M. MAKES WARNER BROS. DEBUT WITH *GREEN*

FANS OF THE ATHENS, Georgia, rock group R.E.M. have an embarrassment of riches this fall. *Green,* the band's debut album for Warner Bros., is due this month, while *Eponymous,* a best-of set culled from the band's previous albums, has just been released by its former label, I.R.S.

"We can't stop it," says R.E.M. bassist Mike Mills, regarding the near-simultaneous release of *Eponymous* and *Green*. "It's I.R.S.'s right to put that together and release it. I'm not much for anthologies like that, but as far as it goes it turned out well."

Green is "a little more upbeat, lyrically as well as musically," says Mills. "But the songwriting is a continuation of a direction we've taken before. We start playing with no real idea where we're going, and the songs literally evolve out of nothing."

The eleven songs on *Green* also make more use of odd instrumentation and sound effects. The opening track, "Pop Song," employs a six-string fuzz bass, while "Get Up" harnesses the cacophony of a dozen music boxes. "Orange Crush" has helicopterlike whirs, and "You Are Everything" uses the sounds of crickets from outside the Bearsville, New York, studio where the song was recorded.

Sixteen songs were recorded over three months last summer for *Green*. And while some were scrapped before completion, others, such as "Memphis Train Blues," will be used as B sides for singles.

Mills says much of *Green* is more accessible than earlier R.E.M. works. Aside from a few numbers, like the oblique "Hairshirt," most of *Green*'s songs are direct, with Michael Stipe's trademark murmured vocals replaced by clearly enunciated lyrics. "I think Michael has grown so much as a lyricist that it's natural for the words to become more and more prominent," says Mills.

R.E.M. is planning to embark on a world tour this winter, with U.S. dates set for March and April.

Rumors circulated in England recently that I.R.S. also plans to release a boxed retrospective and a live album, which was taped during a September 1987 show in the Netherlands province of Utrecht. But the band's manager, Jefferson Holt, says that the British reports contain "erroneous information." He claims the poor quality of the Utrecht tapes would prevent their release, while a boxed set is only a remote possibility.

■ **YEAR-END RANDOM NOTES** December 15-29, 1988

Although R.E.M. left I.R.S. for the big bucks at Warner Bros., the band members can't be accused of selling out. *Green,* their Warners debut, shows no sign of compromise. The album is slightly more upbeat than previous R.E.M. releases—with the exception of the song "Hairshirt"—and it makes good use of some creative sound effects, such as chirping crickets.

■ **RANDOM NOTES** (June 2, 1988)

On their last tour, 10,000 Maniacs opened for **R.E.M.**, and there was a widely reported romance between Merchant and **Michael Stipe**. "Nah," she says, laughing. "I think he's homely. He's an impossible person, but I love him, and we get on really well. We're *really* the best of friends."

■ **RANDOM NOTES** (June 16, 1988)

"Bugs Bunny," says **Michael Stipe**, is the reason **R.E.M.** signed with Warner Bros. Records. Bassist **Mike Mills** is a bit less cartoonish in his account of the band's new deal. "They're an artist's label more than anything else," he says. This summer the band goes back into the studio with producer **Scott Litt**. In other R.E.M. news, guitarist **Peter Buck** recently wed **Barrie Greene** in Mexico.

■ **RANDOM NOTES** (September 8, 1988)

R.E.M.'s **Michael Stipe** joined **10,000 Maniacs** onstage during their recent concert at the Pier, in New York City, to sing "The Campfire Song" with longtime friend **Natalie Merchant**. "When I looked out and saw Miss Merchant and the battleship *Intrepid* side by side, I had to jump up and join in," says Stipe, referring to the warship that is docked near the outdoor venue.

Stipe is now back in Athens, Georgia, working on the next R.E.M. album. "We've just made this big jump in our career, and it's pretty certain we're going to get raked over the coals whatever we put out," he says. The album's title? *"Problems of the Homeless,"* he says, joking. "It will change."

■ **RANDOM NOTES** NOTABLE NEWS (December 1, 1988)

R.E.M.'s **Michael Stipe** did his bit for the cause before this year's presidential elections. Along with working as a volunteer for the **Dukakis** campaign, he took out ads in various college papers that read, "Stipe says: Don't get Bushwhacked. Get out and vote. Vote smart. Dukakis." "I'm just trying to do some good," he says. "If there are people that listen to songs and eke things out of those, then certainly if I make a statement, they might listen to that." Any political songs on R.E.M.'s new album, *Green?* "One of the first songs is pretty political," he says. "It's called 'Orange Crush.' "

MICHAEL AZERRAD

GREEN ALBUM REVIEW
★ ★ ★ ½

The greening of R.E.M.

O N 'GREEN,' R.E.M. DARES to think positive. Songs like "Stand," "Get Up," "World Leader Pretend" and "The Wrong Child" are a continuation of the upbeat call to arms sounded on *Document*'s "Finest Worksong." It was no coincidence that such a hopeful record was released on an election day whose outcome was a foregone conclusion. Now is not the time for despair, R.E.M. seems to be saying, but for a redoubling of efforts.

Having made the leap from a small label, I.R.S., to a monolithic major one, Warner Bros., R.E.M. hasn't sold out; rather, the band has taken the opportunity to crack open the shell it's been pecking at since it recorded its first album. On *Green,* R.E.M. acknowledges the outside world with a slew of musical references and some relatively pointed lyrics.

As Michael Stipe's vocals get more distinct, so does his message— instead of meaning almost anything you want them to, his noticeably improved lyrics seem to be about at most two or three different things. Stipe even makes an effort to enunciate. And perhaps more remarkable, this is the first R.E.M. album with printed lyrics—actually, it provides the lyrics to just one song, "World Leader Pretend," but with this band you take what you can get.

Green reveals a much wider range than previous efforts, including a playfulness that wasn't there before. Some songs have a downright bubble-gummy feel: on "Stand," Peter Buck lets fly with a ridiculously wanky wah-wah guitar solo. Still others reveal more emotion than the band has shown in the past; "You Are the Everything" and the untitled track that closes the album are frank love songs with few strings attached.

Except for those tender ballads, R.E.M. has completely lost its folk inflections. A heavy guitar sound has replaced the old Byrdsy jangle (which scores of college bands continue to ply). The trademark asymmetrical song structures are gone, too; now, verses are repeated for maximum catchiness.

The band's last two albums—*Lifes Rich Pageant* and *Document*—seemed very much of a piece, but *Green* is a distinctive record with a new feel, at once slightly synthetic and deeply felt, with Stipe conveying strong conviction without shouting and subtle emotion without disappearing into the woodwork. (*Green* was coproduced by Scott Litt, who also coproduced *Document,* the band's commercial breakthrough.)

"Turn You Inside-Out" includes percussion by former Sugar Hill Records house drummer Keith LeBlanc, but it's no rap jam—rather, it's the heaviest rock these guys have yet recorded. R.E.M. won its reputation as a great rock & roll band as much with its live shows as with its earnest, evocative records, and this album begins to approach the concert experience—not necessarily in its visceral impact, but in its stunning contrasts: the song that follows "Turn You Inside-Out," the mandolin-laden "Hairshirt," is the most delicate and affecting thing the band has ever done. "I am not the type of dog who could keep you waiting for no good reason," Stipe fairly croons.

Musically, *Green* quotes a lot of sources. Listen closely and you can hear references to the Doors, Led Zeppelin, Sly Stone and others. If R.E.M. were any more calculating, one might suspect this is the band's sneaky way of squeezing into tightly formatted AOR radio, with its emphasis on classic rock bands.

Just as it's fascinating to watch elder statesmen like Keith Richards reconcile rock & roll with middle age, it's fascinating to see how R.E.M. handles fame and commercial success. On paper, this looks to be the band's biggest album ever—strong singles material ("Get Up," "Stand" and "Orange Crush"), a major label, a more accessible sound. So it's not for nothing that the album is titled *Green,* although environmental concerns, naïveté and the generally positive attitude of the record must also have something to do with it.

R.E.M. may be dangerously close to becoming a conventional rock & roll band, but *Green* proves it's a damn good one.

■ RANDOM NOTES (February 9, 1989)

Most artists would likely jump at the chance to headline a major tour. Not so **R.E.M.**'s **Michael Stipe**. "I'm violently opposed to forced travel," he says, "but then I'm violently opposed to washing dishes, and I overcame that." The band, which is currently touring Japan, Australia and New Zealand to promote its latest release, *Green,* will hit these shores on March 1st in Louisville, Kentucky. "We start out with a bang in Louisville," he says with a laugh. "We always start our tours in the strangest places." **Peter Holsapple** of the **dB'S** will be joining the band for the entire tour to play guitar and keyboards. (The dB's have decided not to make any more records, but they may do some live gigs.) There's no word as to whether R.E.M. will be playing any dB's covers on the tour, but Stipe says he'd like to do "The Anchor," by the **Minutemen**.

Three different acts will be opening for R.E.M. in the U.S.: **Robyn Hitchcock and the Egyptians**, the **Indigo Girls** and **Drivin' and Cryin'**. Asked if these acts were chosen because they're the group's favorites, Stipe deadpans, "No, they were just the most convenient to get." Oh. "No, seriously, they're all really good bands."

Stipe says he hasn't gotten much feedback on the album per se. "The local critic wasn't very complimentary," he says. "He hadn't received his free copy of the album, and he mostly complained about that."

ANTHONY DeCURTIS

R.E.M.'S BRAVE NEW WORLD

OKAY, LISTEN! WE NEED everybody here to act like professionals. We don't want to step on anybody's toes."

One of the few adults on the scene, Randy Terrell is trying to preserve order at the Basement, the Atlanta teen club that, to everyone's amazement, is about to be visited by R.E.M. Some sixty high-school photographers are standing in a roped-off area, cameras poised and hormones pumping, awaiting the band's arrival with barely suppressed hysteria. Crews from CNN, MTV and local television stations are also at the ready.

Located behind the Lindbergh Plaza shopping center on Piedmont Road—the site, ironically enough, of the Great Southeast Music Hall, where the Sex Pistols had begun their volcanic American tour over a decade earlier—the Basement was opened last fall by Atlanta parents so their kids could have a place to go to hear music and hang out without the temptations of drink and drugs. Somewhat predictably, those high-minded origins have hardly made the Basement the hippest spot in town for older teens.

Terrell, the Basement's youth director, and the rest of the club's staff hope that today's event will change that. "We needed something that would attract the senior high-school kids, something that would make this place cool," says Miriam Lockshin, the Basement's promotion director. "Obviously, in Atlanta, R.E.M. is king, especially right now, because their album has just come out."

A call from one of the Basement's board members to Jefferson Holt, R.E.M.'s manager, elicited a quick agreement. Since R.E.M. was regularly coming to Atlanta to rehearse for its upcoming world tour, the group would stop by the Basement for fifteen minutes on the afternoon of January 19th to autograph a mural dedicated to the band. Pictures of R.E.M. at the Basement in school newspapers and other publications around the city would increase the club's cachet, and the members of of the band, who live sixty-five miles away, in Athens, Georgia, would have done a bit of community service.

Suddenly, the R.E.M. boys—singer Michael Stipe, guitarist Peter Buck, bassist Mike Mills and drummer Bill Berry—appear. They saunter in, their casualness and mild bewilderment a funny contrast to the jolt of energy that surges through the kids, who are crackling as if they'd been plugged into a live socket. After Terrell provides a brief tour of the club's facilities and explains the day's purpose—"We still haven't gotten to the kids who drink," he tells a politely nodding Buck—the band members seat themselves at a card table to sign autographs, pose for pictures and chat with the students.

Then it's time for what Berry calls the Wall Scrawl. Berry and Buck hoist Stipe high into the air, and the singer begins writing with a black Magic Marker near the top of the mural, which is a light-green square inscribed with the orange letters R.E.M. When Stipe, who is still being held aloft by his band mates, turns around, raises his fist in the air, flashes a huge grin and reveals his message—STIPE SAYS STRENGTH + PEACE—the room explodes with flashes. After a couple of short interviews—"I think it's a great idea, and I'm really glad we were able to do this," Mills says to a television reporter, while Buck laments that "there's too many tragedies that happen with drinking and driving"—the group heads for its van.

And what do the students think of their illustrious visitors? Fourteen-year-old Travis Peck of Pace Academy is only too eager to provide the answer: "R.E.M. is awesome!"

IT'S BEEN A LONG, strange trip for R.E.M., since the release of "Radio Free Europe" on a minuscule independent label in 1981 first brought the group to national attention. Once the darlings of the underground, they are now solicited by parents' groups to improve the social habits of the young. College-radio perennials, they have now graduated—into high schools. Having signed a five-record deal with Warner Bros. last year for a reported $10 million, the members of R.E.M. are approaching the status of—can it be?—superstars.

Meanwhile, on the far less complicated trip across town to an industrial section of northwest Atlanta—where the band is renting the largest room at a studio complex called Rehearse Too Much—the mood is a bit charged. It's Thursday evening, and early Monday morning the band is flying to Japan to begin a yearlong world tour—R.E.M.'s first live shows in sixteen months—and nerves are somewhat frayed. The band members hadn't been told that the Wall Scrawl would include big-time media like CNN, and they are still bemused by the horde of younger fans they picked up after "The One I Love," from their 1987 album *Document,* became their first Top Ten hit.

During the ride, Stipe, whose political outspokenness tends to elicit the most painfully serious questions, laughingly recounts how one student asked him, "We just had a big argument in class about whether we should worship Karl Marx. What do you think, sir?" Munching on nuts, the singer, who is unshaven and characteristically decked out like a Beckett hobo, with the Eighties touch of a long, thin braid down his back, wonders, "Do I really merit the *sir?*"

At Rehearse Too Much, a stage is set up at the far end of a bleak, unadorned warehouse-style space with cinder-block walls. "About twenty-eight bands rehearse here, most of them thrash and metal," Stipe explains as he smokes one of his hand-rolled cigarettes and strolls through the corridors of the complex. That may account for the question one musician, whose band was rehearsing down the hall, asked R.E.M.'s crew while listening to the group run through its set one night. "Who is this fucking R.E.M. cover band?" he asked, his voice dripping contempt. "They play one R.E.M. song after another!"

"What! *Who* said that?" Stipe asks in mock horror when told of the comment. The singer was sufficiently concerned about rigidities in R.E.M.'s sound that, according to Mills, he told the other members of the band "not to write any more R.E.M.-type songs" when they began working on *Green,* the now-platinum album they released in early November. Consequently the remark has just enough of a point to sting Stipe a tad. He shakes his head as he walks away and says, "It's a perfect circle."

On the cramped stage, equipment is being readied for R.E.M.'s last rehearsal before the tour. Buck is huddling with Peter Holsapple, the former main man of the now-defunct dB's, who has been drafted to play guitar and keyboards for R.E.M. on this tour. They are sorting out an arrangement for "Academy Fight Song," a Mission of Burma tune that R.E.M. is covering in its shows. The other band members are cracking open cans of beer and soda and pulling slices from the eight pizzas that were ordered for dinner.

Bertis Downs IV, the band's lawyer and longtime friend, has torn himself away from last-minute tour preparations and driven over from Athens to catch the final rehearsal. R.E.M.'s set includes a healthy dose of songs from *Green,* and Downs, whose fresh-faced enthusiasm belies his profession, says, "I just had to come by to hear how the new songs sound." "After you hear 'Get Up,' " Holt assures him, "you're going to want us to make a live album."

Indeed, hearing R.E.M. power through some twenty-five songs in a space smaller than most clubs is undeniably, as Travis Peck might put it, awesome. Undistracted by an audience, gripped by the challenge of the impending tour, the band is totally concentrated in its musical force.

Dressed simply in black workout pants, a green shirt and a black cloth cap, Stipe stands virtually still, but his voice is strong and resonant. The band crunches the staccato rhythms of "Academy Fight Song" and then leans into muscular versions of "Pop Song 89" and "Stand," from *Green*. Buck's body rocks in emphatic time with his playing, and Berry and Mills build a solid bottom that gives the songs a tougher sound and a greater propulsion than they have on record.

After "Stand" closes, the band confers onstage, and Holt, ever protective of his charges, says to the four or five people sitting near him, "It must be pretty weird, playing these songs with everyone sitting around talking. We should all stand up and scream after they finish the next one." So when the group ends "Maps and Legends," an eerie tune from *Fables of the Reconstruction* that is much enriched by Holsapple's keyboards, it is greeted by a burst of shouts and raucous clapping from the dozen or so people hanging around the room.

The band members stare uncomprehendingly and then break into smiles. Buck waves, and Stipe says, "My first applause of the new year. Thank you!" Then he recalls that this night is the eve of George Bush's inauguration and adds, "My last applause of the Reagan era." Another volley of applause follows. "You've got to fuck with them every now and then," Holt says, satisfied.

The rehearsal resumes as R.E.M. fires up fierce versions of "Finest Worksong" and "These Days." The proceedings come to a brief halt when Buck pops a string during a particularly ferocious rendition of "Turn You Inside-Out"; and then "Sitting Still" and "Driver 8" follow, with Buck and Holsapple ringing out the signature guitar jangle of R.E.M.'s early sound.

The evening ends with "I Remember California," "You Are the Everything," another pass at "Academy Fight Song," the pleasing, untitled song that closes *Green* and "Time After Time (Annelise)," the evocative ballad from *Reckoning*. As the equipment is being loaded, Mills elects to stay in Atlanta, where his mother is about to undergo surgery. Stipe, Buck and Berry climb into the van for the late-night drive back to Athens.

After they arrive, Buck drops in at the 40 Watt Club, which he describes as "purposely kind of a rock & roll dump," to catch the end of a set by an Athens band he produced called the Primates. "Their favorite bands are George Thorogood, Hank Williams and the Minutemen," he says, "and they kind of sound like a combination of all three." Buck's wife, Barrie, a tall, dark-haired beauty who co-owns the 40 Watt, is behind the bar, and the guitarist orders a beer.

After the nightcap, Buck's mind drifts back to the rehearsal. "That's the way to see a band," he tells a visitor, "the way you saw us tonight."

BACK IN ATHENS FOR their last weekend before flying off, the band members and Holt are desperately trying to dispatch all the details that need to be dealt with before departure. Due to a bureaucratic snafu, a crew member's visa may not be ready in time, and Holt and Downs are pulling strings to make sure he is able to leave on schedule. At this point, R.E.M. is a sufficiently important Georgia industry—as he tries to check a friend into an Athens hotel, Buck unselfconsciously refers to the group as "our corporation" while negotiating with the desk clerk—that a U.S. senator intervenes in the band's behalf.

Stipe, who handles most of the band's visual imagery, needs to approve tour T-shirts. Mills is motoring back and forth to Atlanta to visit his mother and say goodbye to his family. Buck and Barrie are trying to find time to run off to the mall to buy luggage.

Finally, Holsapple and his girlfriend, Ilene, have agreed to headline a benefit at the 40 Watt for the Athens Pro-Choice Action League on Friday night. Buck rehearses with Holsapple earlier in the day and joins the duo onstage for ragged but right versions of such numbers as Marvin Gaye's "Sexual Healing," Dion's "Drip Drop" and the Flying Burrito Brothers' "Do Right Woman." A cheerful-looking Stipe drops in to catch the action, with a group of bohemian pals, known to more cynical locals as "diStipels," in tow.

With all the hubbub, it hardly seems only sixteen months ago that R.E.M. announced that the band would take a break from performing live and possibly even recording. R.E.M.'s steps forward have always been careful—the result of an intriguing blend of deliberation, intuition and a staunch sense of integrity. The popularity that came in the wake of the platinum *Document* annihilated whatever vestiges remained of R.E.M.'s insulated cult status. The consequences of that change had to be analyzed and absorbed before the band could define a suitable direction.

"One thing that was affecting us was this blind acceptance and enthusiasm for anything that was said or done onstage," Mills says about the tour that followed the release of *Document*. "People are so frantic by the time you get into these larger halls that it's just a party no matter what you do. It makes you feel kind of weird about *meaning* what you do. You may put your heart and soul into something, but it doesn't matter because those people can't hear it anyway. Since it's something that we did love to do so much, we wanted to step back before we got burned out on it."

Another issue R.E.M. had to confront was the end of its contract with I.R.S. Records, the label that signed the band after the release of "Radio Free Europe." I.R.S. very much wanted to re-sign the group, and R.E.M. felt a great deal of loyalty to the label, which from the first endorsed and committed itself to the band's insistence on total creative control and progress at the band's own pace. When R.E.M. was first shopping for a contract, according to Buck, the folks at I.R.S. were "the only ones who didn't say, 'Boy, if you guys cut your hair and stop wearing dirty clothes, I can turn you into the Go-Go's.' " The band members all say that leaving I.R.S. was the hardest decision they ever made.

The key factor from the band's perspective was that I.R.S. and its overseas distributor, CBS International, had been unable to expand R.E.M.'s audience outside the U.S. Says Berry, "We got really tired of going to Europe and pretty much being given an ultimatum by the record companies over there, the affiliates of I.R.S., who were saying, 'If you don't come over and tour, we're not going to promote your record. You won't even see it on the shelves.' Then we'd get over there, and there'd be absolutely no promotion at all." The band's core of followers never grew significantly.

Needless to say, news that R.E.M. was thinking of leaving I.R.S. excited interest from virtually every major record company. Ultimately, the band was impressed both by the assurances given by Warner Bros. that R.E.M. would be a top priority of the company's overseas division and by the label's artist-oriented reputation.

"They've had some of my favorite artists on the label for years and not really bothered them so much about selling records," Buck says of Warner Bros. "Van Dyke Parks still puts out records. Randy Newman, sometimes he has hits, sometimes he doesn't—he makes great records. We figured that just looking at people's track records, you can understand what kind of business they're going to run." That Lenny Waronker, president of Warner Bros. Records, was himself a producer also weighed heavily with the band.

Still, it may be hard, at least in the public's estimation, for R.E.M. to maintain what Holt calls the "small, homey, hokey, *Mayberry R.F.D.* kind of feel to the way we live our lives" while earning millions of dollars, selling millions of records, pursuing international markets and working with one of the largest entertainment conglomerates in the world.

From the questions they asked, according to Berry, the kids at the Basement seemed to "think of Warner Bros. as literally like a monster, just something that consumes and spits out. I think a lot of kids wonder how we fit." Sitting in his office, Holt halts a conversation about the move from I.R.S. to Warner Bros., saying, "I feel completely uncomfortable discussing that situation, because I just don't think that anything said about it is going to translate, that there's any way for people to understand. It seems like you're either biased toward 'Well, they did what they had to do and went for the money' or 'God, they really did the underdog dirty.' "

In fact, nothing riles R.E.M. quite like the charge that the band has sold out. "My response is, like, Guns N' Roses," Berry says. "Great band, by the way. I love 'em. But it's like they've got this 'fuck you,' 'rock & roll kid' attitude, and they sell seven million records. Their *first* record. And here we are on our sixth record—*Document* was our fifth full LP, it sells a million records, and 'R.E.M. has sold out.' But Guns N' Roses gets all these accolades. I don't know what we're supposed to do. I really don't."

Never known for pulling punches, Buck hits the question dead on. "Pretty much all the extreme opinions about us I think are wrong," he says. "We're not the best band in the world—nobody is—so who cares about that? And all the people who think we've sold out, I don't really care much about them either.

"I know what I do, and I'll set my job up against anyone else's any day and say that I make less concessions to what people tell me to do than anyone else around—I mean, no matter *what* job they do. But, then, no one's going to believe that.

"There are a lot of people who like bands when they're smaller—and *I'm* one of them," he says. "I really love the Replacements, but I don't go see them now. I saw them in front of twenty people fifty times, and the same with Hüsker Dü. The last time I went to see Hüsker Dü, I was, like, 800 people back and getting elbowed in the gut by a fat guy with a leather jacket.

"So whenever people say, 'You're just too big, I don't enjoy going to your shows,' I say, 'That's fine.' I understand the people who say, 'You're too popular. I'm going to go follow the Butthole Surfers.' That's valid.

"Of course," Buck says, with a wry grin, "now the Butthole Surfers are getting a little too popular."

AT A LITTLE AFTER six o'clock on Saturday evening, Michael Stipe, driving a gray Volvo station wagon, pulls up in front of the two-story building R.E.M. has restored in downtown Athens for its offices and rehearsal studio. The street is deserted, the weather is uncommonly cold for Georgia, and the sky is darkening. Stipe, who is wearing his cloth cap and a long coat, suggests a cup of coffee, but when the coffee shop proves loud, brightly lit and, most problematic, crowded, he wants to leave after about a minute.

Unlike Buck, Berry and Mills, who are exactly the people they seem to be, Stipe, at twenty-nine the youngest member of the band, is much harder to fix—a fact that leads many people to dismiss him as pretentious or worship him as a mysterious god. With people he doesn't know very well, he is by turns remote and friendly. Anyone who grows used to one aspect of his personality is hurt or pleased, but always surprised, by the unexpected flash of the other. The emotional distance he seems to require, the imminence of departure that eases the threat of intimacy, is eloquently captured in lines from the song "Good Advices," on *Fables:* "I'd like it here if I could leave / And see you from a long way away."

It's the perfect attitude for a performer, and Stipe—perhaps inevitably and perhaps as a means of protecting himself—has made his personality part of his art. After climbing into a chair in Jefferson Holt's office and pulling his knees up to his chest, he says, "I can easily say, 'Which Michael do you want today?'"

The room is dim, and the window behind Stipe, lit with the day's last light, frames him, a dark silhouette surrounded by a waning brightness. As the interview continues and it grows darker outside, Stipe emerges more clearly among the room's shadows.

"It's so odd, I really don't have any idea how people look at me," he says, a cigarette in his hand and a cup of hot tea on the desk at his side. "I mean, I've always thought that the worst thing would be to be the court jester of a generation, and sometimes I feel like that, especially with the hats and tails onstage. But those are pretty simple devices, and they really stem from something that is a necessity for me. They also stem from an admiration and understanding of theatrics and the fact that you are in the public eye or the media and being able to utilize that."

During the week before November's presidential election, Stipe tried to utilize the fact that he was in the public eye by buying advertisements in college newspapers in Georgia and California that read, STIPE SAYS / DON'T GET BUSHWHACKED / GET OUT AND VOTE / VOTE SMART / DUKAKIS. *Green,* with its suggestions of optimism, environmentalism and innocence, was released on election day. The singer meant for the album to be a gesture of hope and encouragement.

"I decided that this had to be a record that was incredibly uplifting," Stipe says of *Green*. "Not necessarily *happy*, but a record that was uplifting to offset the store-bought cynicism and easy condemnation of the world we're living in now."

One dimension of Stipe's decision is that after years of being accused of obscurantism, he chose to print the lyrics to "World Leader Pretend"—a song that takes emotional honesty and directness of expression as its very subjects—on *Green*'s sleeve. A number of the other songs on *Green*, like "Pop Song 89," "Stand" and "Get Up," are similarly straightforward and bracing.

But frustration over misreadings is another reason why Stipe went for greater sonic clarity and linear meaning on *Green*. "There was frustration," Stipe admits, "to the degree that I rewrote 'Green Grow the Rushes' two times—as 'The Flowers of Guatemala' and 'Welcome to the Occupation'— where I actually ghostwrote the bio that went out to the press, so that they would say that 'this is a song about American intervention in Central America.'"

Despite the general sense of uplift on *Green*, the album doesn't lack disturbing moments. "Orange Crush," about the herbicide Agent Orange that was used in Vietnam, was originally written around the time of *Document*. The haunted travelogue "I Remember California" chronicles the human wreckage, the "nearly was and almost rans," of the L.A. fast lane. The harsh, metallic "Turn You Inside-Out" also provides a menacing note.

"I understand that all high school boys think it's about fucking," says Stipe with a chuckle. "That's the report I've gotten back from the grade schools. It's about manipulation and power. To me, it had a great deal to do, emotionally, with what a performer can do to an audience. A performer could be myself, it could be Martin Luther King, it could be Jackson, it could be Reagan, it could be Hitler—any preacher that is able to manipulate a large group of people."

Despite the urgency of his concerns, one of Stipe's more appealing qualities is his occasional willingness to poke fun at himself. He catches himself in the middle of an intense explanation of how "Oddfellows Local 151," on *Document*, was a "debunking" of the rural mythologizing of *Fables of the Reconstruction*. "Are you there?" he asks, laughing, and then admits, "I always get so serious in interviews, I think people think I'm a really serious person from that. My voice always drops way down to here, and I take on this Buckminster Fuller persona where the world hinges on my words."

On the other hand, Stipe *is* unquestionably a rather serious lad. Asked about R.E.M.'s impact, he says, "It's very hard for me to look at rock & roll and think of it as important in the world, because I just don't think that way. It's important in my life, because it's the arena I've chosen to move in.

"How serious can you be about a pop band?" he asks. "And then on the other hand, I see how music completely and totally affects people and affects their lives. It's nothing. On the other hand, God, look what it did for me, how much music has changed my life."

Buck comes at the issue of R.E.M.'s impact more frontally. "The influence that I'd like to think we have is that people saw that there's a way to go about doing this on your own terms," he says. "The thing is, you have to *not* worry about success. You can't do it and say, 'I want to make a million dollars tomorrow,' or 'I want to be as big as Madonna.' There's different ways to chase that. One of the things that's overlooked in music is that it's totally honorable to be a musician who does what he wants and doesn't make a lot of money.

"People tend to think, 'If you don't sell a million records, you're a failure.' Well, we didn't sell a million records until last year, and we were really successful. We didn't have a gold record until *Lifes Rich Pageant,* and that was five years down the line. We'd been touring, lots of people were coming to see us, and we were making a living. So I've never judged success in those kinds of terms, and hopefully we're an example that you don't have to be judged that way."

BUCK LIVES ABOUT A mile outside of town in a large white Southern-style house, filled with books, magazines, guitars and records, including a definitive collection of R.E.M. bootlegs. Against his better judgment, he recently purchased a "bottom of the line" CD player—his first—so that he'd be able to listen to the Mission of Burma CD compilation he just picked up. In his driveway sits a fancy Dodge jeep, a '57 Chevy and a hearse.

Through the heyday of the Athens scene, when the B-52's, Pylon, R.E.M. and a seemingly endless stream of other bands managed to turn a sleepy Southern college town into a nonstop dance party, Buck lived in a single room that looked like a hip record store after an explosion. His house now, for all its beauty and tasteful appointments, is simply that room writ large. And while R.E.M. has achieved a prominence that none of the other Athens bands could attain, in their home town, Buck, Berry and Mills are rarely bothered. Before he went onstage at the Pro-Choice benefit, the extent to which the patrons of the 40 Watt club permitted Buck to stand undisturbed at the bar seemed almost willful.

"The mayor says hello now" is how Berry describes how R.E.M.'s life in Athens has changed over the years. "It is real normal, except in the fall when the first batch of freshmen come in. They'll see us in the bars, and that gets a little weird, as far as people groping at us. That lasts for about two weeks, because then everybody realizes that we're out in the bars every single night!"

Stipe's life in Athens tends to be a bit more problematic, though even he can move around undisturbed much of the time. For all that the town's music scene has made Athens seem like a swinging place in the popular media, it's essentially still a small Southern backwater dominated by a conservative, football-crazed university. To the school's more Neanderthal frat boys, Stipe is not a mystical poet or a political progressive—or even a cool rock singer—but a geek to be abused. A recent column in a town paper that criticized Stipe prompted the following personal reply from him to the author: "Please cut the shit out. No matter what you think, I have to live in this town too. This is a reflection on me, not my 'image.' It's hard enough as it is."

On the opposite end of the spectrum, Stipe's enigmatic lyrics and romantic persona often inspire slightly unhinged types to read their own emotional difficulties into his songs. Such people are generally very interested in discussing the connections between his work and their lives when they run into him—to chilling effect. For the record, Stipe refuses to discuss his life in Athens and is said to maintain a residence out of state.

O N THE BRIGHTER SIDE, tending a fire in his fireplace, sipping a beer late on Saturday night, Peter Buck seems very much the contented lord of Buck Manor, the affectionate name a fellow musician gave the guitarist's digs. The impending tour recalls for Buck the days in the early Eighties when R.E.M. first hit the road—the four members of the band in a small van with Holt as their driver—for endless tours that have now become the stuff of legend. The pilgrimage was gaining momentum, and for a considerable number of people across the country—in Nowheresville towns and New Wave hotbeds—it was sometimes possible to believe that there was nothing more important in the world than R.E.M.

Earlier in the evening, Stipe had described those days as "harrowing—but a blast." "If there's an extension of *On the Road* and that whole Kerouacian"—he began laughing—"Can I possibly use that term, Kero-*whack*-ian? If there's an extension of that, probably forming a rock band and touring clubs is the closest you could get. Peter and I certainly had romantic ideas along those lines, and damned if we didn't do it. And damned if it didn't pay off."

For his part, Buck says, "We really soon got the reputation of 'Well, they'll do anything.' I mean, we're not going to do commercials, and we wouldn't go on television and lip-sync, but as far as playing real places—we had to. We were broke and we had to sell some fucking records, so 'Yeah, sure, we'll play the pizza parlor.' In the South there's a big thing where every Tuesday gay bars would have New Wave Night, so we played more gay bars than you could shake a stick at.

"If you ever saw *Spinal Tap,* we lived all of that, except for we're not quite as ignorant," he says. "We played that same place where they were second bill to the puppet show. It's Magic Mountain, I recognized it. And we had the exact same crowd—people who would sit in front of us *only* to give us the finger through our entire set."

The sort of experiences that would have broken up many bands—and that did break up most of R.E.M.'s contemporaries—have managed to bind R.E.M. together. The four band members and Holt and Downs still show a remarkable ability to close ranks, shut out the rest of the world and make decisions based solely on their personally determined criteria. And they take nothing about their relationship and their good fortune for granted.

"I most of the time feel like I'm not going to have a job next week," Holt says. "I always thought, 'They're going to get fed up, break up, and I won't have a job.' And I am amazed that it's however many years later and here we are. There's not a day that goes by that I don't think how incredibly lucky and thankful I am that things have worked out the way they are. And it wouldn't surprise me if they broke up tomorrow."

And yet there's a dizzying sense of a new beginning with R.E.M. "For me, *Green* had so many connections to *Murmur,*" Stipe says. "It was very much in the back of my head the whole time we were working on it. From the album cover to the topics of the songs and the way the songs were carried out, to me, there's a great connection there. Signing to another label was a new start for us. It did offer us an opportunity to sit back, scratch our temples and wonder, 'Where are we and where do we want to go?' "

With those questions answered for the moment, the pilgrimage is under way again. The members of R.E.M. are standing on the cusp of a brave new world they don't yet know. And they feel fine.

■ RANDOM NOTES (May 4, 1989)

Robyn Hitchcock says he first met R.E.M.'s Peter Buck four years ago in England. "He was trying to buy a cat, and he was a bit drunk, so I dissuaded him, and we went off to a bar," he says. "I lent him one of my cats while he was in Europe, and he gave it back to me intact when he went home." The friendship has led to Buck's appearances on Hitchcock's albums with the Egyptians (including the new *Queen Elvis*). And during Hitchcock's recent stint opening for the R.E.M. tour, he and Buck did a few shows with Peter Holsapple, Andy Metcalfe and Morris Windsor. "We've formed Nigel and the Crosses," says Hitchcock. "It's like anticipating the Traveling Wilburys. Rather than waiting, we thought we'd do it while we're still in reasonably good shape."

■ MUSIC IN BRIEF June 1, 1989

The civic-minded **R.E.M.** recently donated $5,000 to its home town of Athens, Georgia, in hopes of saving the city's historic warehouse district. The money will help a research project aimed at preserving the area's industrial buildings, many of which boast architectural designs dating back to the late 1800s.

■ RANDOM NOTES (June 15, 1989)

Michael Stipe and his R.E.M. colleagues are not afraid to take a stand. On the *Green* tour, the band had Greenpeace booths set up at every show, and Amnesty International representatives were present at several dates. "On this tour we concentrated on the environment," says Stipe. "It's a hot issue, and because of *Green,* it made sense."

Stipe recently spoke at a press conference in Columbia, South Carolina, to protest the Savannah River Plant, which manufactures tritium for use in nuclear warheads, and to plug *Building Bombs,* a documentary about the plant.

■ MUSIC IN BRIEF (July 13, 1989)

R.E.M. drummer **Bill Berry**, suffering from a bronchial infection, collapsed in Munich in May, causing the band to cancel the remaining dates of its German tour.

■ RANDOM NOTES NOTABLE NEWS (August 10, 1989)

Michael Stipe says he had the censors in mind when he made the video for R.E.M.'s "Pop Song." The clip features a topless Stipe, playfully dancing around with three topless women. "It's meant to provoke," says Stipe of the clip, which he directed. "It's in response to videos which objectify and berate women, which equate nudity with vulgarity." The self-censored version—an uncensored version is airing in Europe—features black bars across everyone's chests, including Stipe's. "I decided that a nipple was a nipple," he says.

Having members of U2, Hothouse Flowers and R.E.M. in the audience on the opening night of a tour would make most performers more than a little nervous, but **Maria McKee** describes her solo stint at Dublin's Mother Red Cap's Tavern as something like a family reunion.

DAVID FRICKE

YEAR-END REVIEW OF *GREEN*

WITH THEIR WARNER BROS. debut, the onetime underground ringleaders in R.E.M. consolidated their position overground, hitting big with one of the year's most infectious singles, "Stand," and reaching out from behind their familiar veil of enigmatic jangle with a striking directness and refined studio attack. Like *Document,* the band's '87 platinum breakthrough, *Green* is a welcome distillation of R.E.M.'s stage magic and love of extremes; the album incorporates elements as divergent as the bubblegum delight of "Get Up," the subtle ballad bite of "Hairshirt," the frank romanticism of the untitled closing track and—dare we say it?—the slow Zeppelinesque grind of "Turn You Inside-Out." Singer-lyricist Michael Stipe's new interest in enunciation and his more explicit approach to personal and political affairs—in "You Are the Everything," "Pop Song 89" and "World Leader Pretend"—also give *Green* a firm, emotive kick that shows how the older, wiser R.E.M. has adapted rock & roll convention to its own purposes. The result: accessibility without compromise.

1989 MUSIC AWARDS

READERS PICKS

ARTIST OF THE YEAR	BEST BAND	BEST TOUR
The Rolling Stones	The Rolling Stones	The Rolling Stones
Tom Petty	**R.E.M.**	The Who
Paula Abdul	U2	**R.E.M.**
R.E.M.	Fine Young Cannibals	Bon Jovi
Fine Young Cannibals	Guns N' Roses	Metallica

■ **RANDOM NOTES** (February 22, 1990)

It was the first thing we ever did together," Amy Ray says of "I'll Give You My Skin," the song the Indigo Girls co-wrote with R.E.M.'s Michael Stipe for an album (tentatively titled *Tame Yourself*) to benefit People for the Ethical Treatment of Animals (PETA). "Michael saw us at the Uptown Lounge, in Athens," says Ray, "and he just walked up to the stage and said, 'I have to write a song for PETA.' " *Tame Yourself*—which is expected to include tracks by Belinda Carlisle, Erasure, the B-52's and k.d. lang—is due in August.

DAVID FRICKE

PETER BUCK Q & A

In a special issue that surveyed the music of the Eighties, ROLLING STONE featured an interview with R.E.M. guitarist Peter Buck.

R.E.M., POSSIBLY THE MOST commercially successful and critically applauded new American rock band of the last decade, was born as the rock & roll clock struck 1980. It was in late January of that year, in the small, swinging college town of Athens, Georgia, that guitarist Peter Buck, singer Michael Stipe, bassist Mike Mills and drummer Bill Berry rehearsed together for the first time. The following April 5th, they made their concert debut—without a name—at a free beer blast in the old, converted Episcopalian church where Stipe and Buck lived.

Playing a mixture of hip covers and their own hastily written originals, the future members of R.E.M. lurched through their set with a lusty abandon fully in keeping with the Athens art-and-party tradition already established by the B-52's and Pylon. But R.E.M. was destined for greater things. That show marked the beginning of the band's remarkable and sometimes troubled passage from local notoriety to mainstream acceptance and, with it, the rise of America's postpunk underground.

"I hate to hearken back to the 'good old days,' because they weren't," Buck, 34, says now, with an ironic chuckle. "But it was a real interesting time. I lived in a town where a lot of stuff was going on, and no one knew that it was different for a town to have a scene: 'Oh, everybody plays in bands, and everybody has a friend who made a record.' "

R.E.M. did not change the face of U.S. rock in the Eighties single-handedly; the band shares that honor with the likes of X, Black Flag, the dB's, Hüsker Dü, the Minutemen, Mission of Burma, Sonic Youth, the Replacements, the Dream Syndicate and, of course, R.E.M.'s fellow Athenians. But R.E.M. was in the thick of the fight from the very start. The band revitalized the independent recording scene with the success of its stirring 1981 vinyl bow, "Radio Free Europe" b / w "Sitting Still," issued on the tiny Hib-Tone label. *Murmur,* the group's 1983 album debut, set *the* standard for new American guitar rock, with its masterful blend of gauzy, lyrical impressionism and driving folk-rock passion. With the support of college radio and the fanzine press, R.E.M. was also instrumental in creating an alternative club circuit that catered to the growing market of young fans disgruntled by arthritic AOR programming and formulaic arena-rock spectacle.

"We played cheap, *anywhere,*" Buck says proudly. "We'd always get more people every time we went back. We were fairly decent, and if nothing else, our show was a nice way to spend an evening for a dollar."

The venues are bigger now; the ticket prices have gone up. But R.E.M. (which cracked the platinum barrier in 1987 with *Document* and again in 1988 with *Green*) has not lost any of its renegade enthusiasm over the years. Between R.E.M. tours and recording projects, Buck, for instance, has become an in-demand freelance producer specializing in young, outlaw bands. He also remains an insatiable record collector and a keen observer of the American underground—or what, in his opinion, is left of it as the clock strikes '90.

"Now Athens is a real professional scene," says Buck, who was interviewed at Bearsville Studios, in upstate New York, during a break in overdubbing sessions for R.E.M.'s next album. "People move down to form a band, they do a demo tape, make an independent single, tour the East Coast—same places we used to play, if they're still in business.

"In those days, there were different ways to do it," Buck says. "Pylon would only play New York and Georgia. They never went up and down the East Coast unless they had to. They just didn't want to tour.

"We, on the other hand," he adds, laughing, "had nothing better to do."

*W*HEN R.E.M. STARTED REHEARSING *in January 1980, what were your ambitions and expectations? Did the dawn of a new decade hold any particular meaning for you?*

I never thought of it that way. To me, the Seventies ended in 1977. You have to remember, growing up at the time I did, there wasn't anyone who made records like us. Rock & roll was full of superrich guys that had mustaches and were ten years older than me. I was twenty-one, and it didn't make any sense to me.

So for you, the punk uprising of 1977–78 was the demarcation point.

That was the beginning of the Eighties for me. Because there was a realization that there were ways to work outside the music business. In my scene, it was predominantly white kids doing it. But I think it was liberating for everybody. I never lived in New York, and I wasn't there when they invented rap and scratching. But I started listening to that in 1979, '80, and I went, "Wow, this is really interesting." For me, the Seventies were over early, and I was really glad, too.

Did you see the Sex Pistols' U.S.-debut show in Atlanta?

Yeah. I gave my mother the money because she had a credit card, you needed a card to reserve the tickets. Then I got down there, and they'd sold all the tickets. I was with this crazy guy, a friend of a friend who didn't know anything about the Sex Pistols. But he was so incensed—I was supposed to be in there—that he kicked the door in, and we got in. He got to see the whole show. They caught me and dragged me out. I saw one song. But it was pretty great.

No one really got it. There were guys with big bellbottoms, beards and safety pins three feet long. When I went to see all the weird bands in Atlanta in 1975, there wasn't a dress code. Mostly people wore whatever weird clothes they had laying around. And there were people doing odd stuff— the Fans, the Brains, the B-52's when they started. Then all of a sudden in '77, you suddenly had all these guys in brand-new leather jackets with safety pins in them.

Even in the beginning, the Athens scene exhibited a remarkable diversity. Where did R.E.M. fit into the mix?

The point was, nobody sounded like a punk band. There were the B-52's, who made up their own rules. Pylon was a weird, angular dance band. The Method Actors were a two-piece psycho-funk band. And then there was us. We were sort of considered the "pop" band. Which was sort of weird, because we're not all that poppy. Then when we went out of town, everybody thought we were really weird.

Like the Seventies independent singles by Patti Smith and Television, the Hib-Tone 45 of "Radio Free Europe" was a major turning point for the underground record industry. Were you surprised by the success, and influence, of that single?

It was mind-boggling. It was supposed to be a demo tape, so we could get jobs. And we met this guy who said he'd put it out. It wasn't very good mastering; we were all young, and we didn't know what the hell we were doing. We sent 200 promo copies literally to any magazine we thought of. We sent one to *Womens Wear Daily*—I swear to God. Then we started getting letters from people at record companies.

Did you feel there was an audience out there for R.E.M.?

It wasn't so much that there was an audience for us, but that there was a lot of dissatisfaction. We weren't sure where our place in the business was, or even if we had one. But we did realize something was going on when there seemed to be so many people, the *smart* ones in town, who would come up and say things: "Have you heard this band or that record?" Sometimes the towns we went through didn't have any bands of their own. Or the local New Wave band would do Cars covers. But people would go see that because "well, at least it isn't Eagles covers." And in every town, no matter how small or how weird, there would always be from twenty to a hundred people who would say the same thing: "The radio around here sucks." The idea that we were kind of successful meant that there were other people who felt like we did.

When you started touring, what were some of the other cities and scenes that impressed you?

Minneapolis was very good to us from the beginning. We played to twenty people on Thanksgiving 1981, and every one of them came up to us afterwards and invited us to their house for a party. Nashville was always real good. There was stuff going on in Washington, D.C.

But there were clubs everywhere. There was a place in Greensboro, North Carolina, called Friday's. It was a pizza parlor, and the guy had bands play. It was an L-shaped room; you could see through the bar to the ovens, with the guy with the long stick with pizzas on it, and see us, too. He'd charge a dollar, we'd get 150 people in there, and we'd get the door. People would let us sleep on their floor. There were clubs like that in every city.

Even in New York, the audiences at your early gigs were mostly made up of rock critics who loved the single.

The first time, it was *all* rock critics. We opened for the Bloods at the Pilgrim Theater, and the PA broke halfway through the third song. So we played instrumentals. And we took requests. People were laughing, shaking their heads and thinking, "This is really unprofessional."

Critics and fanzines helped an awful lot. At the time, there were not a lot of ways to hear this music. When radio is confused and there isn't a way for something to be heard, it becomes a point where words mean a lot more. Today you have MTV. You hear about Pussy Galore on MTV. But in those days we were considered so out there by that area of the business that there was no way we were going to be heard of.

Did you consider yourselves "underground"?

It's an oft-abused phrase. But there was a definite difference between the showcase clubs and the dumps we played. And the dumps were more fun. Also, it wasn't just something that was only for rock & roll bands. Dwight Yoakam used to play a lot of the same clubs in L.A. that we used to play.

Underground is such a weird term. Because *above-ground* is dead most of the time, anyway. Most of us were out of the public eye, and that was fine. There were these alternatives—the small clubs, the independent record stores. None of us expected it to ever be anything but this small alternative. Until three or four years ago, I never heard any of these bands say, "Man, I really want a hit single. I want to sell a lot of records." That just wasn't considered, because it didn't seem possible. What you hoped for was to make enough money to make another record.

When you made 'Murmur,' how did you cope with the business of recording professionally, with its emphasis on technology and "name" producers?

We wanted to use Mitch Easter and Don Dixon as our producers. And I.R.S. said, "It would be nice if you tried this guy, Stephen Hague." Okay, he was a nice guy; he just wasn't what we needed. When we eventually did *Murmur,* every song on it was a first take. But Hague had us do songs thirty-five times. And then he'd put together an edit of, say, the chorus from the thirteenth with the bridge from the twenty-ninth. I got to the point where I didn't know what we were doing. Two days in the studio, and we didn't finish even one song.

We like technology, too. Every record I've ever done, I overdubbed guitars. But the one thing people were always interested in then was a big drumbeat and synchro stuff. And I never really got that. For us, the early records were essentially uptempo folk songs. What do you mean, "a big drum sound so they can dance to it"? They're not gonna dance to this.

How did you feel about your synth-pop contemporaries, like Soft Cell and the Human League?

I loved "Tainted Love." "Don't You Want Me" is a great song. Some of my favorite music is totally manufactured. Some of my favorite records of last year—like the Public Enemy album—there's actually nobody playing on them. I know guys who can make a record with just a computer. Michael [Stipe] is working with the Boogie Down Productions guy, KRS-One. They tap a key, sample some stuff. Great—you can make records really cheap. And it's put the technology right in the hands of the kids. That's what punk was all about. Punk was never about buying a leather jacket and singing songs about Ronald Reagan. It was about liberating yourself from the strictures of the music industry.

Yet you were forced to operate within certain strictures of the music industry when you signed with I.R.S. Records.

When we were looking for a label, I.R.S. was the one we wanted. They had the Buzzcocks at the time, the Cramps, the Fall, Wall of Voodoo. They were doing a lot of the kinds of records I was listening to. And it was the perfect label for us. It was small enough so that we could go and talk to people and tell them what we wanted. And they helped us with marketing things—like touring. We'd just go, "Let's go out and play." And they'd say, "Why don't you play here, because your records are doing well on the radio?" Things that I never would have thought of. They didn't totally leave us alone, but they didn't suggest really stupid things, either.

By the time R.E.M. finally cracked the Top Ten with "The One I Love," in 1987, your I.R.S. deal was almost up. Was the label frustrated by your inability to get hit singles during the preceding years?

Not necessarily. We made those records for so little money that they made tons of money off of us. Maybe not the first day. But *Murmur* cost $25,000. It's gold now.

They would have liked hit singles. But we didn't come up with any. We talked about it, and sometimes Jay [Boberg, president of I.R.S.] had good input. We would never have put "9-9" on the first record if he hadn't said, "I really like that song, would you please record it for me?" That was a cool thing to say, because it obviously wasn't going to be a single. Sometimes he'd say, "If you remix this, it will have a lot better chance to be on the radio." And I'd go, "They're not gonna play this anyway." But they never put a lot of pressure on us. I mean, every album we made sold more than the one before it. You can't say anything bad about that.

Yet the success of "The One I Love" and "Stand" showed not only that you were quite capable of making hit singles but also that both AOR and Top Forty radio had become more receptive to your sound and style.

Radio changed a lot. At the time we had a hit single, Los Lobos had hit singles and Tracy Chapman had a hit single. Who would have thought in 1982 that the biggest hit of '87 or '88 was going to be a black woman with a guitar doing songs about social injustice? There were a lot of us plugging away. Black and white and folk and rap and pop and jangling guitar—we all changed, a little bit, the way people looked at what could get on the radio. Radio is so much more open now than when I was young. I mean, "Personal Jesus" sold a million copies.

R.E.M. has long been seen as the archetypal Eighties college-radio band. How important was college radio to the band's survival and success?

In the beginning, it was very important, because we weren't getting on radio anywhere else. It never made us rich, but it got us to the point where we could play and know that in most cities a hundred people were gonna show up. The playlist was a lot more open then. College stations I go to now are fairly button-down. It's become more of a training ground for AOR radio. There's some great stations, but I get really tired of turning on the radio and hearing only major-label releases. We're on a major label—I have nothing to say about that one way or the other. But college radio has turned into fun music for college kids who want to hear the new Depeche Mode. I always like to think that you should be able to learn something by listening to college stations.

The albums 'Murmur' and 'Reckoning' also triggered the rise of the "college-radio sound," with a host of bands making records with jangling guitars, oblique lyrics and moody pseudo-Stipe vocals. Were you flattered by the imitations or annoyed?

Well, you know, it goes in phases. There was a year and a half where I heard a lot of *Murmur*-esque bands. I mean, whenever anyone says a band sounds like R.E.M., they don't say they sound like *Green*. It's the first record, because that was a kind of different thing.

Two years after that it was the Replacements, and I still see a lot of Replacements bands. Right now it's Sonic Youth. That's what white, middle-class kids are playing now: noise-influenced kind of songs, textured noise stuff. It comes and goes. We had our two years of being imitated.

You've also outlasted many of your original contemporaries, like X, Hüsker Dü and the Dream Syndicate. Where did they go wrong, and how did you beat the odds?

I have no idea. I can never understand why X wasn't the biggest band in the world. They had everything—really great songs, they looked great. They were really literate, but you could also just sit there and bang your head and not pay attention to the lyrics. But I actually bumped into John Doe not long ago, and he said it was the dreaded *p* word: *punk*. They were seen as punks, and it doesn't matter what their influences were, whether it be Hank Williams or French symbolist poetry. They're seen as punks in leather jackets.

I don't think we were ever hindered with that scary image. Our image was four guys who don't have an image. We don't have to fight against any past, any looks. I think the problem with a lot of our contemporaries is that when they wanted to sell records, a lot of them made really big mistakes. I don't think the Dream Syndicate or Hüsker Dü did that. But a lot of our contemporaries, they made the first record, and then they made the second record that they hoped would sell. Then they made the third record where they were really frightened and didn't know what to do. I couldn't tell you how many people I know that made three records, and the third record has nothing to do with what made the band good the first time. Musically, our records are fairly different, but we're still the same songwriters.

How would you describe the musical and emotional dynamics at work within R.E.M.?

What holds us together as a force is working together as songwriters and players. We write songs together and play them together. We haven't ever been in a position where someone's been pissed off about making less money or not having his songs on the record. We're the only band I know that fights *not* to be in our own videos.

We have a real socialist democracy. We sit around tables and vote just about as much as we write songs. We vote on where we're going to play, where we're gonna make the record, who's gonna produce it. We each have equal say and input when we bring songs into the studio. Everything is a total compromise between the four of us.

How do you break a tie?

We have a rule of no. If we can't make up our minds, then we don't do it. It has to be all four in one direction. If one person really thinks that something is wrong and is passionate about it, even if we think he is wrong, we agree with him. Like on the new record, we were playing with some-thing where there's a little sample in it. I like when people sample records. Mike [Mills] is against it. He really hates the idea. So we're gonna make samples of our own stuff to use, because he feels real strongly that it's wrong.

Has the band ever come close to splitting up?

Yeah, several times. But it's just like any marriage. It's when you don't talk about stuff that things get bad. Me and Mike have wrestled on the ground before. We've thrown things at each other and cursed and broken things. But I argue less with the three of them than I do with my parents.

The thing is, we have to be able to look at ourselves in the mirror. You can't really be in a band unless you say at the end of the day, "Everything we did today is okay by me." I hate those meetings. Sometimes they'll go on for four hours, and we still haven't made a decision. And sometimes we'll change our minds three times. But you have to do that. I wouldn't want to do it any other way.

I play with other people all the time, and I realize how fucked up other bands are. There's one guy making decisions, and the rest of the guys don't like it. I wouldn't want to do that. We're still making good music, but aside from that, if we make a really dud record sometime, it's the four of us deciding it.

In recent years, the band has become more outspoken on social and ecological issues. How did growing up in the Reagan decade affect your personal political agenda?

It's not like we, as people, were not interested in that kind of stuff. But it was kind of like being in a deepfreeze. I like America. I live here. I felt totally out of step. It just seemed like a real coldhearted decade. And you go, "Well, I'm a rock & roller guy. This is silly, for me to make any kind of statement." But after a while you realize, "Well, this is my country, too."

I still don't think the president has anything to do with me. I vote in every election, but I always feel defrauded in everything but a local election. But locally we do all kinds of stuff. We go to city-council meetings and vote on things. There are things in Athens that are different now because of people like us.

For example?

Historical preservation. We have curb-side paper recycling, which is pretty cool. Members of the city council who we have involved ourselves with have been very good about trying to protect what is nice about the town. You try to do what you can locally and do the food-bank stuff. All the things that make a small town.

Do you ever have problems deciding which issues to publicly support as a band?

Michael is involved with People for the Ethical Treatment of Animals—we're not. I agree with a lot of their goals, but I wouldn't feel real comfortable supporting them, because I'm wearing suede shoes. I eat meat, you know? I am against most testing on animals, but I have some friends who have AIDS, and I'm not gonna say you should stop using animals for AIDS tests.

So we talk that kind of stuff out. Generally, it's not like we espouse revolutionary platforms. I don't think recycling and helping the homeless is such a shocking agenda. We're gonna do some of the vote stuff. That's probably the main thing people need to realize, that they have the power to vote. And if that doesn't work, they always have where they spend their money.

How would you describe the rock underground of today?

I think that the underground is so overground now that the *real* underground is people who haven't really made a record yet. We've never heard of them. I keep up and get a lot of fanzines. I go see bands. And there are bands that are just brand-new and they have a "career." They have a

T-shirt-merchandising guy, and they have a tour-booking agent. It's a little more career oriented than when we were starting out. As far as underground, I don't know if that means anything anymore. That's the bad thing about what's happened to college radio. There isn't an us-and-them dividing point.

Can you tell whether your original audience has grown with you or away from you over the years?

I think my peer group still listens. I really don't think we've done anything that has really alienated an audience. We were never young guys in hip clothes on the cover of teen magazines and singing about young love, and here, all of a sudden, it's the end of the Eighties and we're *this* kind of band. We've grown steadily and changed. And I'm sure there's a lot of people that listen to Dylan that bought his first or second record.

Do you think the success of R.E.M. helped change the major labels' attitude toward the likes of Sonic Youth and the Butthole Surfers?

I think there's enough people who grew up with us that were college-radio programmers and who are now in A&R. I bump into people all the time who work at record companies, and so many of them say, like, "I was in college when *Murmur* came out." And now they're doing A&R. I think that's great, because the A&R people are always the ones who love what's going on. They're the ones who want to sign bands.

In a way, R.E.M. is engaged in its own A&R campaign. The band has always taken great unknowns out as support acts—like Camper Van Beethoven and 10,000 Maniacs—and you've done production work for bands like the Feelies and Run Westy Run.

If I like a band, I'll take them in the studio and work for free. I don't go in and say, "Let's make a hit single." It's more like "What is this band about?" I did a record with Charlie Pickett; it was this kind of deranged Johnny Thunders blues band. And they'd worry about something being out of tune. I'd just say: "Don't worry about it. It sounds fine. You're not the Doobie Brothers. I guarantee you, nobody is going to return this record and say the guitar is out of tune."

I'm not really sure the things I've done have sold anything because of my name. But I enjoy it, and if it helps kids in bands and it encourages them, great. If for some reason I couldn't write songs anymore or play in a band, I would produce a record a week. Or every other week.

What were your favorite Eighties bands?

I'm just like every other old-timer, in a way. To me, it's colored by who really made your head spin the first time you saw them. My favorite bands? I just remember moments.

What were some of the moments?

We worked with the Replacements a couple of times—before they started getting really drunk all the time. They were just wonderful. Hüsker Dü—the first time I saw them was a great experience. Another really cool moment was seeing the Dream Syndicate. I think they even put a live EP out from it; it was live upstairs at a radio station. We saw the Plugz in Los Angeles, and it was great. In Washington, at the Bayou, the Gang of Four put on probably one of the top three shows I ever saw. I'll never forget that. That was the great thing about the Eighties, that it was *moments*. I'd be so shocked to discover a great band in a place I never thought I'd see one. Who would have known that Minneapolis was just full of really great bands?

What were the biggest disappointments?

I didn't enter the music business with any illusions whatsoever. I hate to sound like Mr. Positive, but I was pleasantly surprised by how many people were nice and had their heads screwed on straight. I was ready for big, fat guys with chains around their necks, and I met some of those. But more often, I met people who really cared about music and did the best they could. One of the things that always moved me was you'd go into a town and there were always a few people keeping the flame going. They might be schoolteachers or janitors or work in a record store. But when I get to this town, I'll call this guy and he'll tell me what band's great, so I can see them.

What are your hopes for the Nineties?

We went through a decade where politically it was the most backwards and screwed-up decade imaginable. A lot of things socially were going wrong. Racism seemed to be on the increase. But things came together in kind of a nice way musically. A lot of the stuff that deserves to be on the radio *is* on the radio. A lot of bands that you wouldn't necessarily think have a lot in common have worked together.

Like the Amnesty tour. For all the imprecise talk about what good it was, it got lots of different music onstage together, and that's kind of where it all ends up for me. A lot of people I respect musically are playing well, making good records and working together. Some of those boundaries are down a bit.

That's my hope for the Nineties. A lot less formal and, musically, a lot more people working together and not paying attention so much to boundaries. Because they're not my boundaries.

MICHAEL STIPE ON THE EIGHTIES

R.E.M. lead singer Michael Stipe contributed the following thoughts on the "Me Decade":

I've BEEN CALLING THE Eighties the Reagan–Garfield era. They're over. That's probably a good thing. We can all praise our various gods for that.

Musically, we saw punk rock becoming more commercialized, black music on the upswing. Personally, I think we came out a little bit ahead. I feel a kind of weird nostalgia. Will people start wearing those same clothes three years after they wore them the first time? But I think that kind of immediate nostalgia is a reflection of the kind of impact American culture has had on the world—that things happen at such an accelerated pace, these clipped parts of our lives. This immediate nostalgia is a really creepy thing.

I don't want to put too much emphasis on those ten years—the decade as a discrete unit—but people tend to, and it seems to work *too* well. It's really odd that those numbers can change things that much. As we move toward the end of the century, that makes a huge difference. I'm optimistic about the Nineties. I think a lot of people will spend the next decade educating themselves and finding out how the world is run.

The last ten years seemed like thirty. Maybe the next ten will seem like sixty.

Some favorite records of the Eighties:

- Anything by Arvo Pärt
- *Mesopotamia*—the B-52's
- Anything by the Cramps
- *Wings of Desire* soundtrack
- *Doolittle*—the Pixies
- *Armed Forces*—Elvis Costello and the Attractions (from 1979)
- *Margin Walker*—Fugazi
- *Songs of the Free*—Gang of Four
- *Surprise Surprise Surprise*—Miracle Legion

- *Talking With the Taxman About Poetry*—Billy Bragg
- *Psychocandy*—the Jesus and Mary Chain
- *Stutter*—James
- *Ghetto Music: The Blueprint of Hip Hop*—Boogie Down Productions
- *Diesel and Dust*—Midnight Oil
- *Viva Hate*—Morrissey
- *I Will Not Be Sad in This World*—Djivan Gasparyan
- *Sign o' the Times*—Prince
- *Wave*—the Patti Smith Group (from 1979)
- *All Hail the Queen*—Queen Latifah
- *What Makes a Man Start Fires?*—Minutemen
- *God*—Rip Rig and Panic
- *The Elephant Man* soundtrack
- *In My Tribe*—10,000 Maniacs
- *Fiyo on the Bayou*—the Neville Brothers
- *Le Mystère des Voix Bulgares*—the Bulgarian State Female Vocal Choir
- *Rain Dogs*—Tom Waits
- *Under the Big Black Sun*—X
- *Gyrate*—Pylon

■ **RANDOM NOTES** NOTABLE NEWS (February 7, 1991)

An all-acoustic R.E.M. (minus drummer Bill Berry) previewed the song "Losin' My Religion"—from the band's forthcoming album—at the 40 Watt Club, in Athens, Georgia.

PARKE PUTERBAUGH

OUT OF TIME ALBUM REVIEW

★ ★ ★ ★

R.E.M. Is in Touch, Out of Time

YES, IT'S A DEPARTURE, but no, it's not so radical a departure that it is unrecognizable as R.E.M. *Out of Time* moves this unconventional band another step forward; a discernible connection to past records remains, but it is not constricting. The point is that R.E.M. has done it again: defied and fulfilled the conflicting expectations of a broad, mainstream audience and a smaller, more demanding—and possessive— cult. This may well be America's best rock & roll band, as this magazine's cover once proclaimed, but the group would probably wave off that honorific. Surely, however, R.E.M. is America's most resourceful rock & roll band.

R.E.M.'s greatest resource is its four members—not their musicianship, in technical terms, so much as the ideas and personalities that they express through their music—and they've remained unerringly true to their instincts. Such fidelity is difficult to maintain amid critical acclaim and climbing sales figures, which you'd expect might lead them self-consciously to break with or replicate a successful formula. But R.E.M., unpredictable and self-invented, has always operated more on intuition than formulas. This band does not carry a map, and not knowing what lies around the next curve is part of the fascination and fun of following R.E.M.

Musically, *Out of Time* is R.E.M.'s most baroque album; it breaks out of the guitar-bass-drums-voice format to make room for everything from harpsichord and strings, on "Half a World Away," to funky, Jimmy Smith-style organ and a cameo rap by KRS-One of Boogie Down Productions, on "Radio Song." The songs are enriched, not cluttered, by these embellishments. Kate Pierson of the B-52's sings on three numbers, shining on the roistering folk-country duet "Me in Honey," and Peter Holsapple, the former dB's leader who accompanied the band on its last tour, lends a hand here and there on guitar and bass.

All of this indicates that R.E.M. is no longer a closed circle, and the outreach allows the group to broaden its scope without diluting its essential character. As on *Document* and *Green,* the band and Scott Litt share the production credit on *Out of Time,* and despite the added flourishes the album is certainly not overproduced. There's no superficial glazing, and the raw, unvarnished content of the songs cuts through. The strings convey emotion, whether they are as sepulchral as doomsday ("Low") or as lithe as springtime ("Near Wild Heaven"). Even when instruments are layered upon one another, as in the subtle swell of strings, guitars and mandolins on the existentially despondent "Losing My Religion," they make a point. That point is "Life gets bigger," and R.E.M. deals with life's billowing complexities throughout *Out of Time.*

The band members, especially bassist Mike Mills, move outside of their prescribed roles to experiment a little. Mills, for instance, pumps up the jam on "Radio Song," ripping into its prickly innards on organ, while guitarist Peter Buck creates sparks with his serrated "Fame"-style attack and drummer Bill Berry syncopates like an honorary Funkadelic. Mills's organ also sets the funereal mood of "Low," on which Berry can be heard tapping congas, and Buck's stinging sustain drenches "Country Feedback" in plaintive, rippling waves of sound.

As the instrumentalists open themselves up, singer Michael Stipe bares his soul. He's long since stopped concealing his identity in an artful murmur, of course, but the extent to which, on *Out of Time,* he unburdens himself of doubt, disappointment and bile—and suggests maybe just a faint ray of cockeyed hope—is nothing short of revelatory. Except for "Endgame" and a strange, fablelike ramble entitled "Belong," all of the album is sung in the first person. Every song has an "I," "me," "my" or "mine" in it, and there's often a "you" as well. Even "Radio Song," an in-your-face number that makes an objective statement about the world outside the self, springs from a subjective reaction: "I tried to sing along, but *damn* that radio's song!"

Most of the time, Stipe waxes downbeat, sounding "low low low" and outcast. He sings, "This could be the saddest dusk I've ever seen," on "Half a World Away," and "It's all the same, the same, a shame, for me," on "Me in Honey." Technically, he has never sounded better, singing with surety, power and control. He dissects interpersonal relationships with a resigned sense of inevitability, filling songs with concrete details and unsparing analysis: "It's crazy what you could have had, crazy what you could have had / I mean it, I need this," he sings with mounting emotion in "Country Feedback." The effect is arresting; his verisimilitude can't be denied, because his voice insists on it.

In contrast, there's the heavenly pop chorale of "Near Wild Heaven" (recalling nothing quite so much as "Good Vibrations"-era Beach Boys) and the breezy, evocative "Endgame," the former largely sung by Mills and the latter mostly played by Buck. Stipe himself gets joyful, or appears to, on "Shiny Happy People," which commences with a sprightly waltz figure, then is yoked by a spunky riff from Buck before Stipe chimes in: "Meet me in the crowd / People, people / Throw your love around / Love me, love me / Take it into town / Happy, happy / Put it in the ground where the flowers grow." These are either the most absurdly sunny or bitingly cynical lyrics he's ever written, and your guess is as good as mine or maybe even Stipe's. More characteristic of *Out of Time* is "Half a World Away," in which urgent, minor-key music is married to doleful words as the singer steels himself "to go it alone and hold it alone, haul it along and hold it."

The songs on *Out of Time* are seemingly small scale in their first-person obsessions, but their meanings spread out to encompass shared feelings of dread, loneliness, anomie and a growing loss of faith. There are no treatises on ecology or foreign policy, no oblique strategies or hidden agendas. There doesn't have to be; all of that is implicit in the atmosphere of entropy, of things falling apart, that's evoked and detailed candidly, with glimmering beauty and unsurpassable sadness, on *Out of Time.*

■ **RANDOM NOTES** NOTABLE NEWS (May 2, 1991)
The video for R.E.M.'s "Losing My Religion" has been banned in Ireland because it contains religious imagery "unfit for broadcast."

ANTHONY DeCURTIS

PERFORMANCE REVIEW

Shocking, Milan, Italy, March 22, 1991

WHEN R.E.M. SIGNED ITS multi-million-dollar, five-album deal with Warner Bros. Records in 1988, part of the group's motivation was to broaden its European following. A three-week promotional jaunt by train across the continent this March in support of *Out of Time* was designed to further that end. In England, France, Germany, Portugal, Spain and Italy, the band gave endless interviews, performed on the notoriously bizarre European-television music shows and glad-handed the local industry heavies.

Though R.E.M. will not be touring this year—in Europe or anywhere else—singer Michael Stipe, guitarist Peter Buck, bassist Mike Mills and drummer Bill Berry were determined to make their presence and their music felt nonetheless. In Milan, that meant performing at an industry showcase for about 200 people at a comfortable, sedate club called—with the typical Italian flair for hyperbole—Shocking.

The eleven-song acoustic set was hardly R.E.M.'s finest moment. Guitarist-keyboardist Peter Holsapple, who had helped out on a similar show in London a few weeks earlier, was not able to join the band for this appearance, and the club's sound man generated what Buck later dryly termed a "dub mix" of the show, dropping instruments and voices in and out of the sound with an incompetence so impressively total that it eventually came to seem a kind of perverse wit, a virtual style in itself.

Still, one turns to R.E.M. for virtues other than technical sheen, and in emotional terms, the band's performance was focused and intense. Though they never mentioned it explicitly, the gulf war was clearly on the band members' minds, and a brooding "Disturbance at the Heron House," from *Document,* with its lyrics about "the followers of chaos out of control," effectively set the evening's tone. The affecting "Half a World Away" followed, and then Stipe introduced "Swan Swan H," the Civil War reflection from *Lifes Rich Pageant,* as "a song about a war our country inflicted on itself a number of decades ago." After that, the delicate, poetic

"Belong," with Stipe and Mills's harmonies floating over Buck's ringing guitar, provided a moment of genuine R.E.M.-style transcendence.

A rousing version of "Driver 8," from *Fables of the Reconstruction*, was followed by "Low," from *Out of Time*, and "Fretless," a powerful song recorded for *Out of Time* but pulled by the band at the last minute. Both songs offered ravaging looks at lives adrift in the wake of lost love. In a charming surprise, Mills, playing a guitar-shaped, acoustic four-string bass, stepped forward to sing the Troggs' sweet 1968 hit "Love Is All Around," with Stipe adding harmonies. "Losing My Religion," the gripping first single from *Out of Time*, came next, with a splendid rendition of "Fall on Me," from *Lifes Rich Pageant*, and a funny, sloppy "Get Up," from *Green*, ending the set on an exhilarating high note.

Throughout the show, the musical experimentalism that makes *Out of Time* sound so fresh was much in evidence. Buck played six-string and twelve-string guitars, as well as mandolin; Mills played bass and organ; Berry moved back and forth between percussion and guitar; and the group's road manager, David Russell, added percussion.

Once the performance was done and the meeting and greeting of media and music-business honchos accomplished, the band went off to a local restaurant for a spectacular Italian dinner. During a brief lull at the table, the memory of all the interviews he'd been doing and the prospect of more to come crossed Buck's mind. "Talking about yourself all the time isn't all it's cracked up to be," he said, obviously weary. "I'd rather be cleaning toilets."

"So would I," Mills agreed, breaking into a sly smile. "At my current salary, of course."

■ **RANDOM NOTES** (June 13, 1991)

It's over. R.E.M. has finished its two-stop tour. After an appearance on *MTV Unplugged*, the band headed to Charleston, West Virginia, to join Billy Bragg and Robyn Hitchcock on APR's live *Mountain Stage*. But once the radios were silenced, the band—inspiring enough hysteria to have the governor declare April 28th R.E.M. Day—played an extra hour and a half, hootenanny-style set with its cohorts, which may have a spillover effect. "Billy's staying at my house, and we're all going into the studio," says Peter Buck. "We'll see what we accomplish in two days."

JEFF GILES

NUMBER ONE WITH AN ATTITUDE

MICHAEL STIPE WAS THE last to know. Hurried, handwritten messages were already scrolling out of a fax machine back at his band's headquarters: "Congratulations, R.E.M., Athens and everyone," "Congratulations to all in the R.E.M. world" and "Congratulations. You deserve it, and as my mother would say, may it be the first of many." Bassist Mike Mills had heard the news. Guitarist Peter Buck had downed a glass of champagne, and his mom had had a good cry. Drummer Bill Berry had said: "Oh, that's weird. I'm gonna sit down."

Stipe, however, could not be found. Later it was discovered that the singer had been out at the creek near his Athens, Georgia, home, walking his three mixed-breed pups. He had then proceeded to city hall, where he had attended a meeting about the historic preservation of some buildings in the sweet-smelling, tree-lined university town of 87,000. Midway through the proceedings, Stipe noticed that a friend was staring at him and jubilantly waving her forefinger. R.E.M. was Number One.

"I sat in the meeting for two and a half hours, and I thought, 'Wow, I'm being pretty calm about this,'" Stipe says of the news that *Out of Time* had become the band's first album to top the *Billboard* charts. "And then I got outside city hall and just screamed and jumped up and down and burst into tears and ran around the block. I'd walked out of the meeting early so there weren't too many people wondering what on earth was wrong."

Just now, Stipe is sitting behind a desk in his lawyer's office. He's wearing a rumpled, auto-mechanic-style outfit, muddy rubber boots and a bright green baseball cap. He's eating an orange. Stipe is asked if he'd like to commemorate R.E.M.'s tenure at the top by talking a little bit about the other bands in the Top Forty. The singer allows as how he doesn't know much about them. He reaches for a copy of *Billboard* and spends a long time trying to find the Pop Albums chart.

"Okay," Stipe says finally, then delivers his countdown in a quiet, earnest voice. "Mariah Carey I've never heard. C + C Music Factory—I think the single is great. Wilson Phillips I've heard. I have no opinion about them. The Black Crowes—they're from Atlanta, right? I have no opinion about them. Enigma have two great videos, and they're kind of floaty, right? Pretty cool. *New Jack City* soundtrack—Ice-T was not bad. Chris Isaak—it's about time. Queensrÿche I've never heard. Rod Stewart we don't need to talk about. ABC [Another Bad Creation] I think is pretty great. Whitney Houston I've never heard. Amy Grant I've never heard. Roxette I've never heard. The Divinyls I've never heard. The Doors—see ya. Not interested. The Rolling Stones—see ya."

Wait a minute. Back up. Stipe has *never* heard Whitney Houston?

"No," he says, his face a picture of innocence. "I couldn't distinguish her from Mariah Carey. I just figured out how to say *Mariah*. You say it like *pariah*."

FOR FOUR YEARS NOW, R.E.M. has been keeping some pretty strange company. The band's albums have always sold well in the first few months after their release—thanks primarily to hard-core fans who have followed the group since it climbed out of the college-radio cellar and became what Bill Berry ambivalently refers to as "the gurus of 1980s mysticism." R.E.M. broadened that fan base considerably by spending most of the last decade on the road. Each of the band's albums sold a little better than the previous one. A graph of R.E.M.'s record sales over the mid-Eighties, in fact, would more or less look like an up escalator.

In 1987 the band found it had a radio-ready Top Ten single on its hands with "The One I Love," and *Document* became the first R.E.M. album to sell a million. The follow-up, *Green,* spawned the hit "Stand," sold a million and a half copies and powered the group's first arena tour. *Out of Time*—helped along by the brooding single "Losing My Religion"—has already sold 1.7 million copies. Even R.E.M.'s back catalog is flying out of record stores. The group's now-legendary debut, *Murmur,* from 1983, sold only 150,000 copies upon release. It is currently hovering around 800,000.

These days, there are R.E.M. fans who think "Stand"—or even "Losing My Religion"—is the first song the band ever wrote. "The people who listen to Top Forty are generally not R.E.M. record buyers—or they weren't until the last year or two," Mike Mills says. "It's kind of surprising to listen to the fourteen-year-old girls call up and go, 'How long have you been together? I like your first record.' And it's like 'No, no. See, the first record came out when you were about *one* year old.' "

IT'S TEN O'CLOCK ON a Wednesday evening, and Peter Buck is sitting on his front porch, trying to make sense of all the above. His house, which is not far from the center of town, is a gorgeous, ornate old mansion. It is full of high-ceilinged rooms liberally strewn with books, records and folk art; it has a widow's walk despite the fact that Athens is hundreds of miles from the sea. Upstairs, a friend of Buck's, the fine, left-leaning songwriter Billy Bragg, is doing some recording on an eight-track that has been set up in an empty bedroom. Mike Mills, who's scheduled to pitch in some backing vocals, is slumped in a chair in the living room. John Wesley Harding, a young British singer who's in town to play a show at the Georgia Theater, is perched atop a stool in the kitchen. Michael Stipe is up in the studio, lending his voice to a soldier's lament called "My Youngest Son Came Home Today."

As Buck talks, Stipe's and Bragg's voices drift down the massive, wooden staircase and through the screen door. Adding further to the mood, there's the fact that Buck's porch lights keep blinking on and off. The guitarist explains: Members of a local fraternity had been stealing things off his porch ("It must be because it's my house; I mean, you can't fence a *plant*"), so he installed motion-sensitive lights. Now his cat trips them off regularly.

"It's sort of crazy here tonight," Buck says, sitting back in a white wicker chair. "But this is how I live."

Unlike Stipe, of whom one's first impressions are that he is a gentle, solicitous person, Buck seems filled with impatience and nervous energy. R.E.M. recently finished an exhausting promotional tour in Europe. For three weeks the band members hopped from city to city, making the press rounds and playing acoustic sets similar to the remarkably thoughtful performance they turned in on *MTV Unplugged* a few months back—a quiet, no-frills concert in which the band recast both old and new material.

On top of that, Buck and Mills just spent another couple of weeks doing interviews at radio stations here in the States. On top of *that,* the band has just learned that the "Losing My Religion" video has been banned in Ireland. Irish promoters were put off in part by what they perceived as the video's "crucifixion" imagery. (Stipe has made it clear the song is not about religion; if there's a crucifixion scene among the video's sixteenth-century tableaux, he says, he can't find it.) Likewise, the Irish weren't prepared for the video's homoeroticism—among the figures seen are an angelic, blond-haired black man and a shirtless, lipsticked young man who has been tied to a tree. ("I didn't think a lot about it," Stipe says of the flap. "If they can't handle it, they don't get to see the video.")

R.E.M. decided to forgo a concert tour this year—the tireless, nine-month *Green* tour dealt a healthy blow to the band's wanderlust—but the lives of its members have not gotten any easier.

Buck bounces his knee incessantly now. He admits to being dead tired of talking about himself. And asked if he's concerned that R.E.M.'s chart-topping success might alienate some of the band's loyal followers, he says flatly, "The people that changed their minds because of 'Losing My Religion' can just kiss my ass."

In general, Buck seems to have a far less romantic view of R.E.M.'s past than many of the band's devotees. "Yeah, I guess I jangled for a while," Buck says. "I can write that kind of stuff in my sleep. I can write 'Driver 8' every day of the week. We all can. In rehearsal it's always easy to fall back on a mid-tempo, minor-key rock thing. And we try not to rely on that. We've got tons of that shit floating around. We'll do it just to get it out of our systems, record it and file it away.

"Every song we used to write in 1982 was really fast, and we'd tear it up," Buck continues. "For me, age brings—if not wisdom—at least a little understanding. I like to play slow songs now. I like to play quiet songs, and I really didn't when I was twenty-one. I don't think I've ever, in the last five years, played the electric guitar for fun. I mean, *plugging in* and all that. I usually play acoustic or mandolin. I really have no interest in going back to being a rock & roll band."

If R.E.M. isn't a rock & roll band, what is it?

Buck muses for a moment. "We're a rock & roll band that plays sitting down, I guess."

BILL BERRY PUTS IT this way: "I'm getting a little bigger around the midsection. The energy isn't the same. I used to be able to go out and party and wake up the next day and do it all over again. My priorities have really shifted. We're in our prime as far as writing songs goes, and that's what we feel like right now—we feel like a studio band."

If *Out of Time* is not the best record R.E.M. has ever made, it's only because every album from *Murmur* onward is awfully good—even *Fables of the Reconstruction,* which some band members have maligned over the years but which Stipe believes is the strongest collection of songs the group has yet written. Still, *Out of Time* is as challenging as anything in the catalog. For every song that sounds unmistakably like R.E.M.—the plaintive "Half a World Away," for instance—there are several that don't: the bare and edgy "Low"; the funky "Radio Song," which includes a guest rap by

KRS-One; and the galloping, folksy duet "Me in Honey," which features B-52 Kate Pierson.

"We've learned to trust each other's instincts," Berry says. "If somebody suggests something, we'll try it. No matter how wacky it is. We couldn't figure out what to do for the middle of 'Get Up.' I had a dream that we should set twelve—not eleven, not thirteen—but twelve music boxes going at the same time. They were all like 'Well . . . okay.' And it worked. I mean, maybe it *didn't* work, but it's there forever now."

Buck agrees. "None of us gets exactly what we want," he says, "and you learn to live with that. It's something that I would never have believed I'd be able to do when I was twenty-four. I used to be like 'Goddamnit, this is *my* song. I don't like that verse. Either you change it or I will.' Now it's like 'Yeah. That's . . . *interesting.*' "

Of "Country Feedback"—a groaning, pedal-steel number that's one of the most compelling tracks on the new album—Buck explains that he and Berry wrote and recorded the music in a couple of hours. "Michael came in the next day and scatted the words," Buck says. "Usually, he has pretty concise words. We get to look them over. We'll say, 'Repeat this. Pull this out. Maybe change this line.' With 'Country Feedback,' he just had two little drawings on a piece of paper—an Indian head and an arrow, I think—and he just kind of shouted."

"I COULD SCAT MY way into the next century," Stipe says the following afternoon, "although I don't know how many people would want to be in the room. Given just the audacity to stand in front of a microphone and amplify yourself to a room of people—you can do pretty much whatever you want. You can read the ingredients off a cereal box." (The "lyrics" to "Voice of Harold," which is on the B sides hoedown *Dead Letter Office,* consist entirely of the liner notes to a gospel album.)

Stipe is clearly uncomfortable with the cult that has grown up around his singular, imagistic lyric writing. Of lyrics like "Swan swan hummingbird, hurrah / We're all free now / What noisy cats are we / Girl and dog, he bore his cross," the singer says, "People need to realize that there's a potential for a great deal of nonsense involved—that's a crucial element in pop songs." Needless to say, Stipe deflects attempts at interpretation. "It's like a Bob Dylan song that you've loved for years and years," says Stipe, "and then you read an interview and he says, 'Oh, it's about this dog that was run over in the street.' You're like 'What! That song colored and altered my opinion of life for three years. What do you *mean* it's about a dead dog in the street!' "

It's a reasonable argument, but it's strange to hear it from a man who once ghostwrote a press release so journalists would know his song "Welcome to the Occupation" (from *Document*) was about U.S. intervention in Central America. In any case, Stipe's writing seems to be wholly intuitive. Even in cases where his source of inspiration is known—the exquisite "Fall on Me" (from *Lifes Rich Pageant*) is "about" acid rain, "Sitting Still" *(Murmur)* is "about" Stipe's sister's working with deaf children, "Camera" *(Reckoning)* is "about" a close friend who was killed in a car accident—it's nearly impossible to link it with the finished song.

Somewhere, all of Stipe's lyrics are written down. "I think our publishing company has them, and they're sealed away in a vault," the singer says. "When I did go back and write them down, I had a pretty good time with it. I got all the crucial words in there, and then I just made some stuff up. I figure someone's going to read it at some point and get a real laugh out of it."

Many fans would put the aforementioned document in league with the Rosetta stone—especially where Stipe's indecipherable early lyrics are concerned—but it's off-limits, of course. "If there's something you want to know," Stipe says by way of apology, "I'll tell you."

He seems to be serious, and he's taken up on his offer. What is the chorus to "Sitting Still"?

"The chorus to 'Sitting Still,' " Stipe says, laughing. The song is on *Murmur,* but the band's been playing it live for years.

Stipe hums to himself for a minute. "It doesn't make any sense," he says. "You really don't want to know."

Come on, out with it.

"On the record or off the record?"

On the record.

"I'm trying to think of it. It's just a little embarrassing because it's very poorly written."

Stipe hums some more. "I can remember the first two lines," he says. " 'Up to par and Katie bar'—'Katie bar the door' is a Southern expression. 'Up to par and Katie bar the kitchen door, but not me in.' That's it."

What's the next line? Is it "City traffic, the big hill"? Is it "Silly to try for the big kill"?

"There's no 'hill' in there, I know that," Stipe says. " 'For the big *something.'* I don't remember. I really don't. I haven't sung that song in five years. I mean, sung the *real* words. I've syllabized it. Is that a word? When we sing it in concert, I wing it. I don't know the words. I know the sounds. I can approximate them."

THAT'S HIM IN THE corner. That's him at the bar, drinking an Amstel Light. It's midnight on Thursday, and while Peter Buck is over at the Georgia Theater playing a few numbers with John Wesley Harding, Michael Stipe is hanging out at the 40 Watt Club. Stipe has come to see Beggar Weeds, a young Jacksonville band that he produced recently. Occasionally, a friend will approach him—Ian McKaye of the iconoclastic hardcore outfit Fugazi, say—but for the most part his presence here goes unnoticed. Stipe looks like any other guy who wears a green baseball hat, shimmies a little and shouts "Yeah!" every so often.

Of late, Stipe has gone to great lengths to convince people that his lyrics are not autobiographical. Still, it's impossible to spend time with him and not have certain lines from "Losing My Religion" run through one's head: "Every whisper of every waking hour / I'm choosing my confessions" or "Oh, no, I've said too much / I haven't said enough." And then, of course, there's always "That's me in the spotlight," of which a frustrated Stipe says, "I wish I'd said, 'That's me in the kitchen' or 'That's me in the driveway.' "

In general, the members of R.E.M. do not discuss their personal lives, past or present. This much is known for certain: Michael Stipe was a globe-trotting army brat who befriended Peter Buck when the former was a University of Georgia art student and the latter was the manager of an Athens used-record store. (The big sellers during Buck's retail days were *Saturday Night Fever* and *Grease*.) Bill Berry and Mike Mills met during high school in Macon, Georgia, when the former was a rebel and the latter was a nerd. They played in sock-hop bands together, then packed off for the university, where they met up with Buck and Stipe. Soon the foursome was living in an abandoned church—of which there remains only a red steeple that sits in front of Steeplechase Condominiums—and playing gigs that involved goofy Sixties covers and a few originals.

Above and beyond all that, this much is rumored to be true: Michael Stipe assumes everyone is thirty-one because *he's* thirty-one. Peter Buck once sneezed twenty-one times. Every time Mike Mills uses his hair dryer, he thinks the phone is ringing. Bill Berry never misses *The Andy Griffith Show* and will often recount episodes for his wife, Mari, saying, "If *I* was Barney . . ."

Of all the band members, Stipe has always been the most closemouthed—for the simple reason that his privacy has been invaded more often than anyone else's. As Stipe puts it: "I've given so much to our audience through being a singer and through writing songs that can be very emotional and I feel like that's enough. And I guess the natural tendency is to get a little defensive about it."

Stipe's public-service work—with regard to the environment and the ethical treatment of animals, among many other things—has brought the singer a great deal of attention in recent years. Now, he says, he'd prefer to work incognito. "I'm in the process of depoliticizing myself," Stipe explains. "I'm glad that people look at the band as politically active. I think that's healthy. But it's a lot to carry, and to quote myself, not everyone can carry the weight of the world. It's enough that people know that R.E.M. are thinking, compassionate people—human beings who support a number of causes, publicly and privately. I don't have to jump on top of a building and scream. I'm not a very good speaker—that's the end-all of it. I'm not a Billy Bragg. I'm not a Peter Garrett."

Though Stipe claims to dislike being thought of as a spokesperson or as R.E.M.'s "resident oddball," as he was once described in these pages, there is clearly a part of him that loves to feed the myth. "He's smart, and he's manipulative, and he'll admit that," Bill Berry says. "He can twist something that's fairly ordinary into something that seems like it just has to be the new order. He's not afraid to churn up the water a little. And especially recently, I think he's actually reveling in the spotlight. He's used the word *poster boy* many, many times in the last six months."

It's true that the once-remote Stipe has been putting himself in the public eye a surprising amount lately—the singer even appeared, all slicked up, on the cover of *Details* not long ago. It's also true that he's been known to leak out bizarre or plainly misleading information. "Talking about yourself—it's not only boring, but who wants to analyze himself that much?" Stipe says. "It's all very Seventies, isn't it? I do what I do. You can't help but be flippant with someone when they ask if you have a refrigerator or not.

"I don't actively lie," Stipe continues, then hedges. "Well, the whole thing about nailing two oranges together—that was a quote I gave someone years ago, about what *Fables of the Reconstruction* sounded like. That was absolutely ridiculous, and I couldn't believe they printed it. I think it was ROLLING STONE, in fact. I had been in the studio twelve hours doing a mix, and to have someone call transatlantic and say, 'What does it sound like?'—

it's like 'Well, I don't know. It sounds like two oranges being nailed together.' "

"Sometimes Michael says things," Berry says of Stipe's occasional flights of fancy, "and the rest of us will be biting our tongues, trying not to laugh."

O N FRIDAY MORNING IT rains, and Berry drives off in search of antiques. "Even at a fairly young age," Berry says, "I had an appreciation for antiques—even when I was a rebellious pot smoker and listened to Deep Purple and stuff. My friends and I would be driving around smoking pot, and they'd be going, 'Hey, man, that's some pretty good shit.' And I'd go, 'Wow, antiques!' "

At a store in Bishop, Georgia, Berry buys a ninety-inch saw upon which a local folk artist named Annie Wellborn has painted a scene called *Peach Valley*. The sixtyish man behind the register—nearly toothless and creaking back and forth in a rocking chair—thinks he knows the drummer from somewhere. He asks Berry if he's from Athens. Berry says, "Yes, sir, I sure am," and they talk about folk art for a few minutes. As Berry is turning to go, the man's face lights up: "You're in that musical group!"

"Yes, sir, I sure am."

"You've got the Number One record in America!"

"Yes, sir, we do."

Back in his Jeep, Berry laughs and shakes his head. "That was *wild,*" he says. "That guy would *never* have recognized me three years ago."

Later, over country ham and iced tea at Ye Olde Colonial diner, Berry talks about the strange fact that R.E.M. suddenly belongs to the world, that Stipe is no longer the only band member whose face gets recognized. "I'll tell you the truth," Berry says. "You can only be a cult band so long. I'm thirty-two years old. I don't want to be a cult fucking hero. We went through that, and it's great and it's flattering, but those people should go out into their clubs and find the next new band. That's what alternative music is all about. It's like 'You were right that time. See if you can do it again.' "

And while some cultists may feel that they have lost R.E.M. to the world at large, very few of the band's alternative-music contemporaries have followed them out of the underground. "The machinery of big music is a very lethal thing," Mike Mills says later. "You have to deal with all the bullshit you get from record companies, from promoters, from writers. None of it is predicated on music. It's all predicated on money. And to maintain musical integrity while dealing with people who only care about money is very tough. The Replacements couldn't do it. They didn't want to put up with the bullshit. They wanted to live the rock & roll life and not have to deal with all the crap. We wanted to be a success doing what we wanted to do."

In regard to their future, the members of R.E.M. remain wary. "There are guys that have had Top Ten hits that are fry cooks right now," Mills says. "They're in prison, or they're digging ditches, or they're living with their mom somewhere. It happens. You don't ever want to get overly confident in this business. The guys in Canned Heat—they had *several* Top Ten hits."

SITTING IN HIS KITCHEN one bright afternoon, the ever-cynical Peter Buck puts it like this: "We're Number One, but I don't think it means anything. For us it's a vindication and it's kind of cool. On the other hand, we'll be Number One for a week and then some woman with really large breasts and a really high voice—someone who hired people to write and produce her record—will be Number One. And so what's the point?

"I think the days of rock & roll bands' being Number One on the charts are over," Buck continues. "Put it this way: A&R people won't sign them. There are no clubs for them essentially. It's *over."*

What about Guns N' Roses?

"Yeah, well, they're a Benny Hill band," Buck says. "They're a Benny Hill parody of what a rock & roll band should be."

Billy Bragg takes an equally dim view of the ways of the music world, but he's not as ready to dismiss R.E.M.'s success. "Is it just about cucumbers down the trousers?" he says of the music industry. "Or is it about genuine people trying to *say* something? Having R.E.M. in the Top Ten means something—it means *a lot* to guys like me who are trying to ride their beast on their own terms."

The members of R.E.M. have certainly done it their way. Some fans groused when the band launched its arena tour, others when Stipe lip-synced in the "Losing My Religion" video—chiefly because the band members had made pretty emphatic promises that they'd never resort to either.

Still, when all is said and done, R.E.M. has never pandered to radio or even come close to making a bad or lazy record. In fact, as Buck is quick to point out, the musicians have rarely heeded anyone's counsel but their own.

"Everyone gave us advice," Buck says of the group's early days. "Every day of the goddamn week, 'Get some hot chicks in bikinis! Get some disco drums!' You go, 'Really? On *Murmur*?' Disco drums! It's obvious that these people didn't listen to the records. It's great—people who have never, *ever* signed a band that has been successful will tell you how to make your band a success.

"I always thought that we were going to live and die on exactly the way that we knew how to make music," says Buck. "Taking advice or having someone tell you what to do—if someone had done that on *Murmur,* we would have just broken up. Man, I spent years cleaning toilets to get to the point where I don't have to take people's advice. Basically, for me, other people's advice is like 'Yeah, fuck you, too.' We always felt we knew better. We *do,* too."

Buck is quiet for a moment, his thoughts returning to the present. "For me, *Out of Time* was the right record to make," Buck says, getting up to leave. "And, good Lord, it's *selling*—that's the weird thing."

Buck walks out of the house, noticing, as he does, his Guns N' Roses WELCOME TO THE JUNGLE welcome mat. He looks up and smiles. "I wouldn't wipe my feet on anything else."

■ RANDOM NOTES (October 17, 1991)

It took about a minute for this year's MTV Video Music Awards to peak. Held at L.A.'s Universal Amphitheater, the gala was christened by Pee-Wee Herman, whose every gawky step was met with a deafening and genuinely moving standing ovation. And once Herman—whose first words were "Heard any good jokes lately?"—had left the podium and the uproar subsided, host Arsenio Hall took the stage to begin the program and serve as a reminder that, as with any awards show, you have to take the good with the bad.

There was plenty of both. But luckily, for every Poison—which tried to compensate for slovenly playing with plenty of hair dye—there was a Metallica, which provided the night's most bone-crushing moment. And for every interminably long-winded acceptance speech by the aerobics-instructors-with-attitude in C + C Music Factory, there was an R.E.M. win. "Losing My Religion" completed a virtual sweep for the band and the video's director, Tarsem, by snagging Video of the Year, Best Group Video, Best Direction, Best Art Direction, Best Editing and Breakthrough Video.

■ YEAR-END RANDOM NOTES December 12–16, 1991

April Fans didn't get too many looks at R.E.M. this year. Two, in fact. Or make that one and a half. After deciding not to tour, the boys popped up on *MTV Unplugged* and *Mountain Stage,* an American Public Radio rave taped in West Virginia. *"Unplugged* was fun, but you're on TV, so you actually have to worry about what you look like," says guitarist Peter Buck, who was joined for the radio show by Billy Bragg and Robyn Hitchcock. "Nobody worries what you look like on the radio."

■ YEAR-END RANDOM NOTES—VIDEO FILES December 12–26, 1991

Thank-yous abounded this year for R.E.M. The clip for the band's "Losing My Religion" was the toast of the small screen and helped to demonstrate the evolution of music video. Beautifully filmed, "Losing My Religion" features provocative religious imagery and enough footage of Michael Stipe's dancing to help young boys everywhere feel less self-conscious about hitting the floor.

YEAR-END REVIEW
R.E.M. *Out Of Time*

W HEN MICHAEL STIPE WROTE the opening lines of "Radio Song"—"The world is collapsing / Around our ears"—he could not have imagined actually hearing them on the radio in the middle of George Bush's Iraqi adventure. But *Out of Time* is about another fight—heart-to-heart combat—and we find Stipe in a rare explicit mood, getting frank about love, obsession, and the inner calm that, when you find it, makes all the pain worthwhile. There is melancholy in the air: in the doleful strings and teardrop mandolin of "Losing My Religion" and in the bittersweet sob of the pedal steel guitar on "Country Feedback." Yet ultimately *Out of Time* is a hopeful, if not celebratory, record. You can hear the sun poking through the cloud cover in "Near Wild Heaven," a delightful three-minute miracle of Sixties Brit-pop zest and *Pet Sounds* majesty. And for all of Stipe's lamenting for what he's lost or aching for what still might be, R.E.M. never surrenders to despondency. "It's crazy / What you could have had," Stipe sings in "Country Feedback." *Out of Time,* an album of rugged, unvarnished beauty and expansive musical verve, is R.E.M.'s way of saying that it's crazy, and way too late, to stop fighting for it now.

1992 MUSIC AWARDS

READERS PICKS

ARTIST OF THE YEAR
R.E.M.
Guns N' Roses
Metallica
Tom Petty and the
　Heartbreakers
Prince

BEST ALBUM
Out of Time, R.E.M.
Use Your Illusion, Guns N'
　Roses
Metallica, Metallica
For Unlawful Carnal
　Knowledge, Van Halen
Empire, Queensrÿche

BEST SINGLE
"Losing My Religion,"
R.E.M.
"(Everything I Do) I Do It for
　You," Bryan Adams
"Enter Sandman," Metallica
"More Than Words,"
　Extreme
"Right Here, Right Now,"
　Jesus Jones

BEST BAND
R.E.M.
Guns N' Roses
Metallica
Van Halen
Tom Petty and the
　Heartbreakers

BEST MALE SINGER
Michael Stipe
Geoff Tate (Queensrÿche)
Axl Rose
Michael Bolton
Prince

WORST ALBUM
Use Your Illusion, Guns N'
　Roses
Spellbound, Paula Abdul
Gonna Make You Sweat, C&C
　Music Factory
Emotion, Mariah Carey
Out of Time, R.E.M.

BEST VIDEO
"Losing My Religion,"
R.E.M.
"Don't Cry," Guns N' Roses
"Enter Sandman," Metallica
"Get Off," Prince
"Into the Great Wide Open,"
　Tom Petty and the
　Heartbreakers

WORST VIDEO
"2 Legit 2 Quit," Hammer
"Rush, Rush," Paula Abdul
"Losing My Religion," R.E.M.
"Promise of a New Day,"
　Paula Abdul
"I Adore Mi Amore," Color
　Me Badd

BEST GUITARIST
Eddie Van Halen
Eric Clapton
Slash
Stevie Ray Vaughan
Peter Buck

BEST SONGWRITER
Michael Stipe
Prince
Axl Rose
James Hetfield (Metallica)
Robbie Robertson

WORST ALBUM COVER
Metallica, Metallica
Out of Time, R.E.M.
Spellbound, Paula Abdul
For Unlawful Carnal
　Knowledge, Van Halen
Use Your Illusion, Guns N'
　Roses

1992 MUSIC AWARDS

CRITICS PICKS

BEST ALBUM
Out of Time, R.E.M.
Achtung Baby, U2
Nevermind, Nirvana
Use Your Illusion 1, Guns N'
    Roses
Everclear, American Music
    Club

BEST SINGLE
"Losing My Religion," R.E.M.
"Smells Like Teen Spirit,"
    Nirvana
"O.P.P.," Naughty by Nature
"Cream," Prince
"Right Here, Right Now,"
    Jesus Jones

BEST BAND
R.E.M.

BEST VIDEO
"Losing My Religion," R.E.M.

DAVID FRICKE

MICHAEL STIPE:
The ROLLING STONE Interview

FOR R.E.M., THE PAST twelve months have been the Year of the Big Music Biz Awards, and there's a small mountain of them piled in a corner of the band's office, in Athens, Georgia. There are gold and platinum sales plaques from around the world for the album *Out of Time* and a half-dozen MTV Video Music Award statuettes for "Losing My Religion," including one for Video of the Year. They're all still wrapped in their cardboard packing, gathering dust, and they're all addressed to R.E.M. vocalist Michael Stipe, who couldn't care less.

"I'm actually going to take the MTV things home and put them on top of my TV—which I never use," Stipe says, glancing at the boxes with a puckish grin. "The gold records go to charity auctions or to my grandmother. I don't need that to tell me what I have achieved. I feel pretty good looking at the record cover and thinking, 'That has that great song on it, and I can still listen to it.' That's achievement."

By that yardstick, Stipe, guitarist Peter Buck, bassist Mike Mills and drummer Bill Berry can be justly proud of their entire first decade together. From the catalytic jangle of their 1981 independent seven-inch debut, "Radio Free Europe" b / w "Sitting Still," to the urgent pop kick of 1988's *Green,* R.E.M. created a body of work rich in exploratory songcraft, emotional depth and timeless garage-rock drive, ascending to mainstream popularity without caving in to record-industry dictums or betraying its original college-radio constituency.

The across-the-board success of *Green* guaranteed a warm reception for *Out of Time.* But R.E.M. was unprepared for the triple-platinum sales and broad public acclaim—including a dramatic sweep of the ROLLING STONE Readers Poll—that followed. The day after Stipe sat down in the R.E.M. office for this rare, in-depth interview, the group received seven Grammy nominations, among them Record of the Year and Song of the Year for the Top Five hit "Losing My Religion."

"I described R.E.M. once as a bunch of minor chords with some nonsense thrown on top," Stipe says, crossing his legs yoga-style on a swivel chair and thoughtfully stroking hs week's-plus worth of beard. " 'Losing My Religion' has that quality. 'Fall on Me' [on *Lifes Rich Pageant*] had it, too. You always want to sing along, and you always want to keep singing when it's over. And maybe every couple of years we hit on one of those.

"I hate to make this comparison, but 'Religion' is similar in theme to 'Every Breath You Take,' by the Police. It's just a classic obsession pop song. I've always felt the best kinds of songs are the ones where anybody can listen to it, put themselves in it and say, 'Yeah, that's me.' "

As R.E.M.'s lyricist, Stipe has been writing songs like that all along: "So. Central Rain (I'm Sorry)," "Fall on Me," "The One I Love." The problem, for hard-core fans and critics anyway, has been trying to distill the "me" that Stipe himself puts into his verse. Yet in striking contrast to his elliptical writing style, Georgia-born John Michael Stipe, now thirty-two, proves to be warm and open in conversation—guarded in spots, particularly about his personal life, but otherwise frank and unpretentious about music, success, the curse of celebrity, his political activism and his wide range of creative interests outside the band. Like Peter Buck, he moonlights as a record producer and indie-rock guru: He recently produced a second album by Athens singer-songwriter Vic Chesnutt, and last summer he sponsored a Deep South in N.Y.C. night at the New Music Seminar to showcase four young Dixie underground bands.

His nonprofit film company, C-00 (pronounced "C-hundred"), co-founded with director Jim McKay, continues to produce striking public-service announcements on AIDS, racism and homelessness. Stipe is also the executive producer of C-00's first feature-length film, *Desperation Angels,* directed by McKay. "It's a road movie," Stipe explains, "a very intense, very smart, very graphic look at the decay of the United States of America in the late Eighties and early Nineties. I've seen dozens of scripts in the last year and a half"—one in ten has a "rock star" in the lead, he groans—"and this one just flew off the desk."

The new year also means a new R.E.M. album, to be recorded in the spring and released in late summer. The night before this interview, R.E.M. held its first practice session of '92, hammering out some of the dozens of song ideas the band has amassed since the *Out of Time* sessions. "Very mid-tempo, pretty fucking weird," Stipe says of the music. "More acoustic, more organ-based, less drums." As for the next R.E.M. tour, he adds: "We'll probably trim it down, lose the lights, lose all the shit, put on a white T-shirt and go onstage. If nothing else, the acoustic shows we did on TV and in Europe really showed that I can sing and the songs are not that weird and enigmatic. They're just pretty good songs, and I've got a good set of pipes."

So good, in fact, that Stipe even won Best Male Singer in our Readers Poll, beating out archetypal belters like Axl Rose and Queensrÿche's Geoff Tate. "I'm blessed, frankly, with really bad sinuses," he explains. "I put up with the snot, because I got a great voice in exchange."

*W*ITH THE HUGE SUCCESS *of 'Out of Time,' have you taken any time to figure out "Why now, why us?"*

I felt really weird that this record is really popular and other records just fell through the cracks. Not just in this country but globally. We were Number One in Israel for nine weeks. Israel! Go figure. It was the first non-Israeli act in five years to go Number One. And that was right after the gulf war.

If I thought a lot higher of myself as a singer and us as a band, then maybe I would be of the mind to think about those kinds of things. But I think we're a good band, sometimes great. A lot of it is just timing and luck. I don't want to sound horribly self-effacing, because we're really proud of what we do and we work real hard at it.

But I just don't think about it in those terms. I don't think I could walk around and purchase toilet paper if I had to think about why people in Bombay and Israel are disco dancing to "Radio Song."

But in the past ten years, you've gone from being an underground rock singer to a major pop celebrity. And compared with your stark stage presence on early tours, you seemed a lot more relaxed in recent appearances, like last year's 'MTV Un-plugged' show. How do you account for the new user-friendly Michael Stipe?

I turned into a performer sometime in the last decade. I quit wearing darker clothes. I let the lights be a little brighter. With the *Green* world tour, ticket prices were so astronomical that I felt guilty that people were paying that much money to sit in the back row and not see a show.

Did you enjoy being a "performer"?

No. It felt real stilted. My haircut on the *Green* world tour should be enough to attest to my taking that to the extreme. That was by far the ugliest haircut of the Eighties. But I just felt an obligation to the audience and the role that I was supposed to be playing. And talk about power—that's a fucking trip. Put your hand up and 20,000 people scream.

I distinctly remember the first time that it hit me really hard. It was at the Wang Center, in Boston. We did two nights there, and the second night we sang "Flowers of Guatemala." I looked out in the audience, and people were weeping openly. It was like "Oh, my God." You could hear a pin drop. It was the most incredible feeling.

You also seem to have this new TV persona—very chatty and all smiles for the cameras, like you've just taken some "shiny happy people" pills.

I am absolutely mortified out of my mind. That's what it translates to. I have this reputation for being an incredibly serious person. And in interviews, I'm desperately trying to think of really good answers. So I come across as this reverent curmudgeon. But when I get in front of TV cameras, I come across like a chipmunk on speed. Cameras make me really animated.

But it's weird being a media figure, to be recognized everywhere by somebody. It's like you walk into someplace and you're playing a game—it's a matter of time until someone whispers to someone else, they look at you and then whisper to someone else.

One reason you're so well known is that in R.E.M.'s videos you have more of a starring role than the other band members, particularly in "Losing My Religion."

I'm the only one who tolerates videos. I love films, and videos are, I think, a great way to get ideas across.

What "Losing My Religion" turned into was a collaboration between my idea and [the director] Tarsem's idea. I wanted to do a very straightforward performance video, much like Sinéad O'Connor's "Nothing Compares 2 U." Almost a static head shot. But I also wanted to get the other guys into it. And Tarsem had this idea, which was to film it in the style of a particular kind of Indian movie in which everything is melodramatic and very dreamlike. It was a good mix.

"Religion" was very much a testing ground. When the others saw how well it turned out, they got more excited about doing other videos.

R.E.M.'s attitude toward videos has changed drastically since "Radio Free Europe." The band was hardly in that one at all.

I almost wish we weren't. Our big experiment was "Can't Get There From Here." We were all in that one and it flopped. And that was my fault. It was my first job as a director and editor. But from there, we went to the other extreme in "Fall on Me," in which I felt the band should not be in the video at all.

But it got to the point where we were making these videos, paying a lot of money to have them made, and they were not being played anywhere. It was dumb. The "anti" attitude was not flying.

You found an effective compromise with "Stand." The focus was on the dancers, but the whole band was in it, and there was that closing shot of you with that coy, embarrassed smile.

The smile that broke a thousand hearts. [*Laughs*] That was not planned. That was a genuine laugh. I don't know what they were doing behind the camera to make me laugh like that, but it worked.

Katherine Dieckmann [the director] had the idea that my public image was a little too staid. She wanted to crack that veneer, and she did. In fact, she sent a copy of the final edit to me and said, "Is that okay with you?" And I said, "Yeah, it's great."

There is a prevailing public image of Michael Stipe as the weird, enigmatic artiste. How much of it is real, and how much is put-on?

The thing is, everybody is like this. But not everybody is projected like this into the homes of millions of people. And that's not to say I'm the most rational-thinking, clearheaded person in the world. I do contradict myself a lot. But I never really believed that to understand or appreciate a good book you have to know who the author is.

There is a degree of projection involved. "This is a projection; this is what I want you to see." But then again, maybe me saying there's a put-on is a put-on in itself. This could go on, like peeling an onion. I don't think so, though. After saying things over and over and seeing them misprinted, you begin to realize that sound bites make sense. You figure out what you feel, you condense it.

But R.E.M.'s success suggests that mainstream-pop fans are quite willing to accept new music and new ideas, that they're much smarter than most bands and record companies take them for.

Yeah. I've always hated the idea that you have to put something on a third-grade level to make most people understand it. I try to rise above it. Early on, I accepted that once a song is pressed and it goes out to people, it's as much theirs as it is mine. Anything anyone wants to see in them is fine.

Like "Fall on Me" is still believed to be about acid rain. Initially, it was. But then I rewrote the song. If you listen to the second verse, there is a countermelody underneath it. That's the original melody to the song; that was the part about acid rain.

In fact, the "Fall on Me" that we all know and love is not about acid rain. It's a general oppression song, about the fact that there are a lot of causes out there that need a song that says, "Don't smash us." And specifically, there are references to the Leaning Tower of Pisa and the guy dropping weights and feathers.

One subject you rarely discuss publicly is your personal background. The standard line in most R.E.M. stories is "Michael Stipe was an army brat who went to the University of Georgia."

That's about it. I had an unbelievably happy childhood. I'm still very, very close to my family.

What did your father do in the army?

Nothing heinous. Let's just say he was in the army. We traveled a lot.

What inspired you to enroll as an art student at the University of Georgia?

I was an art student just because it seemed so simple. I didn't want to get bogged down with books, so I didn't pick English. I didn't want to go into philosophy, because I thought it was a pile of dog shit. I was interested in geology; I could just as easily have taken that. I just happened to pick art because the building was walking distance from downtown Athens, just off Jackson Street.

I actually started with communications in my first quarter. And I had an illegitimate minor in English. I did a lot of reading. I never graduated. I'm a dropout.

Did you have any interest in art in high school?

I love photography. I photographed children for a long time. And buildings. I'm beginning to sound like David Byrne [*laughs*].

Did the big Sixties rock icons like the Beatles and the Rolling Stones mean anything to you when you were growing up?

The Beatles were elevator music in my lifetime. "Yummy Yummy Yummy (I've Got Love in My Tummy)" had more impact on me. I distinctly remember being in a swimming pool and singing along to that song and my father saying, "Don't sing that, it's a nasty song." I was feeling particularly rebellious that day; I continued singing. But I dove into the deep end, so he had to fish me out.

There was a fellow in Texas named Mr. Pemberton, who had a record store. He was really old and looked really mean. But he was really nice, and he used to give me and my sister the singles he didn't need anymore, the ones that wouldn't sell. So we got Tammy Wynette, the Beatles and Elvis. And Roger Miller—he had a song called "Skip a Rope." That song had a profound influence on me.

What did punk, as a movement or an attitude, mean to you?

It was incredibly liberating. I distinctly remember the November 1975 issue of *Creem* magazine. Someone had left a copy in study hall under a chair. And I remember it had a picture of Patti Smith, and she was terrifying looking. She looked like Morticia Addams. And I think it was Lester Bangs or Lisa Robinson writing about punk rock in New York and how all the other music was like watching color movies, but this is like watching staticky black-and-white TV. And that made incredible sense to me.

The Patti Smith record *Horses* came out shortly after that. And then *Marquee Moon,* by Television, came out. And I bought the first Wire album.

Those were the big influences. Their whole *Zeitgeist* was that anybody could do it. And I took that very literally. I read that in an interview with Patti Smith, and I thought, "If she can sing, I can sing." No one's ever really tied in how much I've lifted from her as a performer.

Like what?

She was just real guttural. It was like all the body noises you make. Billy Bragg says that when men wake up in the morning, they have to make every possible body noise they can to assure themselves that they're still alive. Patti Smith's voice was like that. It wasn't a strained, perfect crescendo of notes. It was this howling, mad beast—every noise you can make.

I don't think I've told any reporter this, but actually, the first recording I ever made was when I was thirteen. My sister had one of those secretary's type of tape recorders. One day, everyone was gone from the house. I locked myself in the den in the basement, turned the thing on RECORD and screamed for ten minutes. Man, I wish I had that tape now.

Was R.E.M. your first band?

The first band to ever play out in a club or a bar. The first band worth mentioning. I'd played with a band here in town that played cover songs for a while. I also had this noise band called 1066, after the Norman Conquest, my favorite year in history. And I was in a punk-rock cover band in St. Louis when I was seventeen or eighteen.

None of it was anything, really. I never wrote a song until R.E.M. And then we didn't *really* write a song until "Gardening at Night" [on *Chronic Town*]. I maintain that the first thirty songs we wrote were dry runs, like going to elementary school to learn how to write a song. And with "Gardening at Night," it was suddenly like "Wow, it kind of makes sense."

When did R.E.M., as a band, make sense for you?

We were such a *band* in those early years—just driving around in a truck, pulling into town and wreaking havoc. Being shitty adolescent punk rockers. We were nice about it, but we still tore a lot of shit up. It was as close to a Kerouacian adventure as any of us had ever had. We would drive somewhere, and someone would pay us $200 to make noise for an hour and a half. What could be greater?

It wasn't all that romantic, but we had a lot of fun. We had a great time making *Murmur,* and *Reckoning* was fun. *Fables of the Reconstruction* was a very hard record to make and a real turning point. But *Lifes Rich Pageant* was the reconstruction of the *de*construction that *Fables* became. [Producer] Don Gehman came in with his really big drum sound, and that opened some doors for us.

He was also the first person to challenge me on my lyrics, just saying, "What the fuck is this about?"

How did you react to that?

I crossed my arms and walked out of the room. But I appreciated the challenge a lot. Don just said: "Think about what you're singing. What is this? Why do you want to put that out?"

Did that criticism cause you to rethink your writing style?

No. But with that record, we had a sonic clarity that was technologically miles ahead of anything we'd done before. It made it so you could hear what I was singing.

Actually, I keep trying to get away from that. The vocal on "Belong" [on *Out of Time*], I sang that directly into a Walkman. I don't like the clarity, because it doesn't allow me as much latitude to just flail, to just be a melody and let the words, the meaning, flow out.

Wouldn't you like to have people understand what you're singing?

No. I don't see any reason for it. I think music is way beyond rational thinking. It doesn't have to make any sense. "Half a World Away" [on *Out of Time*] doesn't make sense to anybody but me. And even to me, it's a totally fabricated experience; it's drawn from things that I know or saw on TV or that people I know told me. It's a complete fabrication. But there's *something* there.

What about "The One I Love"? You can't get more plain-spoken than the verse in that ["This one goes out to the one I love / This one goes out to the one I left behind"].

Yeah, but that song has a real twist in it, too: "A simple prop / To occupy my time." That was a little harsh. I didn't want to put that on the record. But I wanted to write a song with the word *love* in it, because I hadn't done that before.

Also, that was the beginning of those songs that the band was getting into, songs that were so pop that I couldn't just sing gibberish over them. I had to come out with something really succinct, like "Pop Song 89" or "Stand." You can't take a melody like that and howl or moan and throw a few hard consonants in. At that point, I flipped back to the "Yummy Yummy Yummy" swimming-pool experience. My immediate response to a song like "Get Up" [on *Green*] is "Great bubblegum!" That's something I understand and something that can really be fun. The other guys just gave me this song for the next record that is so beyond "Stand" it makes "Stand" sound like a dirge.

Have you considered doing a solo record?

I was never a big Rolling Stones fan, but I remember thinking when Mick Jagger put out his first solo record in 1985, "God, the guy's been in the band for twenty-two years, he's the most famous singer in the world, and it took him this long to get it together?" Now I know why. R.E.M. consumes almost every waking hour of my life.

I would love to do a solo record, and I guarantee that it would be very different from R.E.M.

What do you want to do on your first solo record?

The first thing I would do is an album of cover songs. I've actually got a list already: "Paralysed," by Gang of Four, "Talkin' 'Bout a Revolution," by Tracy Chapman, "Gravity," by Pylon, "Hey Jack Kerouac," by 10,000 Maniacs. There was a song called "Drowning," by the English Beat, that I always thought would make a good single. And there are a bunch of songs I know I could really wail on, like "Magic Carpet Ride," by Steppenwolf.

I'd probably do a record of cover songs and then a record of my own stuff that would just be complete incoherency, because I'd want to get all the stuff I can't do in R.E.M. out of my system in one go. I'm sure it would be a horrible mess, although fun to make.

With your heavy load of activities outside of R.E.M.—videos, films, producing bands, political activism—do you ever worry about the "rock Renaissance man" trap?

I'm not going to let that get in the way of things I want to do. The problem is, you're catapulted into this position where your ego is blown up to the size of a major planet. And you begin to believe that you can do anything. And that might not be a bad thing ultimately, except the poor public has to suffer through a lot of it. But as a normal person, it's not a bad thing to feel that nothing is impossible.

What about the "man for all causes" syndrome, like when you pulled off all those politically correct T-shirts on the MTV Video Music Awards show last year?

If it was misunderstood or if people thought it trivialized any of the causes, then I'm very sorry. But I think more people saw it and said, "Wow, I really agree with that." The feedback I've gotten from that alone was more than for anything else I've ever done. I was getting mail from countries that I couldn't even find on the map.

The recent death of Freddie Mercury has increased attention in the music business to the AIDS epidemic. Do you think the rock community has done enough—if anything at all—to combat the disease?

I don't think anyone's done enough, and I don't know what can be done. I plan on being very involved. I have been in the past, maybe less vocally than I have about the environment. With *Green,* I came to be known as the recycle singer. People think of me as this mastermind on toxic-waste incinerators.

But I think this presidential election will prove that the AIDS crisis and dedicating money to research are important issues. If we took one percent of our defense budget—which, according to the info on Ben and Jerry's Peace Pops, is $8 million a day—if we put that money towards AIDS research, that's more than the government has put towards AIDS in ten years.

Will R.E.M. become actively involved in the presidential campaign with a public endorsement or a benefit show?

Not a benefit, because we probably won't play this year. But I supported Dukakis in 1988. Not because of Dukakis, but because of Bush. I was scared and am still scared of him.

The Dukakis stuff I did by myself. As a band, I don't really know. That could turn into a difficult situation, where public support by a rock band could be a real negative instead of a positive thing. But we're talking about a president who's never uttered the words "greenhouse effect," whose comment on AIDS was for people to get behavioral psychiatric help.

'Out of Time' marked the beginning of R.E.M.'s second decade on record. How do you envision the group's future?

Hopefully, we're not going to put out *Chicago XIV.* That would be my worst fear, that we would turn into one of those dumb bands who go into their second decade and don't know how bad they are and don't know when to give it up.

I don't think we're at that point. I think the stuff we're doing now challenges in energy and emotion and feeling anything we've ever done.

How many good years do you think R.E.M. has left? Peter Buck and Bill Berry reportedly made a pact to keep the band going until the year 2000 and then quit.

They decided they wanted to break up at the millennium. There is something poetic about it. I dig that idea. Hey, I can hang in with these guys for another decade.

A grab bag of the most avant of today's avant-rockers—including King Missile, Mr. T Experience and Vic Chesnutt—has contributed to *Surprise Your Pig: A Tribute to R.E.M.* The album of R.E.M. covers is available from Staplegun Records, P.O. Box 867262, Plano, Texas 75086.

DAVID FRICKE

THE "WEIRD" SIDE OF R.E.M.

T HE THING THAT SEPARATES this record from *Out of Time* is that we have some of the weirdest songs in the world on there," says bassist Mike Mills of R.E.M.'s forthcoming album, *Automatic for the People*. "We knew they were weird from the beginning. It wasn't hard to tell."

The album, which was coproduced by Scott Litt and R.E.M., will be released on October 6th and comes only eight months after R.E.M.'s recent Grammy hat trick, which included a Best Alternative Album trophy for 1991's *Out of Time*. But *Automatic for the People* is not the full-tilt rock & roll album the band originally promised. The emphasis is on Southern Gothic balladry and folk-rock torch songs, scored with a fluid mix of acoustic and electric guitars, piano, organ and spacious strings arranged by Led Zeppelin's John Paul Jones and Knox Chandler from the Psychedelic Furs. The album opens with two slow songs—the dark, brooding "Drive" (the first single) and the waltz-time meditation "Try Not to Breathe"—and there are only three uptempo numbers on the entire LP, among them a venomous, fuzzed-up anti-Republican tirade, "Ignoreland."

"We were just as surprised as anybody that the album turned out like this," Mills confesses. "We wrote fast songs. But it's funny: Fast songs are easier to write, but it seems like it's harder to write *good* ones. This time, the slow ones sounded better."

The slow ones are also full of surprises, like the Memphis-via-Athens chamber soul of "Everybody Hurts" and the luscious background vocals in "Star Me Kitten," which bear a strong (and deliberate, Mills concedes) resemblance to 10cc's "I'm Not in Love." Singer-lyricist Michael Stipe adds a few new twists to his vocal palette, including a high, lungbusting wail in the vivacious rocker "The Sidewinder Sleeps Tonight" and a sassy imitation-Elvis gurgle in "Man on the Moon," which sounds like the pop offspring of "Losing My Religion" and "Near Wild Heaven."

The ear candy actually belies the sober undercurrent running through a song like "Try Not to Breathe," in which Stipe sings from the point of view of a person facing the realities of death and old age. "It's a slow, dark record, but it's not depressing dark," Mills insists. " 'Everybody Hurts' is saying, 'Don't get suicidal, don't get depressed, because everybody hurts, you'll come through it.' "

The album title comes from a popular soul-food restaurant in Athens, Georgia. "When they're dishing up the food," Mills explains, "you say, 'I want some pork chops,' and they go, 'Automatic.' " But there was nothing automatic about the making of the album. Mills says that he, Stipe, guitarist Peter Buck and drummer Bill Berry would go on one- or two-week-long writing binges, come up with a few songs and then cut demo versions of them at John Keane's studio in Athens.

After running up about twenty songs that way, "we took a month off and listened to them all," Mills says. "In that sense, it wasn't as planned out. All the ideas for the overdubs came more in the last month or so." Two tracks, "Drive" and "New Orleans Instrumental No. 1," were cut in the Crescent City at Daniel Lanois's Kingsway studio. The rest of the album was recorded at Bearsville Studios, in Woodstock, New York, and Criteria Studios, in Miami, with one track and all the mixing done at a studio in Seattle.

"It's funny—we did this record in the four corners of the U.S. just about, and I feel like I've been on the road enough to have toured," says Mills, which is his way of admitting that R.E.M. will not be going on the road in the near future. "It may be that these songs weren't the ones that kicked us in the butt enough to get us on the road. We want to go out. It's just something that has to be hashed out over a longer period of time."

■ RANDOM NOTES (October 29, 1992)

When you take three years between albums and work almost entirely at home, cabin fever can fuel some pretty strange ideas. At least that seems to be the case for Neneh Cherry, whose sophomore effort, *Homebrew*, sports a duet with the less-than-dance-diva-esque MICHAEL STIPE. "We approached him because we had this weird hunch," says Cherry, who collaborated on the album with her husband and partner, Booga Bear. "There's just something in what he is and the way he sounds. He has this magical kind of quirkiness."

The lyrics to "Trout" stress the importance of teaching sex education in schools, and the song marks Stipe's debut as a rapper—a job he had passed on to KRS-One on R.E.M.'s '91 single "Radio Song." "Michael wanted to do the rap," says Cherry. "I think the whole vibe on the song was going somewhere where neither of us had ever gone before. It was kind of important for it to be like that. It was neither Neneh Cherry nor R.E.M. It was like a place where we could hang together."

PAUL EVANS

AUTOMATIC FOR THE PEOPLE ALBUM REVIEW

★ ★ ★ ★ ★

R.E.M. HAS NEVER MADE music more gorgeous than "Nightswimming" and "Find the River," the ballads that close *Automatic for the People* and sum up its twilit, soulful intensity. A swirl of images natural and technological—midnight car rides and undertow, old photographs and headlong tides—the songs grapple, through a unifying metaphor of "the recklessness of water," with the interior world of memory, loss and yearning. This is the members of R.E.M. delving deeper than ever; grown sadder and wiser, the Athens subversives reveal a darker vision that shimmers with new, complex beauty.

Despite its difficult concerns, most of *Automatic* is musically irresistible. Still present, if at a slower tempo, is the tunefulness that without compromising the band's highly personal message, made these Georgia misfits platinum sellers. Since "The One I Love," its Top Forty hit from 1987, R.E.M. has conquered by means of artful videos, surer hooks and fatter production and by expanding thematically to embrace the doomsday politics of *Document,* the eco-utopianism of *Green* and the sweet rush of *Out of Time.* Brilliantly, the new album both questions and clinches that outreaching progress; having won the mainstream's ear, R.E.M. murmurs in voices of experience—from the heart, one on one.

In a minor key, "Drive" opens *Automatic* with Michael Stipe singing: "Hey kids / Where are you? / Nobody tells you what to do," a chorus that wryly echoes David Essex's glam-rock anthem "Rock On." In its imagining of youth apocalypse, "Drive" upsets the pat assumption that the members of R.E.M. might still see themselves as generational spokesmen. The group then further trashes anyone's expectation of a nice pop record with "Try Not to Breathe." Alluding presumably to "suicide doctor" Jack Kevorkian ("I will try not to breathe / This decision is mine / I have lived a full life / These are the eyes I want you to remember"), the song ushers in a series of meditations on mortality that makes *Automatic* as haunted at times as Lou Reed's *Magic and Loss*. Relief comes in the form of whimsical instrumentation (such low-tech keyboards as piano, clavinet, accordion); political satire ("Ignoreland") that suggests a revved-up Buffalo Springfield; and, on the catchy "Sidewinder Sleeps Tonight," some of Stipe's niftier faux nursery rhymes ("A can of beans / Of black-eyed peas / Some Nescafé and ice / A candy bar / A falling star / Or a reading from Dr. Seuss"). Yet, without a single "Shiny Happy People" among its twelve songs, *Automatic* is assuredly an album edged in black.

Famous ghosts are tenderly remembered. The calypsolike "Man on the Moon" fantasizes holy-fool comedian Andy Kaufman in hip heaven ("Andy, are you goofing on Elvis?"), and a paean to Montgomery Clift, "Monty Got a Raw Deal," exhorts Hollywood's wrecked Adonis to "just let go." Hard grief inspires "Sweetness Follows" ("Readying to bury your father and your mother"), yet compassion wins out: The sorrows that make us "lost in our little lives," the song says, end in an inscrutable sweetness.

A homespun ditty, "New Orleans Instrumental No. 1," and the woozy jazz of "Star Me Kitten" (featuring the weirdest love lyrics imaginable: "I'm your possession / So fuck me, kitten") lighten *Automatic* somewhat, but the darker songs boast the stronger playing. Guitarist Peter Buck dazzles, not only with the finger picking that launched a thousand college bands but with feedback embellishments and sitarlike touches. As always, the rhythm section of bassist Mike Mills and drummer Bill Berry kicks; on about half the numbers, Led Zeppelin bassist John Paul Jones crafts string arrangements that recall, in their Moorish sweep, his orchestral work for the Rolling Stones' *Their Satanic Majesties Request*.

If "Nightswimming" and "Find the River" are R.E.M. at its most evocative, "Everybody Hurts," the album's third masterpiece, finds the band gaining a startling emotional directness. Spare triplets on electric piano carry a melody as sturdy as a Roy Orbison lament, and Stipe's voice rises to a keening power. "When you're sure you've had too much of this life, well, hang on," he entreats, asserting that in the face of the tough truths *Automatic for the People* explores, hope is, more than ever, essential.

We were just as surprised as anybody that the album turned out like this," R.E.M. bassist Mike Mills said of *Automatic for the People,* which the band released in October. The five-star album was recorded in New Orleans, Miami, Seattle and Woodstock, New York, and featured some of the group's darkest music to date. Michael Stipe put down some raw and lovely vocals on "Find the River" and "Nightswimming," and on "Man on the Moon," Peter Buck even came to terms with his mortal enemy the guitar solo.

MARK COLEMAN

AUTOMATIC FOR THE PEOPLE YEAR-END REVIEW

GREAT ALBUMS ARE MADE, NOT BORN. R.E.M. sweated over its tenth—staying off the road, studio-jumping around the country while recording. It paid off. This melancholy gem displays the group at a shimmering peak. Eventually, every song on this deceptively subdued tour de force connects with subtle emotional power—and a melody that can't be erased. The orchestral arrangements (by Led Zep's John Paul Jones) are deployed with care, a steady bass-and-drum heartbeat propels even the quietest passages (except for the beautiful piano-and-voice piece "Nightswimming"), and guitarist Peter Buck employs an array of stringed instruments and amplifier noises. Hard to believe he was once considered a one-arpeggio Charlie: His resourcefulness on *Automatic* is stunning.

But lead singer Michael Stipe provides the driving inspiration for *Automatic*'s inward journey. His richly hued voice illuminates the haunted landscapes of "Everybody Hurts," "Try Not to Breathe" and "Sweetness Follows." Supported by the music's indomitable flow, he exudes hope amid these fearless depictions of mourning and loss. "Monty Got a Raw Deal" and "Man on the Moon" eulogize the doomed Fifties film star Montgomery Clift and the bizarre Seventies comedian Andy Kaufman, respectively, honoring them with warmth and passion. "Ignoreland" surveys the political scene by way of a voice-and-guitar riff that soars like something from *Houses of the Holy*. And, of course, Stipe still has his peculiar way with elusive hooks. "The Sidewinder Sleeps Tonight" exults in the old jangle and stomp—whatever it means. *Automatic for the People* will deliver the goods long after most of its current competition has shut down. It's one for the ages.

■ RANDOM NOTES (January 7, 1993)

The public calendar for the 40 Watt Club, in Athens, Georgia, said the club was closed November 19th—"Thinkin' about fishin' "—but an audience of about 500 had something else on its mind. "The name of the band is R.E.M., and the reason we're here is Greenpeace," said vocalist Michael Stipe. "I hope you enjoy the show." With that the band launched into a one-hour set that featured four songs from *Automatic for the People*.

The event—recorded by a solar-powered mobile studio—will donate a cut to a Greenpeace benefit album. And since R.E.M. isn't touring, the band invited family and fan-club members. "This is it," said guitarist Peter Buck. "This is the tour."

Stipe doubled his exposure a week earlier in Atlanta by joining 10,000 Maniacs—singing John Prine's "Hello in There" and updating his duet with Natalie Merchant on "A Campfire Song."

■ RANDOM NOTES NOTABLE NEWS (January 21, 1993)

Reebok held its Human Rights Awards in Boston—once again a moving and emotionally draining day—honoring a handful of international activists. "It's incredibly inspiring," said Michael Stipe, who presented one award. "These are not extraordinary people. They're ordinary people who have done extraordinary things." The day culminated in a procession and sing-along led by Mickey Hart and Joan Baez. "This has been a great experience," said Peter Gabriel, who serves on the board of advisers. "I'd like to get more people involved. If a few faces get attached to a number of projects, the effectiveness is diminished."

Michael Stipe and Oliver Stone are serving together as executive producers of a politically inspired movie, *Desperation Angels,* which is still in preproduction. "We're interested in showing what we look at as the real America," says director Jim McKay, "because it certainly hasn't been done to our satisfaction."

1993 MUSIC AWARDS

CRITICS PICKS

BEST ALBUM
Automatic for the People,
  R.E.M.
3 Years, 5 Months and 2
  Days in the Life Of . . . ,
  Arrested Development
Kiko, Los Lobos
Dirty, Sonic Youth
Dry, PJ Harvey

BEST SINGLE
"Tennessee," Arrested
  Development "People
  Everyday," Arrested
  Development
"I'd Die Without You," P.M.
  Dawn
"Drive," R.E.M.
"Little Miss Can't Be
  Wrong," Spin Doctors

BEST BAND
R.E.M.
U2 (tie)

BEST MALE SINGER
Michael Stipe

READERS PICKS
ARTIST OF THE YEAR
U2
Pearl Jam

Red Hot Chili Peppers
R.E.M.
Bruce Springsteen

BEST ALBUM
Achtung Baby, U2
Ten, Pearl Jam
Automatic for the People,
  R.E.M.
Blood Sugar Sex Magik,
  Red Hot Chili Peppers
The Southern Harmony and
  Musical
Companion, the Black
  Crowes

BEST SINGLE
"One," U2
"November Rain," Guns N'
  Roses
"Under the Bridge," Red Hot
  Chili Peppers
"Drive," R.E.M.
"Tears in Heaven," Eric
  Clapton

BEST BAND
U2
Pearl Jam
R.E.M.
Guns N' Roses
Black Crowes

BEST MALE SINGER
Bono
Eddie Vedder
Michael Stipe
Axl Rose
Eric Clapton

BEST VIDEO
"Jeremy," Pearl Jam
"November Rain," Guns N'
  Roses
"Digging in the Dirt," Peter
  Gabriel
"Right Now," Van Halen
"Drive," R.E.M.

BEST ALBUM COVER
Achtung Baby, U2
Nevermind, Nirvana
Blood Sugar Sex Magik,
  Red Hot Chili Peppers
Automatic for the People,
  R.E.M.
Angel Dust, Faith No More

BEST DRUMMER
Larry Mullen Jr. of U2
Lars Ulrich of Metallica
Neil Peart of Rush
Alex Van Halen
Bill Berry of R.E.M.

THE 100 TOP MUSIC VIDEOS

ROLLING STONE EDITORS chose the 100 best rock videos of all time for a special issue. Three R.E.M. videos were included.

3 "LOSING MY RELIGION"
1991

The beautifully lit and staged living friezes seen throughout this video are Indian-born director Tarsem's homages to some of his biggest artistic influences: Caravaggio, Soviet constructionist posters, Latin American author Gabriel García Márquez and more (the blink-and-you-miss-it shot of a milk bottle hitting the floor is lifted from just about any film by Russian director Andrei Tarkovsky). Yet during the shooting, Tarsem thought that none of it was working. "I was so nervous, I kept going to the loo to throw up," he recalls. "My assistant director thought I had a drug problem." In his desperation, he hit upon one simple shot: R.E.M. lead singer Michael Stipe dancing on the empty set. Interweaving it with the rest of his footage, Tarsem found "that was what really made the clip come alive." As for what it all means, Stipe ventures that "I think what you're seeing is a bunch of different universes that are all tied together by this empty room that the band is standing in." Standing—and also lip-syncing, something Stipe had previously been dead set against. "I saw [Sinéad O'Connor's] 'Nothing Compares 2 U,' and it moved me immensely," Stipe says. "Her performance was spectacular, and I really had to rethink my stand on lip-syncing, which was that it's totally false. Well, you know, television is totally false, and videos are totally false, so why not go that extra step and delve into lip-syncing?" Oddly enough, despite the eyes he opened with "Losing My Religion," Tarsem hasn't made a rock video since, concentrating instead on commercial work for television. "Nothing freaks me out like doing a video," he says, "and I can't do them unless it's absolutely the right song. People take it very personally when I turn them down, and it's hard for me to explain. I can even like a song very much, but if it doesn't relate to any ideas I have, I can't do it. 'Losing My Religion' just happened to be one of the right songs."

41 "MAN ON THE MOON"
1993

The first and hopefully last video with Michael Stipe doing an Elvis imper-
sonation, "Man on the Moon" is a home movie of the heart—R.E.M.'s
ambling ode to the late performance comedian Andy Kaufman. It's all done
in scratchy black and white, with two or three frames flickering on the
screen at once. While walking around Seattle listening to mixes of the song
on a Walkman, "it kind of occurred to me that it's a real walking song,"
Stipe says. That and "a funny, sad eulogy to a very great man." How much
of it was his idea? "I was doing my messiah-complex thing. The idea was
initially mine, and I took it to Peter." That's director Peter Care, who likes
to take stock images and then, as Stipe says, "fuck them up."

93 "ORANGE CRUSH"
1988

Many of R.E.M.'s clips before "Losing My Religion" don't feature the
reluctant Athens, Ga., rockers at all. "Orange Crush" director Matt Mahurin didn't even meet the whole group until this year's MTV Video Music
Awards—five years after making the clip, the first one from the album
Green. "It was refreshing to work so independently," Mahurin says.
"R.E.M. honors the visual potential of the song more than promoting its
own image." The song, dealing in part with the use of Agent Orange in
Vietnam, received an impressionistic treatment: Darkly lit black-and-white
shots of torsos, screaming faces and flying earth evoke the horrors of war and
its aftermath.

■ YEAR-END RANDOM NOTES December 23, 1993–January 6, 1994

January   In a rap presumably written in the car on the way to the MTV Inaugural Ball, L.L. Cool J treated the audience to this: "93! You and me! Unity! Time to party! With Big Bill and Hillary!" OK, so it was less than inspired—the sentiment was there. At MTV's extravaganza, indisputably the hottest ticket in town, the lineup to salute Bill Clinton ranged from En Vogue to Automatic Baby (R.E.M.'s Michael Stipe and Mike Mills with U2's Adam Clayton and Larry Mullen Jr.). The audience was well-behaved, except for chants of "Chel-*sea!* Chel-*sea!*"

■ RANDOM NOTES (January 27, 1994)

Whoomp! There he was. As long as Michael Stipe was listening to the rough demos of his pal Kristin Hersh's solo outing, *Hips and Makers,* she figured why not put him to work? As the Throwing Muses chanteuse played the unfinished cut "Your Ghost," she says, "the song was playing in one ear, and Michael was talking in the other, and it sounded really nice. So I interrupted him and asked him to sing on it. Michael's voice has almost a keening quality that my voice has, so they blend well together." The pair continued the partnership for a heavy-drama video shoot. "There's fire and haunted houses and big nightgowns and wigs," says Hersh. "I couldn't figure out if it was arty or rockin', then it turned out to just be very beautiful."

1994 MUSIC AWARDS

READERS PICKS

ARTIST OF THE YEAR
Pearl Jam
U2
Soul Asylum
R.E.M.
Aerosmith

BEST ALBUM
"Zooropa," U2
Ten, Pearl Jam
Siamese Dream, Smashing
   Pumpkins

Get a Grip, Aerosmith
**Automatic for the People,
   R.E.M.**

BEST BAND
Pearl Jam
U2
R.E.M.
Aerosmith
Soul Asylum

BEST MALE SINGER
Eddie Vedder
Bono

Michael Stipe
Lenny Kravitz
Sting

BEST SONGWRITER
Eddie Vedder
Bono
Sting
Michael Stipe
Billy Joel

ROBERT PALMER

EVOLVE OR DIE

★ ★ ★ ★ ½

Monster Album Review

NOT SO LONG AGO, ROLLING STONE's David Fricke asked the late Kurt Cobain whom he admired among "established" rock bands. Cobain unhesitatingly named R.E.M., using the occasion to send the band members a virtual mash note for remaining true to their muse and to themselves and for refusing to be swayed by the shifting winds of fashion and commerciality.

The comment was unexpected; R.E.M.'s decade-plus track record surely justified Cobain's praise, but their musical vision and his seemed so different. Cobain wore his heart on his sleeve, wrapping his often angry ruminations in swirls of guitar feedback and distortion. R.E.M.'s music has rarely screamed to make its point and has often seemed deliberately ambiguous. The intricate clarity of their arrangements has been tasteful to a fault.

But now all this is in the past and not just because of Cobain's sad demise. It's too bad he didn't live to hear *Monster.* If the new album isn't exactly a sonic grungefest, it comes a hell of a lot closer than anyone could have anticipated. Imagine earlier R.E.M. favorites like "Ignoreland" or "Radio Song" stripped of acoustic guitars, their lapidary, almost fussily pristine arrangements reduced to slabs of electric-guitar noise and power-chord riffing, and you're only beginning to get the picture. Gone are the manicured interweavings of strings, mandolins and other acoustic instruments, gone the pinpoint definition of instrumental and vocal parts that have characterized so many of R.E.M.'s recorded performances for so long. The two or three softer tunes that might not have sounded out of place on previous outings are pointedly sandwiched in the middle of the disc, surrounded by the sizzle of overdriven amps, snarling distortion and aggressive rhythms. Michael Stipe's singing, so difficult to decipher on early records, so plain-spoken and out in front of the mixes since *Green,* has slipped back into the sonic murk, where it fights to be heard.

Don't misunderstand: R.E.M.'s exceptional pop craftsmanship, their luminous melodic inventions, their sense of mission—in short, everything fundamental—are still there and shining more brightly than ever. What has been jettisoned, at least this time out, is all that tasteful restraint. *Monster* is one urgent-sounding album, and that's as it should be; what the band has to say here is urgent, politesse be damned. *Monster* is concerned, in song after song, with problems of identity. It explores how important having a stable sense of one's own identity can be and how up for grabs identities have become in our postmodern media hothouse, where it's possible to slip on a new persona as easily as a new look and couture can mean anything from Paris fashions to body piercing to a sex change. The concept of reality itself is being called into question: Is this my life or an incredible virtual simulation?

Clearly these issues are of more than academic interest to Stipe, who has arrived at that media plateau where his identity is in danger of becoming public property, and personal reticence inspires unfounded speculation more effectively than it preserves privacy. If Prince (who's no longer Prince) sang lines like "I'm straight, I'm queer, I'm bi" (from *Monster*'s "King of Comedy") or "Do you give good head? / Am I good in bed? / I don't know / I guess so" (from "I Don't Sleep, I Dream"), he would probably be taken literally. Stipe could just as easily be enumerating media guesses as to his own proclivities. He sounds like a man who's delighted to be a bit of an enigma, perhaps pleasantly surprised he has any private life left. But he hasn't held on to his personal space without a struggle. Toward the end of "King of Comedy," he practically snarls: "I'm not your magazine / I'm not your television / I'm not your movie screen / I'm not commodity."

But if the most basic issues of identity are at stake, the solutions are not necessarily cut and dried. In the course of *Monster*'s twelve songs, Stipe goes at it from a variety of angles. In the opener "What's the Frequency, Kenneth?" he quotes director Richard Linklater's dictum "Withdrawal in disgust is not the same as apathy" and sounds ready to withdraw himself. In "Crush With Eyeliner" he decides to lighten up and have a little fun, adapting an oh-so-affected David Bowie / Bryan Ferry croon. "I'm the real thing," he insists archly, aided on the choruses by the practiced anomie of guest Thurston Moore, only to wonder in the next breath, "How can I make myself faker to make her mine?" while the band slams out a glam-rock riff the late Mick Ronson might have appreciated.

These first two songs establish a dynamic that animates *Monster* all the way through: learning to live in an increasingly virtual world without losing your sense of self—or your sense of humor—in the process. Occasionally, Stipe begins to sound not unlike the proverbial rock star, whining about all those fans who just won't let him alone. At least that's what I get out of "Bang and Blame" ("You're laying blame / You know that's not my thing. . . . It's not my fault"). But more often, he tackles the issues with the clearheaded insight and gift for the telling phrase we've come to expect from him. Whether the songs are rocking furiously—like "Star 69," with its garagey, Count Five-ish flavor or the surging hijacked-identity cyber-drama "I Took Your Name"—or shimmering gorgeously like "Tongue" and "Strange Currencies," they're all involving. There isn't a throwaway in the bunch.

What's truly impressive about *Monster* is the way R.E.M. make an album with such potentially grave subject matter so much fun. Earlier R.E.M. albums have been impressive in other ways and not without their own humor, but this one fairly barrels along, sweeping you into its vistas with the sure-footed élan of a band very confident of its considerable powers. It also affirms in no uncertain terms that R.E.M. are a band. *Monster* could be guitarist Peter Buck's finest hour; he's all over this album, proving he can be just as effective without all those overdubs and acoustic fills, playing more from the gut. Mike Mills's melodic bass lines are integral to many of these songs, his piano and organ add a range of textures to the soulful "Tongue," and he locks in with Bill Berry's crisp, incisive drum-ming to make a suitably "monster" rhythm section. If you've been a fan of R.E.M. live and missed the raw power of their gigs on earlier albums, this one's for you.

But really, it's for all of us. Neither a "get back" garage-roots move nor a calculated attempt to win over the Lollapalooza crowd with the Big Guitar Formula, *Monster* is a deeply felt, thematically coherent, consistently in-vigorating challenge to "evolve or die," with all the courage of its convic-tions.

ANTHONY DeCURTIS

MONSTER MADNESS

VERYTHING STOPPED. COLD," SAYS Michael Stipe as he sits in a lounge at Ocean Way Recording, the Los Angeles studio where R.E.M. are attempting to put the finishing touches on their raucous, unsettling new album, *Monster*. It's after midnight—nearly everyone else has left for the day. Stipe speaks softly as he tries to convey the degree to which Kurt Cobain's death last April sucked the spirit out of R.E.M. as they worked on their album.

"We all loved and respected and admired him a great deal," he says. "It was not an incredible shock, because I had been in contact with Kurt. Everybody in the band kind of knew. We were speaking to each other daily, a couple of times a day. . . ." Stipe's voice trails off, and then he chuckles as the zany, flopping sound of someone flexing a cardboard poster wafts through the room. He looks toward the doorway. A visitor has arrived.

"Hey, how's it going," Stipe says, as Anthony Kiedis strides into the room. The Red Hot Chili Peppers have been working in a studio down the hall.

"It's going okay," says Kiedis. "How you doin'? You all right?"

"Yep."

"I'm just getting ready to go have a little midnight snack."

"Where you goin'?"

"Jones."

"Jones!" Stipe exclaims, acknowledging the restaurant's status as the town's hottest eatery. "Get the tomato leek soup. Do you guys know each other?" Stipe asks and then introduces me to Kiedis.

"Oh, I'm interrupting an interview here, my goodness," Kiedis says, genuinely chagrined.

"No, it'll be good," Stipe says, laughing. " 'Michael's dear friend Anthony Kiedis walked in and sat down. They talked about soup.' "

"How blasphemous of me," says Kiedis, slyly. "I'm sorry. I looked into your eyes, and I saw nothing else."

"You're not the first," says Stipe.

"I'll come back and get you another time. What stage are you at here?"

Stipe rolls his eyes, thinking about the state of *Monster.* "We're kind of late. We're on the hind titty. We're supposed to be mixing right now, but I'm still writing," Stipe says. "We're all zoom eyes. Is Flea around?"

"You're sucking the hind titty," Kiedis says absently. "Flea's in a studio about eight blocks away doing bass overdubs. We're doing the double-studio thing to try to crunch in the time. You're still writing? That's gonna be me on this record. I still have crazy stuff to write."

"Well, I'm going to be around for a while, so we should go to Orso or Jones," Stipe says.

"I'll tell Flea to come over, and we'll hang out," Kiedis says on his way out. "I'm terribly sorry to disturb the interview. I'll try that soup. See you, Michael."

Yes, Virginia, there is a rock & roll royalty, and R.E.M.—particularly singer Michael Stipe, whose head is now shaved to a stubble, save for a pair of discreet sideburns and a hint of hair on his chin—are now at the center of it. It has its good and bad aspects. Kurt Cobain calls in his time of most extreme need, and Anthony Kiedis drops by to suggest a midnight snack. And by the way, where's Flea? Shall we go to Orso or Jones? Issues of great seriousness mingle with the standard-issue celeb schmooze. It's heady and fun. But then again, sometimes it's simply harrowing. There are people who die.

Stipe leans back, rolls another of his cigarettes and returns to Cobain. "I had been talking to Kurt, and when he disappeared, I knew it," he says, speaking nearly in a monotone. "We all knew it. For seven days nobody knew where he was. I knew that a phone call was going to come, and I was just hoping that it was going to be a good one. And it wasn't. So we were a little prepared. But it was bad. Really bad."

The sonic-guitar windstorm on *Monster,* "Let Me In," a ravaging plea for contact, was written for and about Cobain. Stipe has also stayed in contact with Cobain's widow, Courtney Love, and accompanied her to the MTV Movie Awards last June. "We've been talking since Kurt's death," Stipe says. "I have a great deal of respect for her. I admire her a whole lot. And I think her record kicks ass."

R.E.M. and Nirvana had discussed the possibility of doing some shows together, and shortly before Cobain's death, Stipe and Cobain had talked about collaborating. "We Fed Exed a few things back and forth, but nothing was ever recorded," Stipe says. "It was in the planning stages. I saw it as a window of being able to get him out of the head that he was in. That was what I threw out to him, like a rope, to try to pull him in—'Let's work on this project together.'

"I knew that he had a great deal of respect for me and for the band. We had spent time together—he came to Athens, he and Courtney and Frances, and stayed at the house. We talked a lot. The truth of the matter is, we really didn't know each other that well. It was more of a mutual respect. He was very publicly an R.E.M. fan, which I think is incredibly daring for someone in his position.

"So that's where that thing came out of. I wanted to get him out of Seattle. I knew that he was there, and he was by himself. Everybody had tried everything they could, and that was my attempt to get him enough out of the head that he was in that he wouldn't kill himself or hurt himself. I thought it was going to be an overdose." Stipe hesitates and can't seem to gather his thoughts: "I wish he had . . . I don't know . . . you can't . . . what if?" He is silent for a moment.

"It was going to be very acoustic—and some organs," Stipe says. "That's the kind of music he wanted to do. He wanted to do something that was really not loud."

WHATEVER STIPE AND COBAIN might have done together—yet another set of possibilities wasted by Cobain's suicide—R.E.M. have moved in decidedly the opposite direction. They have followed up the extraordinary acoustic beauty and warm humanism of their previous album, *Automatic for the People* (1992), with the aptly titled *Monster,* a noisy, abrasive, postmodern, sexually charged maelstrom. Similar in style to the band's more propulsive live shows in the past, although far less genial, *Monster* is easily the edgiest music the band has ever recorded.

That edginess, alas, is also reflected in the atmosphere around Ocean Way. R.E.M. have always been obsessive about meeting deadlines. "It's amazing how far you can get in this business just by showing up for your appointments on time," guitarist Peter Buck once remarked to me early in the band's career. But *Monster* is late, and the band's self-imposed strain is showing. "In terms of the subdued urgency around here, it's always like this toward the end of the process," says bassist Mike Mills. "You always want to make sure that you have time to fine-tune everything as best you can, though we're not going to do as much of that with this record as we have with some. But it's definitely getting toward crunch time. We've lost some time."

Circumstances certainly played a large role in the band's falling behind schedule. When R.E.M. was recording last March at Crossover Soundstage, in Atlanta, Mills took sick and underwent an appendectomy. Then drummer Bill Berry got waylaid by the flu and had to return to his home in Athens to recuperate. On the brighter side, Stipe's sister Lynda had a baby, and Buck's girlfriend, Stephanie, with whom he now lives in Seattle, gave birth to twin girls. Breaks were built into the band's schedule to accommodate those events. Later, Stipe developed an abscessed tooth.

"Because of what was going on with everyone, things were changing," Buck explains over beers one afternoon in a deli around the corner from Ocean Way. "We never changed a schedule in all of our years. We'd do the schedule for a record—start on this day, end on this day—and if we went two days long, we'd be really over. This record we changed the schedule twenty times. That's one of the reasons it's so up in the air."

Another factor contributing to the tension in the studio is the way that *Monster* was recorded. Despite the mishaps that afflicted the band in Atlanta, most of the basic tracks for the songs on *Monster* were recorded live at Crossover, as if the band were playing onstage. The inevitable rawness of recording like that means, as Buck diplomatically puts it, that you have "a lot more options at the end."

"I thought since they hadn't toured in a while, it would be good for them to get into that mind-set—you know, monitors, PA, standing up," says Scott Litt with a laugh. Described by Berry as "the fifth member of the band, as far as recording is concerned," Litt has shared a co-production credit with the band on every new studio album R.E.M. has done since *Document* (1987). "That's why it's been taking so long to mix," Litt says of *Monster*. "We're trying to figure out how raw to leave it and how much to studiofy it."

All that is true, but it also seems as if the members of R.E.M. are having to learn how to be in a band again. Although they've done live shows here and there, R.E.M. have not gone out on the road since their world tour in support of *Green* ended in November 1989. Without the scheduling demands and corps mentality that organizing a tour inevitably brings, the band was able to record *Out of Time* (1991) and *Automatic for the People*—and to some extent, even *Monster*—at a leisurely pace adjusted to the specific demands of each member's personal life.

In the meantime, R.E.M. became a hugely successful band, with the single and video for the Top Ten hit "Losing My Religion" generating quadruple-platinum sales for *Out of Time* in the United States alone. Following that, *Automatic for the People*—with no tour and even with Stipe refusing to do interviews to promote the album—sold more than 2.5 million copies in this country. You could say that since 1989, Berry, Buck, Mills and Stipe have become superstars without really having to be R.E.M.

All this was coming to a head at Ocean Way as the band attempted to wrap up *Monster*. The album had to be finished, but rarely were the four members of the band present in the studio at the same time. They were all staying in different places around town and seemed to be trying to juggle finishing the album with the demands of their individual friends, families and lovers. The last day I stopped by the studio, to say goodbye, all four members of the band were on hand, and the mood was focused, if decidedly grim. "We had a band meeting after the session last night," Mills said. "We have to begin working as a unit again, which we haven't been doing very well lately."

"This would be a lot worse," said Buck with a mixture of hopefulness and exasperation, "if we weren't all such good friends."

WEARING BLACK JEANS, GREEN sneakers and a dark-green T-shirt with a black star on the chest (similar to the shirt he wears in the video for *Monster*'s first single, "What's the Frequency, Kenneth?"), Michael Stipe is standing in a control room at Ocean Way recording the vocal for a track on *Monster* that will eventually be called "King of Comedy." In the studio it is alternately referred to as "Disco Song" or "Yes, I Am Fucking With You." Gripping the mike with both hands, reading the lyrics from a revision-scarred sheet of paper placed on a stand in front of him, Stipe sings: "Make your money with a pretty face / Make it easy with product placement / Make it charged with controversy / I'm straight, I'm queer, I'm bi." Over a driving dance-club beat, his normally warm voice is heavily distorted, a distancing device that runs throughout *Monster*. At the end of the track he snarls: "I'm not the king of comedy / I'm not your magazine / I'm not your television / I'm not your movie screen / I'm not commodity."

The character Stipe evokes on "King of Comedy" is a manipulative, sexually indeterminate power monger who, strangely, is struggling desperately to maintain his sense of humanity. It's like the twin poles of the rock-celeb experience for Stipe—the allure of power over an audience (an idea he has explored since "Turn You Inside-Out" on *Green*) and the danger of losing yourself in the fun-house mirror world of pop stardom.

More specifically, though, *Monster* is filled with what Buck describes as "obsessive-creep love songs." "It's funny," he says. "Sometimes Michael will write songs where I'll go, 'Well, I can see how that's part of Michael's perspective,' even though he's not necessarily writing about his experiences. But there's a lot of songs on this record that are not even his perspective. You can say a lot of things about Michael—and journalists do—but he's not creepy. And these songs, a lot of them are kind of creepy."

For his part, Stipe, 34, professes to be unaware of the sources within himself of the darker emotions on *Monster,* which is dedicated to the late actor River Phoenix, a close friend of Stipe's who died last year of a drug overdose. "I don't know, I just put it out there," he says as we sit on folding chairs in the parking lot outside the studio during a break. He, too, seems a bit surprised by the album's quality of emotional terrorism.

"I wanted to write a record about sex," he continues. "I thought that would be kind of fun, kind of cool. I could come at it from all these different angles. I was thinking about this the other day, because I know that with this record people are going to ask a lot of questions about sex. I've had this pat answer about my idea of sex, that sex is nothing more than friction and ego—and timing. [*Laughs.*] These songs are meant to be in your face. I kind of wanted something that was brash, fucked up and sexy. Dysfunctional. Kind of a gender-fuck train wreck just thrown out there." He smiles. "Hopefully, there's a humanity in it, too."

Part of the gender-fuck element of *Monster* would seem to be Stipe's way of confronting—and playing around with—the widespread speculation about his own sexual orientation. Along with the "I'm straight, I'm queer, I'm bi" nonadmission in "King of Comedy," the tremolo-guitar glam-rock tribute "Crush With Eyeliner"—which Berry terms "that snotty boy-sexy thing"—implies that sexual identity is not determined by nature but can be consciously and constantly created, shifted and re-created.

Singing in a voice that sounds like a combination of the high affectation of Bryan Ferry and Boris Karloff as the Frankenstein monster, Stipe declares: "I'm infatuated / It's all too much passion / She's all that I can take / What position should I wear? / Cop an attitude, fake her / How can I convince her . . . That I'm invented, too?" In another verse he wonders: "How can I make myself be faker / To make her mine?" In this light, Stipe's repeated insistence in the song that "I'm the real thing" (with an obvious nod to Coca-Cola and the identity politics of advertising culture) is hilarious, the ironic opposite of the assertion "I'm not commodity."

On a more disturbing note, however, rumors about Stipe in recent years have centered not only on his sexual preference but also on his health. When R.E.M. announced that they would not be touring after the release of *Automatic for the People*—after not touring two years earlier in support of *Out of Time,* either—and Stipe refused all requests for interviews, people began to wonder if he had AIDS or was HIV positive. A preoccupation on *Automatic* with mortality and dead pop-culture celebrities like Andy Kaufman, Elvis Presley and Montgomery Clift only fueled the concern.

"I don't know how smart it is to say this," Stipe responds when asked about the rumors, "but I purposely did not come forward and say, 'No, I am not HIV positive,' because I thought that it might be good for a lot of people who did respect me or think highly of me to wonder about that and think about it. And think, 'Wow, if it can affect somebody who I really look up to, maybe I should be a little bit more careful myself.' That may be unbelievably naive on my part. I also didn't want to answer to it. It was completely ludicrous. I don't think anybody had anything to base it on.

"On a related issue, in terms of the whole queer-straight-bi thing, my feeling is that labels are for canned food," he says. "People are much too binary in their thinking—I think sexuality is a much more slippery thing than that. I've always liked the idea that I could publicly play with that and not pronounce myself anything and let people . . . not wonder . . . let people take me for what I am. I am what I am—and I know what I am—but I don't really feel comfortable with the labels.

"Going back to the HIV thing," he continues, "I'm not HIV positive. I've been tested many times for various reasons, whether insurance or personal. I've always been of questionable sexuality or dubious sexuality. I've always been skinny, whether people knew it or not—except I got fat once in 1985, when I went nuts, gained 30 pounds, shaved my head and looked like Marlon Brando for a while. But I've always been skinny, I've always had weird hair, and if you put that together with the romance of a public figure and that I wear a hat that says, WHITE HOUSE STOP AIDS, to the Grammys and that I support various AIDS organizations and that I'm queer-friendly, people automatically take all these little things and blow them up into something that they're not."

He pauses. "I guess I'm glad that people are concerned about my health," he concludes with a laugh. "It makes me think that they might want me to stick around. I'm really, really okay."

NEEDLESS TO SAY, IT'S genuinely great news that Michael Stipe is "really, really okay." But given that, at least one question remains unanswered: Why haven't R.E.M., a band whose relentless touring during its early years helped establish its reputation, toured for five years?

"It's '94 now, and we toured right till the end of '89, so really it's four years," says Peter Buck, 37, with uncharacteristic firmness.

Well, the *Green* world tour ended in November '89. R.E.M.'s proposed world tour in support of *Monster* isn't slated to start until January '95 in Australia, so it's really a bit more than five years.

"Wait a minute," Buck says, hesitating. "The end of '89 until January first . . . right, it will have been five years, yeah. Right now, it's four and a half."

Hmm. Feeling a tad defensive?

"Well, yeah," Buck says a little sheepishly. "Because everybody says, 'God, you don't tour,' but U2 didn't even put a record out for three and a half years at one point, and no one said, 'Why aren't you touring?' We've done three records in that time. I am a bit defensive about it. We decided to concentrate on the recording side of it. We did a big tour in '89, and we'd been on the road for ten years full time—up to that point we'd squeezed everything we could out of it in a creative sense. We could have toured after *Out of Time,* and it would have been more of the same.

"I just don't really feel that R.E.M. have to have any rules or boundaries—and not because we've made a lot of money," he continues. "It's more important to do what we feel like. Once you admit that there are rules, then you've lost. And one of those rules is that you tour to promote your record. Well, fuck that—none of us felt we had to. Just coincidentally, we then sold ten million records, which sends us a really weird message like 'Stay home, please.'

"I'm really looking forward to touring," Buck says. "We're all kind of excited by it. It's going to be really great. It'll be different. It'll be fresh. I haven't done it to death."

And for the opposing view, enter Michael Stipe. "I'm dreading it," the singer says bluntly, though with a laugh, about touring. "That's about all the thought I've been able to give it." By this point, Stipe's much-vaunted ambivalence about being a rock & roll frontman onstage, being in the public eye and debating the literal meaning of his lyrics is a source of humor even to him.

"I love performing, and I love traveling," he continues. "But the two combined are pretty poisonous. It's a really hard way to spend a year, moving around a lot. I think Natalie Merchant once said that when you tour, all your friends are jealous because you've been able to travel the world and see all these places, but the fact of the matter is, it's kind of like you're in this bubble floating above everything. At the end of the *Green* world tour, I knew in my heart that I would never do it again. That tour was incredibly hard. At the end of it, I was just blank, a shell. It was really, really, really intense. I just got sick of myself. I wanted to be a human and not so much of a pop star."

He pauses. "Is this going to sound like 'Woe is me, my life is so hard'?" he asks. "All of this has to be couched in my recognizing and completely admitting that I am so unbelievably fucking fortunate. I love my job. I love the position I'm in. I love all the benefits that come with being what I am and doing what I do. I've got everything. Within that, I hate touring. But I'm going to do it. I guess."

But Stipe's reluctance to tour is hardly the only reason R.E.M. retreated from the public eye for a time. All of the band members' lives have changed considerably since the late Eighties. Among other factors, the extraordinary degree of success the band has achieved has understandably had its effect.

"I'd be lying if I said it didn't," says Bill Berry, 36, one afternoon at Ocean Way. "It's changed my life. And it's not just the money, although that's a lot of it. I've moved out of Athens, bought some land, built a nice house out of town, and that's the best thing that's ever happened to me. I went from being the Athens party boy to being the Oconee County hay farmer—which is literally what I do. I wear overalls like this, I have a big John Deere tractor that I ride around in, and I take care of my land when I'm there. That's completely changed my perspective on things. I want to have kids now. My life with my wife, my home life, has shot way up in priority now."

Things have changed as well for Buck—historically the most prototypical rock & roller in the band—since the birth of his daughters Zoe and Zelda. "I think people who say that children change your perspective must have really been fascists beforehand," he says jokingly. "But they're a great thing in my life. I never thought about the future at all. It's not as if I live some crazy, decadent life—I have a couple of beers. But they're a lot more important for me, in perspective, now than the band is. I mean, the band are my friends, and I'm going to be there for them. But if two years ago the band had broken up acrimoniously, it probably would have upset me. Whereas if it breaks up now, it's like 'Well, I've had a good run.' I mean, it's not going to, but in perspective, there are things now that are a lot more important to me. My important part of the day used to be coming into the studio. Now my important part of the day is going home."

"We're all older people," says Mills, 36. "That calms things down a little bit. You're thrown together in the studio, but it's certainly a different feeling than when you're on the road—so who knows how that's going to be. But everybody's still fairly respectful of everybody's space and needs. It hasn't changed that much. Some. [*Laughs.*] Make no mistake, there is definitely some change. But it's not real radical. Everybody's become more like whatever they were. That may sound like a cop-out to say, but that's basically what it is. Everyone's personality has sort of solidified."

SO WHAT DOES R.E.M.'S FUTURE LOOK like? The release of *Monster* and the virtual certainty of a tour that will take them through Asia, Europe and, in the spring of '95, North America, will surely make them one of the most successful bands on the planet. The world is definitely ready for R.E.M. Are R.E.M. ready for the world?

"It will be interesting to see how we feel after this tour," Berry says. "If it's like the last one [*laughs*] . . . you might not hear a record out of us for quite a while. We may break up. This is the first record since *Green* where there's a tour involved, and that's as important as the record itself. When the last two records were released, it was just like 'Well, let's see how it does, sit back at home, write songs, see what happens.' Now it's like 'The record's out—now the real work begins.' Now we go out and see if we still have it onstage live. That's going to be the test. Ask me in a year, and I'll tell you. We haven't been out in the public eye to experience what that new stage of celebrity is going to be like, how wacko it's going to be on tour. So the tour is going to be a real eye-opener."

Buck also sees the end of the upcoming R.E.M. tour as a kind of line of demarcation. "We'll work and do stuff, most likely tour, through the end of '95, and after that it's a matter of what do we want to do," he says. "My guess is that we'll take six or eight months off, still be friends and get back to work again. The way we all feel about it is, 'As long as we're enjoying it, why not keep doing it?' I'd be embarrassed to do bad work, but we haven't done any yet.

"I think we've got a few more records in us," he continues. "If I said three records—that sounds kind of reasonable to me right now. Now we could break up before that or we could make ten more records. At the rate we work, three records is a long time—it's six, seven years. Of course, if we get to the point where we're not popular anymore, then we could do whatever we want to! Some days I think it could last forever, and some days I think it won't last very long."

But Buck's impression is that R.E.M. are in a more comfortable place on the contemporary music scene than they were not so long ago—and that has reinvigorated the band. "If you asked me a few years ago about the future of my musical career," he says, "I probably would have said, 'It will get more and more folky, and I'll end up playing the Bottom Line sitting on a stool when I'm forty-five.'

"There was a period where I didn't really feel that we fit in," Buck says. "It seemed like in 1990 that there wasn't going to be a lot more rock & roll—at least on major labels. The whole Nirvana-Soundgarden-Mud-honey thing was happening, and I had those records, but it was happening in Seattle, and they were playing to 200 kids a night. I wasn't sure, person-ally, how you'd even approach rock & roll anymore. I didn't know what I wanted to do with that kind of music.

"But we all talked about it and realized that we are a rock & roll band, and for better or worse, we wanted to reapproach that," Buck continues. "We decided we wanted to make an uptempo electric record but without using any elements of heavy metal, which none of us ever listened to. So much of what's happening now, all those bands liked the Ramones *and* Black Sabbath. I'm not sure I've ever heard a Black Sabbath record. So we're into a weird, purist, no metal whatsoever, very little blues, white rock & roll thing."

Stipe, too, feels energized by the kind of influence R.E.M. have had. Their effect on younger progressive bands has created a musical and social environment he feels at home in. Still, he's not predicting the future, either.

"It's natural to my personality occasionally to think when I go to our office, 'There will be a day when this office will close, because there will be no reason for it to stay open,' and it is deeply sad to have that thought," he says. "At the same time I look at it, and it's this vibrant, incredible place that amazing things are coming out of—and not just music. It's thrilling to me that I'm at the epicenter of that. From whatever notion that me and Peter and Mike and Bill had fifteen years ago to start a band and stick with it and not buckle under has led to this. And all the amazing people that I've met through this band, because of this band—it's really heartening. And that will never end, of course.

"I've gotten this far and I've maintained my sanity," Stipe continues. "I feel almost big brotherly toward people in rock & roll whom I admire a lot—like Kurt, Sonic Youth and Eddie Vedder. That these people have such an incredible respect for us has really opened my eyes up about what we have done—that these people would give me the time of day as a person and give us any credit whatsoever as a band.

"I feel so much like a contemporary of those guys, and yet I also feel like I've been there a little bit," he says. "I have great sympathy for anybody who's been thrown into . . . *this* as quickly as Kurt and Eddie have been. They got, in a way, the same tag that I did, where I was being positioned as the voice of a generation. It was something that I really, really did not want. It was like 'Wait a minute—I'm a fucking singer in a rock & roll band. I did not ask for this.' It's a lot of pressure. If *Murmur* or *Reckoning* had sold five million copies, I wouldn't be alive to tell the tale."

Stipe looks up then and brightens a bit. "I'm excited that we're in a position to pretty much do what we want to do," he says. "The only real constraint, creatively, is ourselves—and that's enough. We're four very distinct and very different people. But I think that push me / pull you has always been part of our indefinable chemistry. There's an acceptance there."

And maybe even touring won't be so bad. "I'm kind of looking forward to it a little bit, I guess," Stipe finally allows as he begins getting ready to leave for the night. "It's going to be exciting to travel the world again." Then he pulls himself up short one last time. "I always see the person in the audience who's yawning," he says. "The one out of 20,000."

ANTHONY DeCURTIS

MICHAEL STIPE Q & A

In a special issue entitled "Generation Next," ROLLING STONE featured interviews with the leading lights of alternative rock. Michael Stipe was one of the fifteen artists interviewed about the new generation of musicians and their work.

MICHAEL STIPE, 34, SITS at a huge conference table in a meeting room at the Four Seasons Hotel, an expansive New York City vista visible outside the window. Wearing clunky black glasses that simultaneously make him appear comical and serious, Stipe looks like Jean Genet reincarnated as the chairman of a multinational corporation. It's suitable somehow.

Surrounding Stipe is an array of bottles of water, tumblers, cups and pots of coffee and a healthy sampling of semihomeopathic elixirs. R.E.M. threw a party the previous night after the MTV Music Video Awards ceremony, which the group attended. Though in casual conversation none of the band's members could recall exactly which four awards R.E.M. had won, the foursome were happy to celebrate nonetheless. The bash lasted well into the morning, and Stipe—not to mention your intrepid reporter—is hung over.

Still, there's no denying that the singer has rebounded strongly. It's early afternoon, but Stipe, up and working since midmorning, has been doing interviews to promote the new R.E.M. album, *Monster*. Now he's ready to switch gears for an hour to discuss the changing face of the rock & roll scene.

And who better to weigh in on the subject? R.E.M. are pivotal figures in the music's history, a crucial link between the underground pioneers of the Sixties and Seventies and the current crop of innovators rechanneling the mainstream. "We're the acceptable edge of the unacceptable stuff," R.E.M. guitarist Peter Buck once said about the band, but these days the definition of what's acceptable is rapidly broadening—and R.E.M. are an important reason why.

Michael Stipe reflects on those matters and, hangover remedies near at hand, speaks of what's past, passing and to come.

*D*O *YOU FEEL ANY particular generational identification?*
        No. I did not feel at all like a yuppie, although I realize that R.E.M. kind of were the soundtrack to that. We were on the edge of the yuppies, maybe, the ones who wanted to be hip or whatever, but who at the same time were doing the total Eighties thing. I really never grasped that concept. I felt a real division.

Was there a point at which you became consciously aware of the difference between you and elements of your audience?

At one point I just became acutely aware that people my age or a few years older did not have the same values or priorities that I have—at all. Not to say that mine were that well defined, but theirs seemed *very* well defined—but not by them, by someone else. They were just kind of going with it. Of course they looked at me as if I were a scarecrow—unless I was on stage, in which case I was entertaining. But on the street it was like, "Get out of my fucking face. Get off our sidewalk."

Do you feel like there's a generational schism now?

I think there definitely is. Kurt Cobain's death really drew a line between those who got it and those who didn't. Just culturally speaking, removing ourselves from all the personal stuff, an event like that really fucking drew the line.

But even young people aren't unified in what they think of Cobain's death.

There is a lot of contempt. Go on the Internet and there are as many jokes about Kurt's death as there are people affected by it.

Last night this guy sitting behind me screamed out during the Cobain memorial, "He was a junkie."

"And you're an asshole." But mythologizing Kurt is really something that he would abhor. It's something *I* abhor. But everything that we're talking about really happened. As a person, as an artist, it's not fair to . . . you have to put him up pretty high to say that his death had that effect. But it really did.

Would you be willing or interested to offer a definition of alternative?

Neither willing nor interested. [*laughs*] I mean, with songs being co-opted by AT&T and Pizza Hut within three weeks of hitting radio, the turnaround is so quick that there probably really is no alternative. What is alternative is probably something that's very slippery and not really covered in the media. I'm not sure we're even aware of it.

Isn't it possible that "alternative" is less a style of music than a way of going about things?

Yeah, I'd go for that. It's more attitude. But I would also say that the term has been so co-opted by the music and entertainment industry that it doesn't mean anything anymore. It's just another way of labeling a group of, say, musicians, or filmmakers or what have you. Models. I mean we now have alternative models. What the fuck? It means nothing now.

There's an older generation of artists that you've talked about a lot—the Velvet Underground, Patti Smith, Iggy Pop. What qualities of theirs inspired you?

Passion, I think. They had their thing, and for whatever reason, they were secure enough in it that they just went forward, damn the consequences. By not listening to whatever the word of the day was, or the sound of the day, these people forged their own paths and became, for that reason, incredible influences. Maybe in the case of the Velvets, ten years later or fifteen years later, not even in their own time.

Speaking of following your own path, R.E.M. has never really conformed to expectations, whether mainstream or underground. For example, while many people associate progressive music with noise and abrasiveness, R.E.M. has never been afraid of beauty and subtlety.

I had a conversation with Tori Amos where she was talking about vulnerability in music. There are artists who leave themselves vulnerable, and that might mean not being afraid of something that's beautiful. The Velvet Underground—some of those unbelievably delicate nursery rhyme songs, with little tiny voices, and a viola playing, or a simple piano figure in amongst all the white noise stuff—there's something about not being afraid of being vulnerable that really sets those people apart.

Beauty can be very challenging, as well. It can really be challenging. It's so much easier to write about angst and anger and fear and darkness and fucked-up feelings than to write about incredible, intense happiness. Happiness just sounds dorky. We've all experienced it, but it's much harder in a pop song to pull that off. It's much easier to pull off the darker stuff.

Along similar lines it seems that as a singer you've been attracted to ballads, another not very fashionable taste.

I like power ballads. "Love Hurts" by Nazareth—that was deeply influential. "Sweet Emotion."

I also remember your performing "Moon River" in concert, and even Lou Gramm's "Midnight Blue," I think while it was still on the charts.

That's a great song.

What attracts you to stuff like that?

Honestly? A clever chord progression. I can hear the melody of a song I don't know in an elevator and I'll hum it all day. That's what the attraction is. It usually has very little to do with the words.

What impressed me, though, was that anybody would expect R.E.M. to treat a song like that ironically, but your version seemed. . . .

Really genuine. Yeah. It wasn't ironic, and it wasn't comic. [*pause*] Do you know why I love "Moon River" so much? Did I ever tell you this? You know the line, "my huckleberry friend"? I always thought it was *Huckleberry Hound,* which was one of my favorite cartoons when I was a kid. [*laughs*]

Perfect. I always thought it was because of some profound Southern connection. Moving right along, have you ever thought that rock & roll was dead?

I believed it when I read it a few times, and I thought, "Uh oh, better find a new job." But it was bullshit. Here comes some great new band, and it's just as alive for me as it ever has been. It doesn't have to be *Never Mind the Bollocks,* it can be one song on the radio. It could be a video.

Did any of the Sixties icons like the Beatles or the Rolling Stones mean anything to you when you were growing up?

[*Shakes his head no.*] I've always referred to the Beatles as elevator music, because that's exactly what they were. "Michelle" in German is the one Beatles song that meant something to me, because I was in Germany when I was seven years old and heard it on the radio and thought it was really pretty. I mean, I didn't know they were the Beatles. I've never sat down and listened to a Beatles record from beginning to end. Those guys just didn't mean a fucking thing to me.

It was exciting last night to see the Rolling Stones, because I know that I will never go see them in concert; I have no desire to watch them perform a two-hour show. But to see the truncated, commercial version of it last night was exciting: I watched Mick Jagger perform—that was kind of cool. But they don't mean a fucking thing to me, either. The Monkees and the Banana Splits meant a lot more to me—and whoever did "Yummy, Yummy, Yummy." I mean, that was the stuff I really knew and loved. "Honey," all the Glen Campbell stuff.

Was there any particular transformative moment in your life, as far as music is concerned?

I remember as a teenager knowing that the 1970s were the dullest, most ridiculous time, that culturally it was just like . . . it was *bankrupt.* There was nothing there, nothing at all. I think that's what punk rock came out of, and why to me at the age of fifteen when I discovered it, it was like, "Holy fucking god, this is *unbelievable*. Nobody knows about this, and here it is."

You were in St. Louis?

I was in St. Louis, yeah. Somebody left a *Creem* magazine under their chair in study hall, and I picked it up and started reading it. I'd never really paid much attention to music magazines or music. I liked "Benny and the Jets," and "Rock On" by David Essex, and "Crocodile Rock," and . . . what else? There *was* nothing else. I picked up this issue of *Creem,* and there was this article by Lisa Robinson about the New York scene. It had a photograph of Patti Smith—she looked like a vampire—and talked about Tom Verlaine and the Ramones. I think Lisa was comparing punk rock to an old static-y black and white television set, and popular music as being lurid color, well formed, glossy. The little, static-y black and white TV was absolutely . . . it was my heart and soul, and I knew it. It was like, "Wow . . . fuck. Fucking wow! This is amazing." At that point I started getting *Rock Scene* magazine and *Creem.* And, then later, *New York Rocker, Trouser Press* and the *Village Voice.* That was when I went, "Something's going on here." It made me want to get on a bus and go to New York.

What did you do instead?

I stayed where I was. But I went to this fucked up hardware store, and they had this discount music section with all these eight-tracks that were marked down that nobody wanted. It was covered with a plastic tarp because the roof leaked, so you had to go under the plastic to get to the stuff. I bought both New York Dolls' albums for 99 cents on eight-track and the Velvet's *Live '69.* I bought *Radio Ethiopia* on eight-track.

That's just incredible.

That was where it was at. When I read about those New York bands, they talked about the Stooges and the Velvets. And they talked about the Doors—Patti Smith went on and on about Jim Morrison, although I never really had much interest in him for some reason. I think the Lizard King thing was just kind of like, "What?" [*laughs*] I didn't really get that. But I read Arthur Rimbaud's entire collected works before I knew his name was not pronounced Rim-bawd, because Patti Smith said he was a huge influence on her. I was sixteen years old. It was pretty wild shit. But that's not to say I stopped wearing bell bottoms, because I didn't. That took another three years. [*laughs*]

One last thing: You once wrote a line in "Little America," "I can't see myself at thirty." Is there a point at which . . .

It's funny, but I can't remember if it was "can't" or "can." I need to listen to the song and try to figure it out.

I think it was "can't."

I don't . . . I mean, I know what I meant by the song, "I don't buy a laquered thirty" . . . Yeah, and here I am at thirty-four. I don't feel very laquered. I don't feel like a bug stuck in amber—which is cool. I don't feel thirty-four. I mean, my friends range from fifteen-year-olds to fifty-five-year-olds. It's weird. It's all attitude, isn't it? Kinship and attitude. I don't really feel like I'm any particular age at all.

I'm going to be forty in six years. It used to be, like, "Oh my god: forty." But forty doesn't seem that weird to me. It seems weird, maybe, to think of being forty and doing what I'm doing now. But I'm sure I'll be doing some version of it—hopefully gracefully—as a forty-year-old.

DISCOGRAPHY

CHRONIC TOWN (EP)
I.R.S., August 1982
Single: Wolves, Lower
Additional tracks: Gardening at Night; Carnival of Sorts (Box Cars); 1,000,000; Stumble

MURMUR
I.R.S., April 1983
Single: Radio Free Europe
Additional tracks: Pilgrimage; Laughing; Talk About the Passion; Moral Kiosk; Perfect Circle; Catapult; Sitting Still; 9-9; Shaking Through; We Walk; West of the Fields

RECKONING
I.R.S., April 1984
Singles: So. Central Rain (I'm Sorry); (Don't Go Back To) Rockville
Additional tracks: Harborcoat; 7 Chinese Brothers; Pretty Persuasion; Time After Time (Annelise); Second Guessing; Letter Never Sent; Camera; Little America

FABLES OF THE RECONSTRUCTION
I.R.S., June 1985
Singles: Can't Get There From Here; Driver 8
Additional tracks: Feeling Gravitys Pull; Maps and Legends; Life and How to Live It; Old Man Kensey; Green Grow the Rushes; Kohoutek; Auctioneer (Another Engine); Good Advices; Wendell Gee

LIFES RICH PAGEANT
I.R.S., July 1986
Singles: Fall On Me; Superman
Additional tracks: Begin the Begin; These Days; Cuyahoga; Hyena; Underneath the Bunker; The Flowers of Guatemala; I Believe; What If We Give It Away?; Just a Touch; Swan Swan H

DEAD LETTER OFFICE
I.R.S., April 1987
Tracks: Crazy; There She Goes Again; Burning Down; Voice of Harold; Burning Hell;

White Tornado; Toys in the Attic; Windout; Ages of You; Pale Blue Eyes; Rotary Ten; Bandwagon; Femme Fatale; Walter's Theme; King of the Road

DOCUMENT

I.R.S., September 1987

Singles: The One I Love; Its the End of the World as We Know It (and I Feel Fine); Finest Worksong

Additional tracks: Welcome to the Occupation; Exhuming McCarthy; Disturbance at the Heron House; Strange; Fireplace; Lightnin' Hopkins; King of Birds; Oddfellows Local 151

EPONYMOUS

I.R.S., October 1988

Tracks: Radio Free Europe; Gardening at Night; Talk About the Passion; So. Central Rain; (Don't Go Back To) Rockville; Can't Get There From Here; Driver 8; Romance; Fall On Me; The One I Love; Finest Worksong; It's the End of the World as We Know It (and I Feel Fine)

GREEN

Warner Bros., November 1988

Singles: Stand; Pop Song 89

Additional tracks: Get Up; You Are the Everything; World Leader Pretend; The Wrong Child; Orange Crush; Turn You Inside-Out; Hairshirt; I Remember California; (Untitled)

OUT OF TIME

Warner Bros., March 1991

Singles: Losing My Religion; Shiny Happy People; Radio Song

Additional tracks: Low; Near Wild Heaven; Endgame; Belong; Half a World Away; Texarkana; Country Feedback; Me in Honey

AUTOMATIC FOR THE PEOPLE

Warner Bros., September 1992

Singles: Drive; Man on the Moon; The Sidewinder Sleeps Tonight; Everybody Hurts

Additional tracks: Try Not to Breathe; New Orleans Instrumental Number 1; Sweetness Follows; Monty Got a Raw Deal; Ignoreland; Star Me Kitten; Nightswimming; Find the River

MONSTER

Warner Bros., September 1994

Singles: What's the Frequency, Kenneth? Bang and Blame; Star 69; Crash with Eyeliner; Strange Currencies

Tracks: What's the Frequency, Kenneth?; Crush With Eyeliner; King of Comedy; I Don't Sleep, I Dream; Star 69; Strange Currencies; Tongue; Bang and Blame; I Took Your Name; Let Me In; Circus Envy; You

VIDEOGRAPHY

SINGLE-SONG VIDEOS
I.R.S. RELEASES:

"Wolves, Lower"
Date: August 1982
Directors: Valerie Faris, Jonathan Dayton

"Radio Free Europe"
Date: July 1983
Director: Arthur Pierson

"So. Central Rain"
Date: May 1985
Director: Howard Libov

"Can't Get There From Here"
Date: June 1985
Directors: Michael Stipe, Aguar Bros. Films, Hartley Schilling

"Driver 8"
Date: August 1985
Directors: James Herbert, Michael Stipe

"Life and How to Live It"
Date: October 1985
Directors: Jackie Slayton, James Herbert

"Feeling Gravitys Pull"
Date: October 1985
Directors: Jackie Slayton, James Herbert

"Fall on Me"
Date: August 1986
Director: Michael Stipe

"Its the End of the World as We Know It (and I Feel Fine)"
Date: February 1987
Director: James Herbert

"The One I Love"
Date: August 1987
Director: Robert Longo

"Finest Worksong"
Date: January 1988
Director: Michael Stipe

"Talk About the Passion"
Date: September 1988
Director: Jem Cohen

WARNER BROS. RELEASES:

"Stand"
Date: October 1988
Director: Katherine Dieckmann
Location: Ithaca, New York

"Orange Crush"
Date: September 1988
Director: Matt Mahurin
Location: New York City

"Turn You Inside-Out"
Date: March 1989
Director: James Herbert
Location: Atlanta, Georgia

"Get Up"
Date: October 1989
Director: Eric Darnell
Location: Various

"Pop Song 89"
Date: April 1989
Director: Michael Stipe
Location: New York City

"Losing My Religion"
Date: February 1991
Director: Tarsem
Location: Los Angeles

"Shiny Happy People"
Date: February 1991
Director: Katherine Dieckmann
Location: Athens, Georgia

"Near Wild Heaven"
Date: June and July 1991
Director: Jeff Preiss
Location: New York City

"Radio Song"
Date: August 1991
Director: Peter Care
Location: Los Angeles

"Drive"
Date: August 1992
Director: Peter Care
Location: Van Nuys, California

"Man on the Moon"
Date: September 1992
Director: Peter Care
Location: Pear Blossom, California

"The Sidewinder Sleeps Tonight"
Date: September 1992
Director: Kevin Kerslake
Location: Los Angeles

"Everybody Hurts"
Date: November 1992
Director: Jake Scott
Location: San Antonio, Texas

"What's the Frequency, Kenneth?"
Date: August 1994
Director: Peter Care
Location: Los Angeles

"Bang and Blame"
Director: Randy Skinner
Location: New York

"Star 69"
Directors: Jonathan Dayton and Valerie Ferris
Location: Australia

"Crush with Eyeliner"
Director: Spike Jonze
Location: New York

"Strange Currencies"
Director: Mark Romanek
Location: New York

ABOUT THE CONTRIBUTORS

Michael Azerrad, a former ROLLING STONE contributing editor, is the author of *Come As You Are: The Story of Nirvana*. He attended R.E.M.'s first performance in New York City in 1980. They sucked.

Mark Coleman is a senior editor at ROLLING STONE.

Christopher Connelly, a former editor at ROLLING STONE, is an executive editor of *Premiere* magazine and the host of MTV's *The Big Picture*.

Anthony DeCurtis is a writer and editor at ROLLING STONE, where he oversees the record review section. He is the editor of *Present Tense: Rock & Roll and Culture* and co-editor of *The ROLLING STONE Illustrated History of Rock & Roll* and *The ROLLING STONE Album Guide*. He won a Grammy for his liner notes for the Eric Clapton retrospective *Crossroads* and has twice won ASCAP Deems Taylor Awards for excellence in writing about music. He holds a Ph.D. in American literature from Indiana University and lectures frequently on cultural matters.

Paul Evans is the co-author of *The ROLLING STONE Album Guide* and *The ROLLING STONE Encyclopedia of Rock & Roll*. His column, "Rollin' & Tumblin'," appears regularly in the magazine.

David Fricke is the music editor of ROLLING STONE. He joined the magazine in 1985 as a senior writer. He is also the American correspondent for the English weekly *Melody Maker* and has written about music for *Musician, People* and the *New York Times*. He is the author of *Animal Instinct,* a biography of Def Leppard, and wrote the liner notes for the box set *The Byrds,* released in 1990.

Jeff Giles is an arts writer at *Newsweek* and the author of a novel, *Back in the Blue House*. He has written ROLLING STONE cover stories about R.E.M., Winona Ryder, Robin Williams and the Spin Doctors, as well as contributing to the *New York Times, The New Yorker* and *Details*.

Jimmy Guterman writes books and produces CDs. He is an editor for Delphi Internet Services.

Glenn Kenny writes about music and popular culture for ROLLING STONE, the *Village Voice, Entertainment Weekly, TV Guide* and the New York *Daily News*.

Rick Marin is a general editor at *Newsweek*. An award-winning television critic, he has written about pop culture for the *New York Times, TV Guide, GQ, Vogue* and *Interview*.

Robert Palmer is a former chief pop music critic for the *New York Times* and a frequent contributor to ROLLING STONE and other publications. His documentary films include *The World According to John Coltrane*, which he wrote and co-directed, and *Deep Blues* (based on his award-winning book of the same name), a tour of Mississippi juke joints for which he served as writer and musical director.

Steve Pond is a ROLLING STONE contributing editor. His work also appears in the *New York Times, Premiere, Playboy, GQ,* and the *Washington Post*.

Parke Puterbaugh is a longtime contributing editor and former senior editor for ROLLING STONE. He writes about music, travel, and the environment for a number of other publications and is co-author of a series of travel books. He lives in Greensboro, North Carolina.

Fred Schruers is a contributing editor at ROLLING STONE.

Andrew Slater has written for ROLLING STONE and other publications. He is now in artist management.